Media Spectacle

In recent decades culture and society have become permeated by the logic of the spectacle. In his fascinating new book, *Media Spectacle*, Douglas Kellner helps bring developments in hi-tech culture and in media-driven society into focus, producing a critical theory of the contemporary moment. The author's case studies engage a range of spectacular forms, including:

- how McDonald's fast-food chain embodies the dynamics of globalization;
- how Michael Jordan and Nike help illuminate global media sports culture;
- how the megaspectacle of the O. J. Simpson trial provides insight into the intersections of gender, race, and class in contemporary US society;
- how TV spectacles like *The X-Files* engage fears of political conspiracy, alien invasions, biotechnologies, and other current worries;
- how presidential politics have become a megaspectacle in an era of media culture.

Kellner engages in close and detailed reading of cultural texts and events to interrogate what they tell us about contemporary reality. This book will be essential reading for students and academics working in the areas of media and cultural studies as well as the sociology of culture.

Douglas Kellner is George F. Kneller Philosophy of Education Chair at the UCLA Graduate School of Education and Information Studies. He is the author of *Media Culture* (1995), *Grand Theft 2000* (2001), and many other books on contemporary theory, culture, and society.

Media Spectacle

Douglas Kellner

Routledge
Taylor & Francis Group

LONDON AND NEW YORK

First published 2003 by Routledge
11 New Fetter Lane, London EC4P 4EE

Simultaneously published in the USA and Canada
by Routledge
29 West 35th Street, New York, NY 10001

Routledge is an imprint of the Taylor & Francis Group

© 2003 Douglas Kellner

Typeset in Times by
Prepress Projects Ltd, Perth, Scotland
Printed and bound in Malta by
Gutenberg Press Ltd

British Library Cataloguing in Publication Data
A catalogue record for this book is available from the British
Library

Library of Congress Cataloging in Publication Data
A catalog record for this book has been requested

ISBN 0-415-26828-1 (hbk)
ISBN 0-415-26829-X (pbk)

Contents

Preface and acknowledgments

As the human adventure enters a new millennium, media culture continues to be a central organizing force in the economy, politics, culture, and everyday life. Media culture drives the economy, generating ebbing and flowing corporate profits while disseminating the advertising and images of high-consumption lifestyles that help to reproduce the consumer society. Media culture also provides models for everyday life that replicate high-consumption ideals and personalities and sell consumers commodity pleasures, solutions to their problems, new technologies, and novel forms of identity. As technocapitalism moves into a dazzling and seductive information/entertainment society, mergers between the media giants are proliferating, competition is intensifying, and the media generate spectacles to attract audiences to the programs and advertisements that fuel the mighty money machines. Yet the terrifying spectacle of September 11 and its aftermath unleashed war and destruction, creating multiplying crises in the global economy and growing insecurity in everyday life.

In the past decades, spectacle culture has evolved significantly. Every form of culture and more and more spheres of social life are permeated by the logic of the spectacle. Movies are bigger and more dazzling than ever, with hi-tech special effects expanding the range of cinematic spectacle. TV channels proliferate endlessly with all-day movies, news, political talk, sports, specialty niches, reruns of the history of television, and whatever else can gain an audience. The music spectacle reverberates through radio, television, CDs and DVDs, computer networks, and extravagant concerts. Media culture provides fashion and style models for emulation and promotes a celebrity culture that provides idols and role models.

Media culture excels in creating *megaspectacles* of sporting events, world conflicts, entertainment, "breaking news" and media events, such as the O. J. Simpson trial, the death of Princess Diana, or the sex, murder, and related scandals of the moment. The megaspectacle has come, too, to dominate party politics, as its heavily dramatized presentations implode into the political battles of the day, such as the Clinton sex scandals and impeachment, the thirty-six-day battle for the White House after the election in 2000, and the September 11 terrorist attacks and subsequent Terror War. "Terror War," in this sense, involves both "the war against terrorism" and the use of aggressive military force and terror as the privileged vehicle of constructing a US hegemony in the current world (dis)order. These dramatic media passion plays define the politics and culture of the time, and attract mass audiences to their programming, hour after hour and day after day.[1]

The Internet, in turn, has generated a seductive cyberspace, producing novel forms of information, entertainment, and social interaction, while promoting a dot.com frenzied boom and bust that fueled and then deflated the "new economy," generating a turbulent new form of creative destruction in the vicissitudes of global capitalism. Ever bigger and more encompassing corporate mergers suggest potential synergies between the Internet and media culture, and thus the information and entertainment industries. These interactions of technology and capital are producing fecund forms of *technocapitalism* and a *technoculture,* both of which promise that the new millennium will be full of novelties, innovation, hype, and instability.

September 11 and the subsequent Terror War intensified uncertainty and unpredictability, disclosed a new vulnerability in the most powerful Western societies, and showed how a set of well-orchestrated terrorist attacks could wreak havoc with the global economy and polity. These catastrophic events and their attendant instability and capriciousness assure a profitable futures market for investments in chaos and complexity theory, as well as in the arms and security industries. Yet it also appears that the "information society" is being put on hold in the interests of eradicating "evil" (i.e. terrorism) from the world. The new forms of war and politics suggest that perhaps there may even be a comeback for postmodern theory,[2] which articulates breaks and ruptures in history and far-reaching novelties in the economy, politics, society, culture, and everyday life. There may also be a return to dialectical theory, as the interconnections between globalization, technological revolution, media spectacle, the Terror War, and the domains of cyberspace and the Internet become central to every sphere of existence, from the dramas and banalities of everyday life to the survival of the human species and life on earth.

In the new millennium, media culture is more important than ever in serving as a force of socialization, providing models of masculinity and femininity, socially approved and disapproved behavior, style and fashion, and appropriate role models (Kellner 1995). The celebrities of media culture are the icons of the present age, the deities of an entertainment society, in which money, looks, fame, and success are the ideals and goals of the dreaming billions who inhabit Planet Earth. As the human species prepares to embark on voyages into outer space, to explore inner space with the miracles of nanotechnology, and to remake the human species with biotechnology, the possibilities emerge that the media, consumer, medical, and other technologies of the present age will propel the human species into a posthuman adventure that may even exhibit the spectacle of the end of humanity in an age of spiritualized and transformative machines.[3]

Whatever the vicissitudes and dynamics of the future, today, media culture continues to arbitrate social and political issues, deciding what is real, important, and vital. Especially spectacular events, such as the 1991 Gulf War, the 2000 battle for the White House, or the September 11, 2001 terrorist attack and its aftermath, bring the TV day to a halt, with cable news channels suspending regular programming to cover the events of the minute. Sometimes megaspectacles such as September 11 and the Terror War take over the TV day in its entirety and dominate news, information, advertising, and entertainment for months on end. At the same time that corporate positioning and relentless mergers reduce the number of news sources and put them under more rigid corporate control, Internet sites propagate information and disinformation. The 'net also provides an interactive sphere where netizens can discover novel opinions and facts and themselves participate in the great dialogue of the contemporary moment (whatever it may be).

In this book, I undertake studies of key media spectacles of the present age in order to illuminate transformations and defining features of the contemporary economy, polity, society, and culture in the new millennium. Chapter 1 provides an overview of defining media spectacles in every domain of contemporary life and stakes out the critical social theory and cultural studies that I will deploy throughout the book. In Chapter 2, I show how analysis of the McDonald's fast-food chain provides insights into the dynamics of globalization, the dialectic of the global and the local, and the ways in which US cultural products are appropriated and made use of throughout the world to provide new forms of global and hybridized culture. Likewise, the study of Michael Jordan and Nike in Chapter 3 helps to illuminate global media culture and NBA basketball and how US sports have become globally popular in the 1990s, while sports deities such as Jordan have developed into worldwide celebrities. The McDonald's study helps to elucidate features of contemporary consumer culture, while the Jordan and Nike readings engage the interconnection of sports, commercialization, and celebrity culture in the present era, wherein sports, business, and spectacle culture merge into one another.

In Chapter 4 the megaspectacle of the O. J. Simpson trial in the mid-1990s provides a case study of the intersections of gender, race, and class in contemporary US society and the ways in which identity politics are fragmenting society into competing groups from which individuals gain their primary identity. The Simpson saga, far from being merely a sordid murder trial, also shows how the logic of the spectacle is permeating the legal system and crime and colonizing everyday life by permeating the TV day, generating endless "breaking news," talk shows, Internet sites, and, later, TV documentaries and docudramas.

Chapter 5 engages the popular TV series and film franchise *The X-Files*, shown in first run on television from 1992 into 2002, which provides an instructive example of the TV spectacle that combines hi-tech aesthetic effects with convoluted allegories of the horrors of contemporary life. Producing a spectacle of government conspiracy, alien invasion, and biotechnological mutations of the human, *The X-Files* puts on display a vast panorama of contemporary fears, fantasies, and conflicts. It allows a diagnostic critique of worries about government conspiracies, aliens and terrorists, medical invasions of the mind and body, and mutations of the human in an era of technoculture and technoscience.

Politics, too, has become a megaspectacle over the past decade as the Persian Gulf TV War dramatized US military power and weapons systems, attempted to save a failing Bush presidency (the first one), and tried to insert the United States as the principal police force in the New World Order (Kellner 1992). A more TV- and media-savvy younger presidential candidate, Bill Clinton, used media spectacle to defeat the aging and disengaged George Bush in 1992. But Clinton then faced the wrath of a resolute Republican opposition that put into play all the media of contemporary culture to create a spectacle of scandal in an attempt to destroy his presidency. Curiously, and unpredictably, the Republican spectacle of moralistic vengeance backfired and Clinton survived (barely) the spectacle of impeachment.

After a lackluster election in 2000 between Son of Bush and Clinton's Vice-President Al Gore, the world was treated to the megaspectacle of a battle for the White House, in which an election was stolen by the Republicans, generating fertile conditions for future political wars and spectacle (Kellner 2001). In an era of spectacle politics, reading political spectacles, such as the Clinton sex scandals and impeachment trials and the battle for the White House in November–December 2000, can illustrate the broad patterns and trajectories of contemporary politics, culture, and society. Indeed, I will argue that these components of recent US political spectacle are inter-related and can best be read in the context of seeing how the cultural wars and presidential politics from the 1960s to the present have played out on the stage of political spectacle. In Chapter 6, I provide a study of *Presidential Politics, the Movie* to discuss the vicissitudes of media and US politics from the 1960s to the present.

Two major spectacles delayed the publication of this book. I had undertaken to conclude my studies for book publication when in November 2000 I got caught up in the battle for the White House in the 2000 US presidential election. Election night provided one of the great media spectacles of all time, as the presidential election went from what appeared as a win for Al Gore, to an announced win for George W. Bush, to an eventual deadlock and the subsequent Florida recount wars, themselves grand political spectacle. I initially wrote up an account of election night that I felt would provide an excellent opening for my studies of media spectacle. The analysis of the battle for the White House became what I envisioned as a chapter in this book, and then eventually became a book in itself, *Grand Theft 2000* (Kellner 2001), when I concluded that the media spectacle of the 2000 election and its aftermath was one of the great political battles and crimes of US history.

Having concluded *Grand Theft 2000* in the fall of 2001, I returned to finish *Media Spectacle,* but the September 11 terrorist bombings and subsequent Terror War generated another major media spectacle, which, over the next months, took over my research energies. Engaging the momentous spectacle as it unfolded, I produced another book-length manuscript, which I am now preparing for publication under the title of *September 11 and Terror War: The Dangers of the Bush Legacy* (Kellner, forthcoming). Hence, I now have a media spectacle trilogy that I present as my gift to understanding society, culture, and politics in the third millennium.

As the present text indicates, I did manage to complete my studies of *Media Spectacle* in a highly turbulent political and cultural situation. In some ways, postponing the publication of *Media Spectacle* while I worked on the major unfolding political spectacles of the era was fortuitous. As Chapter 1 reveals, the opening years of the new millennium were rich in spectacle, making it clear that the construction of media spectacle in every realm of culture was one of the defining characteristics of contemporary culture and society. Likewise, the problems of the specific studies that I was carrying out have been enriched and complexified in the past couple of years. Although up until 2000 McDonald's appeared to be an almost uncontested example of the success of capitalist globalization, around that time the anti-globalization movement began making McDonald's the target of major demonstrations. McDonald's' profits began to fall for the first time in the opening years of the new millennium and McDonald's itself emerged as an increasingly contradictory and contested site in the present age (see Chapter 2).

The Michael Jordan sports spectacle that I have been following for some years took on added dimensions and pathos in 2001–2 as Jordan attempted a comeback and as his failing marriage to his wife, Juanita, added a dimension of tabloid sex scandal to the Jordan saga. The reaggravation of Jordan's knee injuries in March 2002 and his dropping out of play for the season just before the NBA playoffs provided a spectacle of finitude, mortality, and the limitations of the aging body, just as the younger Jordan had presented a spectacle of godlike transcendence and sports idol deity. Hence, the Michael Jordan spectacle also emerges as more complex and contradictory as the millennium unfolds (see Chapter 3).

The O. J. Simpson saga also continued to play out in the new millennium as its celebrity scandal dimension intensified, with new clashes between Simpson and the law. Another round of celebrity sex scandal in his personal life also emerged as Simpson carried out a very public and tumultuous relationship with a lookalike of his murdered wife, Nicole. It was also becoming clearer that the Simpson spectacle was a bellwether event in the transition to a time of tabloid journalism in which, during an age of new media, celebrity scandals and the megaspectacle of the day dominated the news cycle (Chapter 4).

The conspiracy theories concerning the Simpson celebrity murder scandal continued to proliferate and pointed to the growing role of media machination and manipulation in contemporary US society and culture. Although the popular TV series *The X-Files* declined in popularity in its last two seasons, culminating in an announcement in January 2002 that the program would be canceled at the end of its ninth season, the narrative trajectories of the last two seasons make it clear that the alien and conspiracy motif intersects in a major way with fears over cloning, the genetic engineering of human beings, and the creation of a new species that could surpass and eliminate human beings, thus bringing the adventures of the human to a close. I am thus able to provide an overview of the entire TV series and its relevance during an age of cloning and genetic engineering (Chapter 5).

Further, as I noted above, adding the 2000 election, the battle for the White House in the Florida recount wars, and the events of September 11 to my studies of contemporary politics (found in Chapter 6 of this text) provided an enrichment of our understanding of the role of media spectacle in the politics of our time. A new political sex scandal, following the Clinton sex scandals, emerged in 2002 when Chandra Levy, an intern of California Congressman Bill Condit, was found to be missing and the tabloids had a field day uncovering the kinky details and perhaps fateful overlapping of their mutual sex lives. The saturation coverage of the arrest of film and TV actor Robert Blake in April 2002 for the murder of his wife shows that the celebrity murder scandal evident in the O. J. Simpson megaspectacle continues to be of major import and fascination in the present age.

Thus, the theories and models of media spectacle developed in the present book should be handy for years to come. Since I make extensive use of Internet research sources I should make some comments about the application and citation of this material. As is well known, Internet sources often disappear as sites shut down, take material off, or change location. Google.com, alexa.com, and some other search engines have taken to copying and caching files in order to preserve Internet material that often disappears from its original location. Thus, while I cite the Internet URL of actual material used in my text, the specific Internet source cited may disappear. Further, I would recommend that readers wishing to inspect my sources look for them in the "Wayback Machine" at www.archive.org/index.html, or type in key words from the material cited to google.com or other search engines in order to find the original sources that I cited or other related interesting material. The Internet is a cornucopia of research material, although it must, of course, be used with caution.

In some cases, the studies presented here appear in print for the first time; in other cases, I have recast previously published texts to fit into the framework of this book and updated earlier versions. At the beginning of each chapter, I cite previous publication sources and express gratitude to individuals who contributed to each study. For the entire book, I would like to thank Rhonda Hammer, who read, discussed, and was often engaged in the research, as when we spent a year or more watching the O. J. Simpson spectacle go through surprising twists and turns. I would also like to give special recognition to Richard Kahn, who carefully edited every chapter and provided ideas and research material that I utilized in specific studies. I am grateful to Richard for expertly constructing and administering my UCLA website (www.gseis.ucla.edu/faculty/kellner/kellner.html) and designing and helping administer a new blogLeft project,[4] begun in March 2002 as I brought these studies to a close.

Finally, thanks to Mari Shullaw for commissioning the book, putting up with the constant delays signaled above, and giving me solid editorial advice and support throughout this process. For copy-editing support, I would like to recognize Gillian Whytock, David MacDonald, and Ann Grant, and for ideas and stimulation over the years, I am grateful to UCLA students in cultural studies.

And, now, on with the show …

Douglas Kellner, Los Angeles, August 2002

Notes

1   I suppose that this is the place to indicate the US-centric nature of my subject-position and that I am interpreting the world from the lenses of decades at the University of Texas in Austin and then from the vistas of the University of California at Los Angeles. As I now write, I am looking out the window from West Hollywood into downtown LA and the Hollywood hills, into what is perhaps the epicenter of the contemporary media spectacle of our times and during an era of globalization that is more than a merely local

phenomenon. Of course, things look different from variegated class, gender, race, and regional positions. And yet, although the focus of my studies is on salient phenomena of US culture and their planetary proliferations, in a globalized world, technologies, commodities, cultures, ideas, and experiences rapidly circulate throughout the planet. Thus, for those living outside the United States, I might recall what Marx said to all with regard to his analysis of capitalism in England: "De te fabula narratur!" ("The tale is told of you!").

2 For my various takes on postmodern theory and culture, see Best and Kellner (1991; 1997; 2001) and Kellner (1995). In the last text, *Media Culture*, I maintain that the contemporary era is an interim period between a modern and the postmodern epoch. As I try to show in the present text, one of the features of postmodernity is the increasingly important role of media spectacle in the economy, polity, culture, and everyday life.

3 For debates over the vicissitudes of the human in the contemporary era and the possible transition to the posthuman, see Best and Kellner (2001).

4 In 2002, developments of daily weblogs with commentary and URL links, on various topics, known as blogs, became popular (for my own blog, begun in March 2002, see www.gseis.ucla.edu/courses/ed253a/blogger.php).

1 Media culture and the triumph of the spectacle

During the past decades, the culture industries have multiplied media spectacles in novel spaces and sites, and spectacle itself is becoming one of the organizing principles of the economy, polity, society, and everyday life. The Internet-based economy deploys spectacle as a means of promotion, reproduction, and the circulation and selling of commodities. Media culture itself proliferates ever more technologically sophisticated spectacles to seize audiences and increase the media's power and profit. The forms of entertainment permeate news and information, and a tabloidized infotainment culture is increasingly popular. New multimedia, which synthesize forms of radio, film, TV news and entertainment, and the mushrooming domain of cyberspace become extravaganzas of technoculture, generating expanding sites of information and entertainment, while intensifying the spectacle form of media culture.

Political and social life are also shaped more and more by media spectacle. Social and political conflicts are increasingly played out on the screens of media culture, which display spectacles such as sensational murder cases, terrorist bombings, celebrity and political sex scandals, and the explosive violence of everyday life. Media culture not only takes up always-expanding amounts of time and energy, but also provides ever more material for fantasy, dreaming, modeling thought and behavior, and identities.

Of course, there have been spectacles since premodern times. Classical Greece had its Olympics, thespian and poetry festivals, its public rhetorical battles, and its bloody and violent wars. Ancient Rome had its orgies, its public offerings of bread and circuses, its titanic political battles, and the spectacle of empire with parades and monuments for triumphant Caesars and their armies, extravaganzas put on display in the 2000 film *Gladiator*. And, as Dutch cultural historian Johan Huizinga (1986; 1997) reminds us, medieval life too had its important moments of display and spectacle.

In the early modern period, Machiavelli advised his modern prince of the productive use of spectacle for government and social control, and the emperors and kings of the modern states cultivated spectacles as part of their rituals of governance and power. Popular entertainment long had its roots in spectacle, while war, religion, sports, and other domains of public life were fertile fields for the propagation of spectacle for centuries. Yet with the development of new multimedia and information technologies, technospectacles have been decisively shaping the contours and trajectories of contemporary societies and cultures, at least in the advanced capitalist countries, while media spectacle has also become a defining feature of globalization.

In this opening chapter, I will provide an overview of the dissemination of media spectacle throughout the major domains of the economy, polity, society, culture, and everyday life in the contemporary era and indicate the theoretical approach that I deploy. This requires a brief presentation of the influential analysis of spectacle by Guy Debord and the Situationist International, and how I build upon this approach.

Guy Debord and the society of the spectacle

The concept of the "society of the spectacle," developed by French theorist Guy Debord and his comrades in the Situationist International, has had a major impact on a variety of contemporary theories of society and culture.[1] For Debord, spectacle "unifies and explains a great diversity of apparent phenomena" (Debord 1967: Section 10). Debord's conception, first developed in the 1960s, continues to circulate through the Internet and other academic and subcultural sites today. It describes a media and consumer society organized around the production and consumption of images, commodities, and staged events.

Building on this concept, I argue that media spectacles are those phenomena of media culture that embody contemporary society's basic values, serve to initiate individuals into its way of life, and dramatize its controversies and struggles, as well as its modes of conflict resolution. They include media extravaganzas, sporting events, political happenings, and those attention-grabbing occurrences that we call news – a phenomenon that itself has been subjected to the logic of spectacle and tabloidization in the era of the media sensationalism, political scandal and contestation, seemingly unending cultural war, and the new phenomenon of Terror War. Thus, while Debord presents a rather generalized and abstract notion of spectacle, I engage specific examples of media spectacle and how they are produced, constructed, circulated, and function in the present era.

As we enter a new millennium, the media are becoming more technologically dazzling and are playing an ever-escalating role in everyday life. Under the influence of a multimedia culture, seductive spectacles fascinate the denizens of the media and consumer society and involve them in the semiotics of a new world of entertainment, information, and consumption, which deeply influences thought and action. In Debord's words: "When the real world changes into simple images, simple images become real beings and effective motivations of a hypnotic behavior. The spectacle as a tendency *to make one see the world* by means of various specialized mediations (it can no longer be grasped directly), naturally finds vision to be the privileged human sense which the sense of touch was for other epochs (ibid.: Section 18). According to Debord, sight, "the most abstract, the most mystified sense corresponds to the generalized abstraction of present day society" (ibid.).

Experience and everyday life are thus shaped and mediated by the spectacles of media culture and the consumer society. For Debord, the spectacle is a tool of pacification and depoliticization; it is a "permanent opium war" (ibid.: Section 44), which stupefies social subjects and distracts them from the most urgent task of real life – recovering the full range of their human powers through creative practice. The concept of the spectacle is integrally connected to the concept of separation and passivity, for in submissively consuming spectacles one is estranged from actively producing one's life. Capitalist society separates workers from the products of their labor, art from life, and consumption from human needs and self-directing activity, as individuals inertly observe the spectacles of social life from within the privacy of their homes (ibid.: Sections 25 and 26). The Situationist project, by contrast, involved an overcoming of all forms of separation, in which individuals would directly produce their own life and modes of self-activity and collective practice.

The correlate of the spectacle, for Debord, is thus the spectator, the reactive viewer and consumer of a social system predicated on submission, conformity, and the cultivation of marketable difference. The concept of the spectacle therefore involves a distinction between passivity and activity, consumption and production, condemning lifeless consumption of spectacle as an alienation from human potentiality for creativity and imagination. The spectacular society spreads its wares mainly through the cultural mechanisms of leisure and consumption, services and entertainment, ruled by the dictates of advertising and a commercialized media culture. This structural shift to a society of the spectacle involves a commodification of previously non-colonized sectors of social life and the extension of bureaucratic control to the realms of leisure, desire, and everyday life. Parallel to the Frankfurt School conception of a "totally administered" or "one-dimensional" society (Marcuse 1964; Horkheimer and Adorno 1972), Debord states that: "The spectacle is the moment when the consumption has attained the *total occupation* of social life" (1967: Section 42). Here, exploitation is raised to a psychological level; basic physical privation is augmented by "enriched privation" of pseudo-needs; alienation is generalized, made comfortable, and alienated consumption becomes "a duty supplementary to alienated production" (ibid.: Section 42).

Since Debord's theorization of the society of the spectacle in the 1960s and 1970s, spectacle culture has expanded in every area of life. In the culture of the spectacle, commercial enterprises have to be entertaining to prosper and, as Michael J. Wolf (1999) argues, in an "entertainment economy," business and fun fuse, so that the E-factor is becoming a major aspect of business.[2] Through the "entertainmentization" of the economy, entertainment forms such as television, film, theme parks, video games, casinos, and so forth become major sectors of the national economy. In the United States, the entertainment industry is now a $480 billion industry, and consumers spend more on having fun than on clothes or health care (Wolf 1999: 4).[3]

In a competitive business world, the "fun factor" can give one business the edge over another. Hence, corporations seek to be more entertaining in their commercials, their business environment, their commercial spaces, and their websites. Budweiser ads, for instance, feature talking frogs that tell us nothing about the beer, but which catch the viewers' attention, while Taco Bell deploys a talking dog and Pepsi uses *Star Wars* characters. Buying, shopping, and dining out are coded as an "experience," as businesses adopt a theme-park style. Places such as the Hard Rock Cafe and the House of Blues are not renowned for their food, after all; people go there for the ambience, to purchase House of Blues paraphernalia, and to view music and media memorabilia. It is no longer good enough just to have a website, it has to be an interactive spectacle, featuring not only products to buy, but music and videos to download, games to play, prizes to win, travel information, and "links to other cool sites."

To succeed in the ultracompetitive global marketplace, corporations need to circulate their image and brand name, so business and advertising combine in the promotion of corporations as media spectacles. Endless promotion circulates the McDonald's "golden arches," Nike's "swoosh," or the logos of Apple, Intel, or Microsoft. In the brand wars between commodities, corporations need to make their logos or "trademarks" a familiar signpost in contemporary culture. Corporations place their logos on their products, in ads, in the spaces of everyday life, and in the midst of media spectacles, such as important sporting events, TV shows, movie product placement, and wherever they can catch consumers' eyeballs, to impress their brand name on potential buyers. Consequently, advertising, marketing, public relations, and promotion are an essential part of commodity spectacle in the global marketplace.

Celebrity too is manufactured and managed in the world of media spectacle. Celebrities are the icons of media culture, the gods and goddesses of everyday life. To become a celebrity requires recognition as a star player in the field of media spectacle, be it sports, entertainment, fashion, or politics. Celebrities have their handlers and image managers, who make sure that their clients continue to be seen and positively perceived by the public. Just as with corporate brand names, celebrities become brands to sell their Madonna, Michael Jordan, Tom Cruise, or Jennifer Lopez product and image. In a media culture, however, celebrities are always prey to scandal and thus must have at their disposal an entire public relations apparatus to manage their spectacle fortunes and to make sure that they not only maintain high visibility but keep projecting a positive image. Of course, within limits, "bad" and transgressions can also sell, and so media spectacle contains celebrity dramas that attract public attention and can even define an entire period, as when the O. J. Simpson murder trials and Bill Clinton sex scandals dominated the media in the mid- and late 1990s.

Entertainment has always been a prime field of the spectacle, but in today's infotainment society, entertainment and spectacle have entered into the domains of the economy, politics, society, and everyday life in important new ways. Building on the tradition of spectacle, contemporary forms of entertainment from television to the stage are incorporating spectacle culture into their enterprises, transforming film, television, music, drama, and other domains of culture, as well as producing spectacular new forms of culture, such as cyberspace, multimedia, and virtual reality.

For Neil Gabler, in an era of media spectacle, life itself is becoming like a movie and we create our own lives as a genre like film, or television, in which we become "at once performance artists in, and audiences for, a grand, ongoing show" (Gabler 1998: 4). In Gabler's view, we star in our own "lifies," making our lives into entertainment acted out for audiences of our peers, following the scripts of media culture, adopting its role models and fashion types, its style and look. Seeing our lives in cinematic terms, entertainment becomes, for Gabler, "arguably the most pervasive, powerful and ineluctable force of our time – a force so overwhelming that it has metastasized into life" to such an extent that it is impossible to distinguish between the two (ibid.: 9). As Gabler sees it, Ralph Lauren is our fashion expert; Martha Stewart designs our sets; Jane Fonda models our shaping of our bodies; and Oprah Winfrey advises us on our personal problems.[4]

Media spectacle is indeed a culture of celebrity which provides dominant role models and icons of fashion, look, and personality. In the world of spectacle, celebrity encompasses every major social domain from entertainment to politics to sports to business. An ever-expanding public relations industry hypes certain figures, elevating them to celebrity status, and protects their positive image in the never-ending image wars. For there is always the danger that a celebrity will fall prey to the hazards of negative image and thus lose celebrity status, or become a negative figure, as will some of the players and institutions of media spectacle that I examine in these studies.

Sports have long been a domain of the spectacle, with events such as the Olympics, World Series, Super Bowl, soccer World Cup, and NBA Champion-ships attracting massive audiences while generating sky-high advertising rates. These cultural rituals celebrate society's deepest values (i.e. competition, winning, success, and money), and corporations are willing to pay top dollars to get their products associated with such events. Indeed, it appears that the logic of the com-modity spectacle is inexorably permeating professional sports, which can no longer be played without the accompaniment of cheerleaders, giant mascots that clown with players and spectators, and raffles, promotions, and contests that feature the products of various sponsors.

Sports stadiums themselves contain electronic reproduction of the action, as well as giant advertisements for various products that rotate for maximum saturation – previewing environmental advertising, in which entire urban sites are becom-ing scenes to boost consumption spectacles. Arenas such as the United Center in Chicago, the America West Arena in Phoenix, or Enron Field in Houston are named after corporate sponsors. Of course, following major corporate scandals or collapses, such as the Enron spectacle, the ballparks must be renamed!

The Texas Rangers' Ballpark in Arlington, Texas, supplements its sports arena with a shopping mall, office buildings, and a restaurant in which, for a hefty price, one can watch the athletic events while eating and drinking.[5] The architecture of the Texas Rangers' stadium is an example of the implosion of sports and entertainment and postmodern spectacle. An artificial lake surrounds the stadium, the corridor inside is modeled after Chartres Cathedral, and the structure is made of local stone that provides the look of the Texas Capitol in Austin. Inside there are Texas longhorn cattle carvings, panels depicting Texas and baseball history, and other iconic signifiers of sports and Texas. The merging of sports, entertainment, and local spectacle is now typical in sports palaces. Tropicana Field in Tampa Bay, Florida, for instance, "has a three-level mall that includes places where 'fans can get a trim at the barber shop, do their banking and then grab a cold one at the Budweiser brew pub, whose copper kettles rise three stories. There is even a climbing wall for kids and showroom space for car dealerships'" (Ritzer 1998: 229).

Film has long been a fertile field of the spectacle, with "Hollywood" connoting a world of glamour, publicity, fashion, and excess. Hollywood has exhibited grand movie palaces, spectacular openings with searchlights and camera-popping paparazzi, glamorous Oscars, and stylish, hi-tech films. Although epic spectacle became a dominant genre of Hollywood film, from early versions of *The Ten Commandments* through *Cleopatra* and *2001* in the 1960s, contemporary film has incorporated the mechanics of spectacle into its form, style, and special effects. Films are hyped into spectacle through advertising and trailers that are ever louder, more glitzy, and razzle-dazzling. Some of the most popular films of the late 1990s were spectacle films, including *Titanic*, *Star Wars – Phantom Menace*, *Three Kings*, and *Austin Powers*, a spoof of spectacle, which became one of the most successful films of summer 1999. During the fall of 1999, there was a cycle of spectacles, including *Topsy Turvy*, *Titus*, *Cradle Will Rock*, *Sleepy Hollow*, *The Insider*, and *Magnolia*, with the last featuring the biblical spectacle of the raining of frogs in the San Fernando Valley, in an allegory of the decadence of the entertainment industry and its deserved punishment for its excesses.

● The 2000 Academy Awards were dominated by the spectacle *Gladiator*, a mediocre film that captured the best picture award and the best acting award for Russell Crowe, thus demonstrating the extent to which the logic of the spectacle now dominates Hollywood film. Some of the most critically acclaimed and popular films of 2001 were also hi-tech spectacle, such as *Moulin Rouge*, a film that itself is a delirious ode to spectacle, from cabaret and the brothel to can-can dancing, opera, musical comedy, dance, theater, popular music, and film. A postmodern pastiche of popular music styles and hits, the film uses songs and music ranging from Madonna and the Beatles to Dolly Parton and Kiss.

Other 2001 film spectacles included *Pearl Harbor*, which re-enacts the Japanese attack on the United States that propelled the country to enter World War II, and which provided a ready metaphor for the September 11 terrorist attacks. Major 2001 film spectacles ranged from David Lynch's postmodern surrealism in *Mulholland Drive* to Steven Spielberg's blending of his typically sentimental spectacle of the family with the vision of Stanley Kubrick in *AI*. And the popular 2001 military film *Black Hawk Down* provided a spectacle of US military heroism, which some critics believed sugar-coated the real problems with the US military intervention in Somalia. This created fears that future US adventures involving the Bush administration and the Pentagon would meet similar problems. There were reports, however, that in Somalian cinemas there were loud cheers as the Somalians in the film shot down the US helicopter, and pursued and killed US soldiers, attesting to growing anti-US sentiment in the Muslim world against the Bush administration's policies.

Television has been, from its introduction in the 1940s, a promoter of consumption spectacle, selling cars, fashion, home appliances, and other commodities along with consumer lifestyles and values. It is also the home of sports spectacles such as the Super Bowl or World Series, political spectacles such as elections, scandals, and entertainment spectacles such as the Oscars or Grammies, and its own specialities such as breaking news or special events. Following the logic of spectacle entertainment, contemporary television exhibits more hi-tech glitter, faster and glitzier editing, computer simulations, and, with cable and satellite television, a diverse array of every conceivable type of show and genre.

Television is today a medium of spectacular programs such as *The X-Files* or *Buffy, the Vampire Slayer* and spectacles of everyday life such as MTV's *The Real World* and *Road Rules*, or the globally popular *Survivor* and *Big Brother* series. Real-life events, however, took over TV spectacle in 2000–1 in, first, an intense battle for the White House in a dead-heat election that arguably constitutes the greatest political crime and scandal in US history (see Kellner 2001). After months of the Bush administration pushing the most hardright political agenda in memory and then deadlocking as the Democrats took control of the Senate in a dramatic party reaffiliation of Vermont's Jim Jeffords, the world was treated to the most horrifying spectacle of the new millennium, the September 11 terrorist attacks and unfolding Terror War. These events promise an unending series of deadly spectacles for the foreseeable future (see Kellner, forthcoming).

Theater is a fertile field of the spectacle, and thus contemporary stage has exploited its dramaturgical and musical past to create current attractions for large audiences. Plays such as *Bring in 'Da Noise, Bring in 'Da Funk*, *Smokey Joe's Cafe*, *Fosse*, *Swing!*, and *Contact* draw on the history of musical spectacle, bringing some of the most spectacular moments of the traditions of jazz, funk, blues, swing, country, rock, and other forms of pop entertainment to contemporary thespian audiences. Many of the most popular plays of recent years on a global scale have been musical spectacles, including *Les Misérables*, *Phantom of the Opera*, *Rent*, *Ragtime*, *The Lion King*, *Mama Mia*, and *The Producers*, a stunningly successful musical spectacle that mocks the Nazis and show business. These theatrical spectacles are often a pastiche of previous literature, opera, film, or theater, and reveal the lust of contemporary audiences for nostalgia and participation in all types of cultural extravaganzas.

Fashion is historically a central domain of the spectacle, and today producers and models, as well as the actual products of the industry, constitute an enticing sector of media culture. Fashion designers are celebrities, such as the late Gianni Versace, whose murder by a gay ex-lover in 1997 was a major spectacle of the era. Versace brought together the worlds of fashion, design, rock, entertainment, and royalty in his fashion shows and emporia. When Yves Saint-Laurent retired in 2002, there was a veritable media frenzy to celebrate his contributions to fashion, which included bringing in the aesthetic and images of modern art and catering for the demands of contemporary liberated women as he developed new forms of style and couture.

In fashion today, inherently a consumer spectacle, laser-light shows, top rock and pop music performers, superstar models, and endless hype publicize each new season's offerings, generating highly elaborate and spectacular clothing displays. The consumption spectacle is fundamentally interconnected with fashion, which demonstrates what is in and out, hot and cold, in the buzz world of style and vogue. The stars of the entertainment industry become fashion icons and models for imitation and emulation. In a postmodern image culture, style and look become increasingly important modes of identity and presentation of the self in everyday life, and the spectacles of media culture show and tell people how to appear and behave.

Bringing the spectacle into the world of high art, the Guggenheim Museum's Thomas Krens organized a retrospective on Giorgio Armani, the Italian fashion designer. Earlier, Krens had produced a Guggenheim show exhibiting motorcycles and showing plans to open a Guggenheim gallery in the Venetian Resort Hotel Casino in Las Vegas with a seven-story Guggenheim art museum next to it. Not to be outdone, in October 2000, the Los Angeles County Art Museum opened its largest show in history, a megaspectacle "Made in California: Art, image, and identity, 1900–2000," featuring multimedia exhibitions of everything from canonical Californian painting and photography to Jefferson Airplane album covers, surf boards, and a 1998 *Playboy* magazine with "the babes of Baywatch" on its cover. In 2001, the Los Angeles County Art Museum announced that it would become a major spectacle itself, provisionally accepting a design by Rem Koolhaas that would create a spectacular new architectural cover for the museum complex. As described by the *Los Angeles Times* architectural critic, the "design is a temple for a mobile, post-industrial age … Capped by an organic, tent-like roof, its monumental form will serve as both a vibrant public forum and a spectacular place to view art" (December 7, 2001: F1).

Contemporary architecture too is ruled by the logic of the spectacle, and critics have noticed how art museums are coming to trump the art collection by making the building and setting more spectacular than the collections.[6] The Frank Gehry Guggenheim Museum in Bilbao, Spain, the Richard Meier Getty Center in Los Angeles, the retrofitted power plant that became the Tate Modern in London, Tadao Ando's Pulitzer Foundation building in Saint Louis, and Santiago Calatrava's addition to the Milwaukee Museum of Art all provide superspectacle environments in which to display their art works and museum fare. Major architectural projects for corporations and cities often provide postmodern spectacles whereby the glass and steel structures of high modernism are replaced by buildings and spaces adorned with signs of the consumer society and complex structures that attest to the growing power of commerce and technocapitalism.

Popular music is also colonized by the spectacle, with music-video television (MTV) becoming a major purveyor of music, bringing spectacle into the core of musical production and distribution. Madonna and Michael Jackson would never have become global superstars of popular music without the spectacular production values of their music videos and concert extravaganzas. Both also performed their lives as media spectacle, generating maximum publicity and attention (not always positive!). Michael Jackson attracted attention in 2001 in a TV spectacle in which he reportedly paid hundreds of thousands of dollars to digitally redo the concert footage he appeared in. Jackson had his images retooled so that he would be free of sweat and appear darker than the "real" image, in order to blend in better with his family members, who were performing with him, and to appear as a cooler black to appeal to his fans. In June 2002, the Michael Jackson spectacle took a bizarre turn when the onetime superstar called the president of Sony records a "racist," in a rally with African American activist Al Sharpton, for not releasing a September 11 single that Jackson had helped to produce and for not adequately promoting his recent album. Within days, there were reports, however, that Jackson was co-producing the September 11 fund-raising song with a child pornography producer, that McDonald's had dropped its sponsorship when it learned of this, and that Sony too had issues with the project.[7] In a culture of the spectacle, public relations and image can thus make or break its celebrities. Indeed, one cannot fully grasp the Madonna phenomenon without analyzing her marketing and publicity strategies, her exploitation of spectacle, and her ability to make herself a celebrity spectacle of the highest order (Kellner 1995).

In a similar fashion, younger female pop music stars and groups, such as Mariah Carey, Britney Spears, Jennifer Lopez, or Destiny's Child, also deploy the tools of the glamour industry and media spectacle to make themselves spectacular icons of fashion, beauty, style, and sexuality, as well as purveyors of music. Male pop singers, such as Ricky Martin, could double as fashion models, and male groups, such as 'N Sync, use hi-tech stage shows, music videos, and PR to sell their wares. Moreover, hip-hop culture has cultivated a whole range of spectacle, from musical extravaganzas to lifestyle cultivation to real-life crime wars among its stars.

Musical concert extravaganzas are more and more spectacular (and expensive!) and the Internet is providing the spectacle of free music and a new realm of sound through Napster and other technologies, although the state has been battling attempts by young people to utilize P2P (peer to peer) technologies to decommodify culture. Indeed, films, DVDs, sports events, and musical spectacles have been circulating through the Internet in a gift economy that has generated the spectacle of the state attacking those who violate copyright laws that some would claim to be outdated in the culture of hi-tech spectacle.

Food too is becoming a spectacle in the consumer society, with presentation as important in the better restaurants as taste and substance. Best-selling books such as Isabel Allende's *Aphrodite* and Jeffrey Steingarten's *The Man Who Ate Everything* celebrate the conjunction of eroticism and culinary delight. Magazines such as *Bon Appetite* and *Saveur* glorify the joys of good eating, and the food sections of many magazines and newspapers are among the most popular parts. Films such as *Babette's Feast*, *Like Water for Chocolate*, *Big Night*, and *Chocolat* fetishize food and eating, presenting food with the pornographic excesses usually reserved for sex.

Eroticism has frequently permeated the spectacles of Western culture, and is prominently on display in Hollywood film, as well as in advertisements, clubs, and pornography. Long a major component of advertising, eroticized sexuality has been used to sell every conceivable product. The spectacle of sex is also one of the staples of media culture, permeating all cultural forms and creating its own genres in pornography, one of the highest-grossing domains of media spectacle. In the culture of the spectacle, sex becomes shockingly exotic and diverse through the media of porn videos, DVDs, and Internet sites that make available everything from teen–animal sex to orgies of the most extravagant sort. Technologies of cultural reproduction, such as home video recorders (VCRs), DVDs, and computers, bring sex more readily into the private recesses of the home. And today the sex spectacle attains more and more exotic forms with multimedia and multisensory eroticism, as envisaged in Huxley's *Brave New World,* on the horizon.[8]

The spectacle of video and computer games has been a major source of youth entertainment and industry profit. In 2001, the US video game industry hit a record $9 billion in sales and it expects to do even better in the next couple of years (*Los Angeles Times*, January 1, 2002: C1). For decades now, video and computer games have obsessed sectors of youth and provided skills needed for the hi-tech dot.com economy, as well as for fighting postmodern war. These games are highly competitive, violent, and provide allegories for life under corporate capitalism and Terror War militarism. In the game *Pacman*, as in the corporate jungle, it's eat or be eaten, just as in air and ground war games, it's kill or be killed. *Grand Theft Auto 3* and *State of Emergency* were two of the most popular games in 2002, with the former involving high-speed races through urban jungles and the latter involving political riots and state repression! While some women and game producers have tried to cultivate kinder, gentler, and more intelligent gaming, the best-selling corporate games are spectacles for predatory capitalism and macho militarism and not a more peaceful, playful, and co-operative world. Indeed, in 2002, the US military developed a highly popular and critically acclaimed computer game, freely available to anyone online for downloading and playing upon registration with the US Army (www.goarmy.com/aagame/index.htm). Promoted as "The Official Army Game," it allows the user to participate in simulated military basic training activities. The *Go Army* spectacle provides at once propaganda for the military, a recruitment tool, and participation in simulated military action. As military activity itself becomes increasingly dependent on computer simulation, the line between gaming and killing, simulation and military action, blurs, and military spectacle becomes a familiar part of everyday life.

The terrifying spectacle of fall 2001 revealed that familiar items of everyday life, such as planes or mail, could be transformed into instruments of spectacular terror. The al-Qaeda network hijacking of airplanes turned ordinary instruments of transportation into weapons as they crashed into the World Trade Center twin towers and the Pentagon on September 11. Mail delivery evoked fears of disease, terror, and death, as the anthrax scare of fall and winter 2001 made ordinary letters threatening items. And rumors spread that terrorist networks were seeking instruments of mass destruction, such as chemical, biological, and nuclear weapons, to create spectacles of terror on a hitherto unforeseen scale.

The examples just provided suggest that media spectacle is invading every field of experience, from the economy to culture and everyday life to politics and war. Moreover, spectacle culture is moving into new domains of cyberspace that will help to generate future multimedia spectacle and networked infotainment societies. My studies of media spectacle will strive to contribute to illuminating these developments and to developing a critical theory of the contemporary moment. Building on Debord's analyses of the society of spectacle, I will develop the concept in terms of salient phenomena of present-day society and culture.

But while Debord's notion of spectacle tended to be somewhat abstract and theoretical, I will attempt to make the concept concrete and contemporary. Thus, whereas Debord presents few actual examples of spectacle culture, I develop detailed analyses that strive to illuminate the present age and to update and develop Debord's notion. Moreover, although Debord's concepts of "the society of the spectacle" and of "the integrated spectacle" (1990) tended to present a picture of a quasi-totalitarian nexus of domination,[9] it is preferable to perceive a plurality and heterogeneity of contending spectacles in the contemporary moment and to see spectacle itself as a contested terrain. Accordingly, I will unfold contradictions within dominant spectacles, showing how they give rise to conflicting meanings and effects, and constitute a field of domination and resistance.

These "dialectics of the present" will disclose both novelties and discontinuities in the current epoch, as well as continuities with the development of global capitalism. The in-depth studies that follow in this book attempt to articulate defining features of the existing and emergent society, culture, and everyday life in the new millennium. Yet my studies suggest that novel and distinctive features are embedded in the trajectory of contemporary capitalism, its creation of a global economy, and ongoing "creative destruction," which has been a defining feature of capitalist modernity from the beginning. Hence, the cultural studies in this book will be rooted in critical social theory and will themselves contribute to developing a critical theory of society by illuminating key features and dynamics of the present age. The studies will illustrate, in particular, the dynamics of media spectacle and an infotainment society in the current stage of technocapitalism.[10]

The infotainment society and technocapitalism

Today the society and culture of spectacle is creating a new type of information–entertainment society, or what might be called the "infotainment society." The changes in the current conjuncture are arguably as thoroughgoing and dramatic as the shift from the stage of market and the competitive and *laissez-faire* capitalism theorized by Marx to the stage of state-monopoly capitalism critically analyzed by the Frankfurt School in the 1930s. Currently, we are entering a new form of *technocapitalism* marked by a synthesis of capital and technology and the information and entertainment industries, all of which is producing an "infotainment society" and spectacle culture.[11]

In terms of political economy, the emerging postindustrial form of technocapitalism is characterized by a decline of the state and enlarged power for the market, accompanied by the growing strength of transnational corporations and governmental bodies and the decreased strength of the nation-state and its institutions. To paraphrase Max Horkheimer, whoever wants to talk about capitalism must talk about globalization, and it is impossible to theorize globalization without addressing the restructuring of capitalism. Culture and technology are increasingly important constituent parts of global capitalism and everyday life in the contemporary world and permeate major domains of life, such as the economy and polity, as well as constituting their own spheres and subcultures.

The term "infotainment" suggests the synergies of the information and entertainment sectors in the organization of contemporary societies, the ways in which information technologies and multimedia are transforming entertainment, and the forms in which entertainment is shaping every domain of life from the Internet to politics. It is now well documented that the knowledge and information sectors are key domains of our contemporary moment, although how to theorize the dialectics of the present is highly contested. While the theories of Harvard sociologist Daniel Bell (1976) and other postindustrial theorists are not as ideological and far off the mark as some of us once argued, the concept of "postindustrial" society is highly problematic. The concept is negative and empty, failing to articulate positively what distinguishes the alleged new stage. Hence, the discourse of the "post" can occlude the connections between industrial, manufacturing, and emergent hi-tech industries and the strong continuities between the previous and present forms of social organization, as well as covering over the continued importance of manufacturing and industry for much of the world.

Yet discourses of the "post" also serve positively to highlight the importance of significant novelties, of discontinuities with modern societies, and thus force us to rethink the original and defining features of our current social situation (see Best and Kellner 1997; 2001). Notions of the "knowledge" or "information" society rightly call attention to the role of scientific and technical knowledge in the formation of the present social order, the importance of computers and information technology, the materialization of biotechnology, genetic engineering, and the rise of new societal elites. It seems wrong, however, to characterize knowledge or information as *the* organizing or axial principles of a society still constructed around the accumulation of capital and maximization of profit. Hence, in order to avoid the technological determinism and idealism of many forms of postindustrial theory, one should theorize the information or knowledge "revolution" as part and parcel of a new form of technocapitalism. Such a perspective focuses on the interconnections between new technologies, a networked global society, and an expansion of the culture of spectacle in an emergent mode of the "infotainment society," rather than merely obsessing about "new technologies" or "globalization," without seeing the articulations of these phenomena.[12]

The limitations of earlier theories of the "knowledge society," or "postindustrial society," as well as current forms of the "information society," revolve around the extent to which they exaggerate the role of knowledge and information. Such concepts advance an idealist vision that excessively privileges the role of knowledge and information in the economy, in politics and society, and in everyday life. These optics downplay the role of capitalist relations of production, corporate ownership and control, and hegemonic configurations of corporate and state power with all their massive and momentous effects. As I argue below, while discourses of the "post" help describe key defining features of contemporary societies, at least in the overdeveloped world, they neither grasp the specificity of the current forms of global technocapitalism, nor do they sufficiently mark the continuities with previous stages of societal development.

Consequently, to grasp the dynamics of our current social situation, we need to perceive the continuities between previous forms of industrial society and the new modes of society and culture described by discourses of the "post," *and* also grasp the novelties and discontinuities (Best and Kellner 1997; 2001).[13] In the studies in this book, I argue that current conceptions of the information society and the emphasis on information technology as its demiurge are by now too limited. The new technologies are modes of information *and* entertainment that permeate work, education, play, social interaction, politics, and culture. In all of these domains, the form of spectacle is changing areas of life ranging from work and communication to entertainment and diversion.

Thus, "new technologies" are much more than solely information technology, and involve important components of entertainment, communication, and multimedia, as well as knowledge and information, in ways that are encompassing and restructuring both labor and leisure. Previous forms of culture are rapidly being absorbed within the Internet, and the computer is coming to be a major household appliance and source of entertainment, information, play, communication, and connection with the outside world. To help grasp the enormity of the transformation going on, and as indicators of the syntheses of knowledge and cultural industries in the infotainment society, I would suggest reflecting on the massive mergers of the major information and entertainment conglomerates that have taken place in the United States during the past decades. This process has produced the most extensive concentration and conglomeration of these industries in history, as well as an astonishing development and expansion of technologies and media products.

During the 1980s, television networks amalgamated with other major sectors of the cultural industries and corporate capital, including mergers between CBS and Westinghouse; MCA and Seagram's; Time Warner and Turner Communications; Disney, Capital Cities, and ABC; and GE, NBC, and Microsoft. Dwarfing all previous information/entertainment corporation combinations, Time Warner and America On-Line (AOL) proposed a $163.4 billion amalgamation in January 2000, which was approved a year later. The fact that "new media" Internet service provider and portal AOL was initially the majority shareholder in the deal seemed at the time to be the triumph of the new online Internet culture over the old media culture. The merger itself called attention to escalating synergy among information and entertainment industries and old and new media in the form of the networked economy and cyberculture. But the dramatic decline of its stock price after the merger and a reorganization of the corporation in June 2002 called attention to the difficulties of merging old and new media and complexities and uncertainties within the culture industries that are producing spectacle culture.

These amalgamations bring together corporations involved in TV, film, magazines, newspapers, books, information databases, computers, and other media, suggesting a conflictual and unpredictable coming together of media and computer culture, and of entertainment and information, in a new networked and multimedia infotainment society. There have also been massive mergers in the telecommunications industry, as well as between cable and satellite industries, with major entertainment and corporate conglomerates. By 2002, ten gigantic multinational corporations, including AOL–Time Warner, Disney–ABC, GE–NBC, Viacom–CBS, News Corporation, Vivendi, Sony, Bertelsmann, AT&T, and Liberty Media controlled most of the production of information and entertainment throughout the globe.[14] The result is less competition and diversity and more corporate control of newspapers and journalism, television, radio, film, and other media of information and entertainment.

The corporate media, communications, and information industries are frantically scrambling to provide delivery for a wealth of services. These will include increased Internet access, wireless cellular telephones, and satellite personal communication devices, which will facilitate video, film, entertainment, and information on demand, as well as Internet shopping and more unsavory services such as pornography and gambling. Consequently, the fusions of the immense infotainment conglomerates disclose a synergy between information technologies and multimedia, which combine entertainment and information, undermining the distinctions between these domains.

The constantly proliferating corporate mergers of the information and entertainment industries therefore call for an expansion of the concept of the knowledge, or information, society into concepts of technocapitalism and its networked infotainment society. In this conception, the synthesis of global corporate capitalism and information and entertainment technologies is constructing novel forms of society and culture, controlled by capital and with global reach. In this context, the concept of the *networked infotainment society* characterizes the emergent technocapitalist project in order to highlight the imbrications of information and entertainment in the wired and wireless multimedia and information/entertainment technologies of the present. Together, these corporate mergers, and the products and services that they are producing, constitute an emergent infotainment society that it is our challenge to theorize and attempt to shape to more humane and democratic purposes than the accumulation of capital and corporate/state hegemony.

The syntheses of entertainment and information in the creation of a networked infotainment society are part and parcel of a global restructuring of capital. Few theories of the information revolution and the new technologies contextualize the structuring, implementation, distribution, and use of information technologies and new media in the context of the vicissitudes of contemporary capitalism and the explosion of media spectacle and the domain of infotainment. The ideologues of the information society act as if technology were an autonomous force. They often neglect to theorize the interconnections of capital and technology, or they use the advancements of technology to legitimate market capitalism (i.e. Gilder 1989; 2000; Gates 1995; 1999). More conventional and older sociological theories, by contrast, fail to grasp the important role of entertainment and spectacle in contemporary society and culture. Likewise, other theories of the information society, such as those of Daniel Bell (1976), exaggerate the role of information and knowledge, and neglect the importance of entertainment and spectacle.

Thus, Guy Debord's concept of the "society of the spectacle" in which individuals are transfixed by the packaging, display, and consumption of commodities and the play of media events helpfully illuminates our present situation. Arguably, we are now at a stage of the spectacle at which it dominates the mediascape, politics, and more and more domains of everyday life. In a culture of the technospectacle, computers bring escalating information and multimedia extravaganzas into the home and workplace through the Internet, competing with television as the dominant medium of our time. The result is a spectacularization of politics, of culture, and of consciousness, as media multiply and new forms of culture colonize consciousness and everyday life, generating novel forms of struggle and resistance.

The dramatic technological revolution has resulted in groundbreaking forms of technoculture, such as the Internet and cyberculture, and vast technological sophistication and development of media forms, such as radio, television, film, and video. Digitization has deeply transformed culture, producing new modes of spectacle and new domains of technoculture. The studies collected in this book interrogate contemporary culture to illuminate major trends, possibilities, dangers, and conflicts of the present age. In the following sections, I will, accordingly, elucidate the methods of cultural studies that I am developing and their conjunction with critical social theory to signal the goals and context of this book.

From media culture to media spectacle

My earlier book, *Media Culture* (1995), appeared following an era of Reagan/Bush/ Thatcher conservatism and was shaped by its dispiriting politics and culture. *Media Spectacle* was informed, in turn, by the triumph of neo-liberalism in what now appears as an era of Reagan/Bush I/Clinton/Bush II, marked by the unleashing of market forces and the curtailment of the welfare state and social services. While Clinton and Blair purportedly offered a "Third Way" between state socialism and unrestrained market capitalism, in retrospect the past decades exhibit the triumph of global capitalism and the corporate spectacle. The turn-of-the-millennium period was one of dramatic technological revolution, exhibiting ever-expanding globalization with both celebrations and assaults on the bludgeoning global economy. It was also a time of profound political struggle between liberals and conservatives (with radicals continuing to fight on the margins). There were intense cultural wars, which began in the 1960s, between feminists and anti-feminists and those who would promote racial justice and an inclusive multiculturalism against those who asserted class, gender, and race privilege and who fought to preserve tradition and to oppose liberal social change.

The US 2000 election already appears as a retro back to the future with the ascension of George W. Bush, son of the former CIA Director and President George H.W. Bush II has assembled his father's legion of doom for new domestic and global adventures and after the September 11 terrorist attacks is now engaging in an ongoing Terror War, suggesting that the spectacles of the new millennium will be frightening and violent. Bush's blasts from the past create a brave new world of *déjà vu* all over again. Like those of Reagan and Bush I, the Bush II administration has used tax cuts for the rich and escalating military spending to destroy the budget surpluses that had accrued in the prosperous Clinton years, thus forcing cutbacks in government spending and social welfare.

As the new millennium unfolds, the domestic US and global economy appears highly unstable and Western countries are threatened by new enemies within and without. The combination of a crisis-ridden global economy with ever-proliferating media and technology, and a global Terror War within a highly contested and combustible political domain, promises an increase in apocalyptic spectacle into the new millennium. The culture industries are also multiplying media spectacle for mass distraction, entertainment, and profitability in one of the few expanding domains of the "new economy." These developments suggest promising futures for the study of media spectacle and a growing need for cultural studies to help unpack their production, meanings, circulation, and effects.

This book is not per se a polemic against media spectacle, although I certainly note some of its disturbing features and sharply criticize some of the effects of specific media spectacles, such as the McDonald's commodity spectacle. Critics of the dramatic expansion of the media and their incursion into the new realms of cyberspace and virtual reality have worried about the obliteration of the real and the substitution of an ersatz, contrived, and manufactured pseudo-reality for the ordinary experiences of everyday life. Others fret that with the glut of information and entertainment citizens will become extremely distracted from the trials and travails of ordinary life and will increasingly seek escape in the realm of hi-tech entertainment. Yet other critics obsess about the vulgarization of culture, of its dumbing down and banalization in an era of special effects, spectacular media extravaganzas, tabloid journalism, and the glitter and glitz of competing hi-tech media.

All of these critiques of media culture have been articulated many times before. Yet the expansion and technological development of media spectacle provide new life to these old fears, as well as growing worries that the Internet and cyberspace may generate. While I will certainly be critical of many of the media spectacles that I interrogate, and level criticisms at the general structure and direction of the society and culture of the spectacle, I am also interested in providing concrete readings of specific media spectacles, in order to see what they tell us about contemporary life as we enter the third millennium.

My conception of cultural studies involves critical interrogations of what key examples of media spectacle reveal about the contemporary condition, combined with critiques of the ways that certain media spectacles promote oppression of various sorts. Thus, I attempt to discern what media culture discloses about contemporary society, as well as carrying out ideological critique of the specific politics of a text or artifact. Thus, while engaging the politics of representation and ideological critique in reading cultural texts, I also go beyond the texts to interrogate the context in which they are produced and received. My studies thus evoke social context and history to help read the texts of media spectacle, and deploy cultural texts to illuminate the more general social and cultural milieu of the present, one that I have sketched out in this introduction and will flesh out in the studies that follow.

This dialectic of text and context was developed by Walter Benjamin and T. W. Adorno in their conceptions of cultural texts as hieroglyphics or prisms that provide a source of critical knowledge of the contemporary era.[15] Adorno and Benjamin deployed a micrological and hermeneutical method of deciphering cultural phenomena ranging from newspaper astrology columns to television programs to twelve-tone music or the poems of Holderlin. During the same epoch, Siegfried Kracauer (1995) read the dominant modes of culture and society from phenomena such as the Tiller Girls dance reviews and the mass ornament – analyses which anticipated, I might note, German fascism, just as Kracauer (1966) claimed that German expressionist film anticipated the rise of Hitler. So, too, can one interrogate the phenomena of media spectacle today in order to appraise the current forms of contemporary society, the prevailing dreams and nightmares, and the regnant values and ideologies.

I would therefore suggest that media spectacle provides a fertile field for cultural, political, and ideological analysis. Following these models of critical theory, I closely examine some salient phenomena of media spectacle in order to provide insight into the vicissitudes of the contemporary moment. As I try to demonstrate, critical inter-rogation of cultural texts and phenomena can tell us a lot about the conditions of the world as we enter a new millennium. Reading the spectacle of some of the popular texts of media culture helps to provide insights into current and emergent social realities and trends. Popular texts seize the attention and imagination of massive audiences and are thus barometers of contemporary taste, hopes, fears, and fantasies. Let me, then, briefly illustrate this argument with some examples of how critical decoding of popular media spectacles of the era can provide critical insights into the present age. I then explicate the concept of diagnostic critique that guides my particular version of cultural studies.

Signs of the times *Semiolic -*

During the summer of 2000, dinosaurs became a megaspectacle with the release and popularity of the DreamWorks film *Dinosaur*, accompanied by concurrent museum exhibitions of dinosaurs, always a popular exhibit, to complement the film and an explosion of TV documentary specials and news reports about these extinct species. Indeed, a megaspectacle encompasses several media such as film, television, the Internet, and cultural life; it is a focal point for attention and provides clues to the social psyche. W. J. T. Mitchell has written a book on the history of dinosaurs (Mitchell 1998), highlighting our cultural awareness and construction of the species, and the different meanings attached to these strange beasts. I bring up the example to suggest that hermeneutical deciphering of such figures can provide insight into contemporary social and political dynamics and concerns.

Dinosaurs can be read as a polysemic spectacle that encompasses a wealth of images and meanings. The extinct beasts are a sign of radical otherness, of a species that no longer exists. Dinosaurs are dramatically different from any exist-ing species and thus are a figure of difference and altereity. Dinos are, as well, figures of monstrosity, of the power of nature over humans, and of the violence and menace within nature (the DreamWorks movie, by the way, was deemed too violent for young children and there were debates over whether young children should or should not see the film). And, perhaps most telling, dinosaurs are a figure of finitude, extinct species that were extinguished by natural catastrophe. Thus, dinosaurs point to the finitude of the human species itself, and constitute a figure of warning in an era of nuclear bombs, biological–chemical weapons of mass destruction, global Terror War, emergent nanotechnology, and scientific awareness of cosmic and interplanetary cataclysm (for systematic discussion of these issues, see Best and Kellner 2001).

Television presents spectacles on a daily basis for mass consumption and some of the most popular programs of the past years have adopted a spectacle form. ABC's *Who Wants to be a Millionaire?* emerged as the most popular new US TV program of 2000–1. Itself modeled after a UK TV series, the phenomenon reveals the global obsession with instant wealth and the transformation of knowledge into information. Making a spectacle out of the gaining of easy money, the series is highly ritualistic in its posing of questions, its illuminated and blinking set and portentous music, and its host's repetitive intonation of the fatal question, "Is that your final answer?" The show rewards those who, in particular, possess a detailed knowledge of the trivia and minutiae of media culture, registering a transformation of the cultural ideal of knowledge into information. Whereas the classic quiz shows of the 1940s and 1950s rewarded contestants who had absorbed a body of knowledge and allowed them to choose areas to which they had devoted the hard work of education to gain mastery of their field, *Millionaire* focuses on questions concerning the trivia of media culture, rewarding those who have devoted themselves to absorbing the picayune detail of the spectacle culture, of which television is a crucial component.

A popular new form of "reality" television, *Survivor,* was also based on a UK series which had become globally popular and a model for shows around the world. The CBS *Survivor* series, broadcast in summer 2000, involved a dangerous endurance contest among sixteen contestants on a deserted island off Borneo and quickly became a major ratings success. On this show, contenders voted each other off each week, with the winner receiving a million dollars. The competition elicited complex sets of alliances and Machiavellian strategies in a social Darwinian passion play, in which an overweight, gay, middle-aged "corporate trainer," Richard Hatch, became a national celebrity. The series outdrew the Republican convention and its concluding show was deemed by *TV Guide* to be the number one event of the television season (January 8, 2001).

Big Brother, another form of "reality" TV spectacle, presented a positive spin on Orwell's dystopia of a society under total surveillance. Following the model of a wildly successful Dutch TV series, a group of volunteers lived in a house under the unrelenting surveillance of TV cameras. The denizens were not allowed to have contact with the outside world, and viewers voted on which characters should stay or go, until only one remained and won a cash prize. CBS bought the rights to air a US version of the series and broadcast the show in summer 2000.[16] Like the Dutch version, each week viewers voted on which contestant would be eliminated and the "winner" took home a half-million-dollar bonanza (during the second season of the US version the contestants voted each other out). The sight of dozens of microphones and cameras everywhere, including the CBS logo of an open eye, recalls the Orwellian nightmare, transmuted into fluff entertainment in the society of the spectacle. Quite possibly *Big Brother* helps to acclimatize people to surveillance, such as is exercised by the FBI "Carnivore" program, which can intercept private e-mail, or round-the-clock video surveillance at work, in public spaces, and perhaps even at home.

Upping the ante of spectacle culture, CBS played an even more dangerous *Survivor* series in the Australian outback for spring/summer 2001, a *Survivor Africa* series for fall/winter 2001–2, followed by *Survivor Thailand*. Meanwhile, the Fox TV network, which seemed to have reached a new low with its embarrassing *Who Wants to Marry a Millionaire?*,[17] devised a reality TV series, *Temptation Island,* for 2001 in which four unmarried couples would be subjected to the temptations of an attractive array of dating and sexual partners to "test" the couples' relationship; it was a hit and a second season played out in 2002, offering more sex and spectacle.

Following this formula, ABC series *The Bachelor* emerged as the big hit of 2002. A single and eligible male was provided with twenty-five potential mates and as the weeks went by he eliminated the competing women, until one was chosen, a ritual of humiliation which was, however, hugely popular with female and male audiences. A more militarist 2001 reality TV series concocted by ABC, *The Mole*, inserted a plant in a group, providing a chance for potential CIA agents to gain experience of infiltration and exposure, while meeting complex challenges. Fox's reality show *Boot Camp* (2001), in turn, provided training for would-be marines to head off to trouble spots around the world for adventure and endurance tests, thus providing excellent training for US participation in Operation Enduring Terror War.

Demonstrating the psychopathology of the spectacle, contestants on these "reality" shows are driven by a lust for money and, perhaps more so, the 15 minutes of fame and celebrity promised to them by Andy Warhol. Buffeted by the machines of publicity, there appears to be no losers, as those voted off return to instant renown and receive invitations to become TV guest hosts, VJs, or even to appear in *Playboy* (though one contestant on the Swedish *Big Brother* committed suicide after his exile, and it is not clear what the long-term effects of celebrity withdrawal on participants in these experiments may be).

Hence, whereas Truman Burbank, in the summer 1998 hit film *The Truman Show*, discovered to his horror that his life was being televised and sought to escape the video panopticon, many individuals in cyberworld choose to make televisual spectacles of their everyday life, such as the Webcam "stars" or the participants in the MTV "reality" series *Real World* and *Road Rules*. Even PBS got in on the act in summer 2000 with its reality-based show *The 1900 House,* which featured another survival endurance trial, this time involving a family suffering without the amenities of the consumer society and technoculture in a Victorian-era British middle-class house. The Brits also produced a more civilized reality series, *Castaway,* which forced a group of people marooned on a Hebridean island to co-operate in order to survive the rigors of bad weather and isolation.

The mushrooming popularity in 2002 of a MTV faux-reality series on Ozzy Osbourne's family and work life marks a new phase of "realitainment" in which celebrity lives, documentary, and staged events are collapsed into a voyeuristic exposé of the lives of the rich and famous. A long-time heavy-metal rocker fabled for his dissolute lifestyle and stunts, such as biting off the head of a bat on stage, Ozzy's rather ordinary family life became a subject of immense fascination to massive television audiences, constituting the surprise hit of the season.

These reality TV series and their websites seem to be highly addictive, pointing to deep-seated voyeurism and narcissism in the society of the interactive spectacle. It appears that individuals have a seemingly insatiable lust to become part of the spectacle and to involve themselves in it more intimately and peer into the private lives of others. Moreover, the (pseudo)reality series exemplify what Daniel Boorstin (1961) referred to as "pseudo-events," in which people pay more attention to media-produced spectacles than to pressing concerns in the sociopolitical world and everyday life. As Baudrillard (1983a) astutely observed, postmodern media society revolves around an "obscenity" that implodes public and private spheres and puts on display the most banal and intimate aspects of everyday life – be it the sex games of Bill Clinton or the melodramas of ordinary "real-life" drama participants.

In the fall of 2001, reality television lost its luster when the TV news dramatically overshadowed its banal intrigues with the megaspectacle of the September 11 terror attacks and the succeeding Terror War. As the United States began its retaliatory bombing in Afghanistan on October 7, the war news was suddenly interrupted by the spectacle of a videotape of Osama bin Laden, the leader of the al-Qaeda terrorist network believed to be behind the attacks. Bin Laden appeared in his now familiar turban and camouflage jacket, an assault rifle by his side, in an Afghan landscape with a cave behind him. In ornate Arabic, translated erratically by the network translators who were trying to render his speech into English, bin Laden praised the September 11 strike on the United States that "destroyed its buildings" and created "fear from north to south," praising God for this attack. Calling for a jihad to "destroy America," bin Laden assailed the "debauched," "oppressive" Americans who have "followed injustice," and he exhorted every Muslim to join the jihad. The world was now divided, bin Laden insisted, into two sides, "the side of believers and the side of infidels," and everyone who stands with the United States is a "coward" and an "infidel."

Remarkably, bin Laden's Manichean dualism mirrored the discourse of Israeli President Ariel Sharon, George W. Bush, and those in the West, who proclaimed the war against terrorism as a holy war between good and evil, civilization and barbarism. Each dichotomized its "other" as dominated by fear, Bush claiming that his holy war marked freedom versus fear, citing Islamic extremists' animosity to Western values and prosperity. Bin Laden's jihad, in turn, positioned the fearful United States against his brave warriors, also characterizing his battle as that of justice versus injustice. Both appealed to God, revealing a similar fundamentalist absolutism and Manicheanism, with each characterizing the other as "evil." And both sides described their opponents as "terrorists," convinced that they were right and virtuous while the other side was villainous.

Bin Laden was quickly elevated into an international media megaspectacle, reviled in the West and deified in parts of the Islamic and Arab world. Books, artifacts, and products bearing his name and image sold around the globe. For his followers, he personified resistance to the West and fidelity to Islam, whereas to his enemies he was the personification of evil, the Antichrist. Needless to say, entrepreneurs everywhere exploited his image to sell products. On the Internet, one could purchase toilet paper decorated with bin Laden's visage and choose from three slogans: "Wipe out bin Laden," "If he wants to attack he can start with my crack," or "If your butt gets to cloddin' just wipe with bin Laden." In addition, condoms, shooting targets, dartboards, golf balls, voodoo dolls, and violent video games featured bin Laden's now iconic image. Websites presented bin Laden porn, tasteless cartoons, and computer games in which the player could dismember the al-Qaeda terrorist leader.

Documentaries and news reports circulated endlessly every extant image and all footage of bin Laden, portrayed in either negative or positive contexts, depending on the media venue. Viewing the countless video and other images of Osama bin Laden, one is struck by his eyes. The al-Qaeda terrorist leader never seems to look into the eyes of others or the camera when he speaks. Bin Laden seems to be in another sphere, above and beyond mundane social interaction. His communiqués are thus ethereal and bloodless in their presentation, even if their content is highly bloodthirsty, as his eyes look up and away into a transcendent horizon. The Iranian leader, the Ayatollah Khomeini, by contrast, always had contempt, mixed with slight fear, in his eyes, which usually turned down and away from Westerners when he encountered them. Whereas Khomeini's lack of eye contact was always dour and rejective, one occasionally sees a twinkle in bin Laden's eyes, betraying a tell-tale worldliness, before they dart back into a beyond that guides and bedevils him.

George W. Bush, by contrast, is known for his propensity to stare directly into other people's eyes and famously claimed he could look into the Russian president's soul by looking him in the eye. Bush is good at making eye contact with the camera, providing the illusion that he is speaking directly to the people, face to face, while bin Laden is staring out into space and speaking to eternity. To be sure, sometimes the camera catches a blank-looking Bush, his small eyes perhaps pointing to the littleness within. At other times, it catches his infamous smirk, which could reveal arrogance and contempt, or shows his eyes darting erratically from side to side, acknowledging insecurity and anxiety.

In a controversial move, the Bush administration put an embargo on bin Laden videotapes, pleading with the US TV networks not to play the tapes, which were seen as propaganda and perhaps vehicles of "secret messages" to followers. In December 2001, however, the administration released a bin Laden videotape found in Afghanistan, which supposedly provided the "smoking gun" that once and for all would determine bin Laden's guilt. The results for the West were disappointing. Although bin Laden seemed to admit to foreknowledge of the September 11 attacks and gloated and laughed over the results, for the Arab world the tape was a fake. Qatar's Al Jazeera television had commentators who immediately insisted that the "tape has been fabricated, it's not real." The father of condemned terrorist Mohammed Atta dismissed the tape as a "forgery" to an *Associated Press* journalist. Obviously, some Arabs were so bound to their belief in bin Laden that they could not recognize the cynicism and viciousness in his distortion of Islam, while others so distrusted and hated the United States that it was unlikely that they would believe anything released by the "Great Satan."

Although George W. Bush blustered on December 14 that it was "preposterous" that anyone could doubt the authenticity of the bin Laden tape, in fact there were fierce debates over its production, translation, meaning, and mode of release. Such debates demonstrated acute differences in the hermeneutical capacities of audiences and critics throughout the world, vindicating the position long argued in British cultural studies that different audiences produce different interpretations of the text. Special effects experts in London "say [that a] fake would be relatively easy to make" (*Guardian*, December 15, 2001). But experts in the United States from Bell Laboratories and MIT (Massachusetts Institute of Technology) concluded that "technology [is] not yet good enough to fake bin Laden tape" (*Associated Press*, December 15, 2001).[18]

The response to the bin Laden tape confirmed French theorist Jean Baudrillard's position that we are currently living in an era of simulation in which it is impossible to tell the difference between the real and a fake, reality and simulation (1983b; 1993). As Hollywood films use more and more computerized scenes, as rock stars like Michael Jackson digitally "cleanse" their image, and as politicians use political image production and spectacle to sell themselves, the difference between the authentic and the real is harder and harder to determine. Is George W. Bush a real president, or is he just acting out the sound bites fed him by his handlers, performing a scripted daily political act that he does not fully understand? Are the frequent warnings of terrorist attacks genuine, or just a ploy to keep the public on edge to accept more reactionary, rightwing law-and-order politics? Is the terrorist threat as dire as the US Department of Homeland Security claims or is it hyping threats to raise its budgets and power? In an era of simulation, it is impossible to answer these questions clearly as we do not have access to the "real," which, in any case, is complex, overdetermined, intricately constructed, and in some cases, as German philosopher Immanuel Kant (1999) discerned in his distinction between phenomenon and noumenon, ultimately impossible to specify.

So far, the year 2002 has been rich in spectacle. While the 2001–2 New Year spectacles and celebrations took place throughout the world, one could hope for a better year and future. In Europe, there were spectacular displays to inaugurate the Euro, ranging from laser-sound-and-light spectacles to fireworks and mass gala festivities. In Pasadena, California, the annual Tournament of Roses parade fêted the theme of "good times" with the usual floats trumpeting corporations, leisure, and the commodity spectacle. But, under heavy security, the parade opened with the US Marine Corps band and closed with the West Point marching band, featuring military floats, and equestrian riders from the US Marshals Service. The festival featured military and patriotic themes and projected war spectacle as the spirit of the new millennium.

As 2002 unfolded, spectacle culture developed apace. The Super Bowl spectacle is arguably one of the biggest world sports events annually – with over 800 million viewers on average from all corners of the globe. To participate in the St Louis Rams and New England Patriots Super Bowl 2002 spectacle, over 160 million US citizens tuned in to the biggest TV event of the year. Mariah Carey sang the "Star

Spangled Banner" in a diva performance, rising to a deafening crescendo at the end, as a flag was unearthed from the rubble of the World Trade Center and put on triumphant display. Whereas single players usually come out on to the field to great individual fanfare, the Patriots defense marched out ensemble, as a team, ready to roll. Sporting red, white, and blue uniforms, the Patriots were a heavy underdog against the powerhouse Rams, but pulled off an upset in the game's final seconds in what sportscasters instantly hyped as the "greatest Super Bowl in history," the biggest upset, and the most exciting finish ever.[19]

Super Bowls are sometimes connected to military events, as when the 1991 spectacle featured Gulf War floats, military marching bands, and a commemoration of George Bush I and the US military. Following this template, Super Bowl 2002 featured Bush I and former US Navy and NFL star Roger Staubach flipping the coin to decide which team would receive the first kickoff. A hi-tech spectacle featured US troops watching live in Kandahar, and military personnel punching in statistical graphics, making the screen appear like a computer in a military system. Stars of each team were periodically shown in front of a waving US flag with a graphic announcing that "they were proud to be a part of SB36, of this great nation, and that they were thankful for the troops' courage in Afghanistan."

Broadcast by the ultra-right Fox network, the computer graphics featured red, white, and blue banners and the transition graphics involved the use of an exploding fireworks scene with the triad of patriotic colors blasting across the screen. The Super Bowl logo in the center of the field was in the shape of the United States, and the Fox network used a patriotic logo with the flag's colors and images, imitating NBC, which had transformed its multicolored peacock into the flag's tricolors after the September 11 terrorist attacks. As always, half-time featured a spectacle of music and entertainment, with Bono, Irish singer and U2 band member, just back from the World Economic Forum. Bono and Bill Gates had tried to persuade the world economic leaders of the importance of addressing the gaps between the haves and the have-nots, and caring about poverty, health, and the environment. Bono screamed, "It's a beautiful day," and the crowd exploded with joy as U2 performed its hit song with the "beautiful day" signature. A more somber performance provided a tribute to the victims of the September 11 World Trade Center bombing. A large banner unfolded with the names of the victims of the attack as Bono and U2 sang their apocalyptic "Where the Streets Have no Name." At the end of the set, the banner collapsed as smoke enveloped the stage in an evocation of the World Trade Center after the attack. When Bono concluded, he opened his jacket to reveal a US flag, and the crowd went wild.

Super Bowls are also spectacles for advertising, with websites collecting the ads and museums putting on the annual display. In an $8 million extravaganza, Britney Spears belted out the Pepsi song to a background of images presenting Spears in a postmodern collage of styles from the previous decades that was a pastiche of Pepsi ads and imagery of the epoch. For the conformist 1950s, Britney appeared as a soda fountain patron in a grainy black and white montage; the 1960s Britney appeared as a white Supreme, circa 1963, and a mid-1960s beach party girl; for the 1970s, Britney appeared as a peacenik flower child; and the 1980s imagery cut to her as Robert Palmer in the 1989 "Simply Irresistible" Pepsi ad format. The flow of retro Pepsi ads and fashion imagery culminated in a contemporary display of Britney in a belly shirt, with a highly futuristic neon-lit diner in the background, positioning the present as a conservative back-to-the-future of the 1950s!

The ad suggested that the Pepsi generation now encompasses multiple generations with icons such as Madonna and Britney representing the Pepsi community. In other ads, Budweiser featured horses bowing to the Statue of Liberty and New York and a highly acclaimed spot in which a falcon swept down from an apartment to cop a Bud for a young man and his two female friends. Altogether ten Bud ads ran, sending the message that beer promoted fun and good times and that it was cool for young people to drink. Ad prices have declined from the top price of $3 million a spot in 2000, with Fox opening bidding at $1.9 million for a 30-second spot this year. While the past couple of Super Bowls had featured a bevy of dot.com ads, this year saw limited entries, such as infect-truth.com, whose ads perhaps inadvertently sent out messages of hope that more truthful and honest corporations would not meet the fate of their predecessors, many of which, like Enron, had gone bankrupt.

A highly propagandistic set of ads, made by the US government and shown as public service announcements, made a connection between drugs and terrorism, sending out a message that if you use drugs you provide money for terrorists. "Where do terrorists get their money?" asks one of the ads, which portrays a terrorist buying explosives, weapons and fake passports while putting a stack of Russian AK-47s into a rental car! Answering its own question, the ad proclaims that half of the twenty-eight organizations identified as terrorist by the National State Security Department are funded by sales of illegal drugs. The implication is that people who use drugs help terrorists, and the ad, costing US taxpayers over half a million dollars for its production, provided the pro-Bush administration Fox network with $3 million in advertising revenues, while serving as propaganda for both the US military and the administration's drug policy.

As for the game itself, it was a cliffhanger. The underdog Patriots took a 14–3 half-time lead, the Rams fought back in the second half to a 17–17 tie, and in the final second the Patriots scored a field goal to gain an upset win, costing Las Vegas gamblers billions but creating a patriotic fervor for New England and much of the nation. The Patriots' owner declared after the game, in a cleverly conceived speech: "We did it with teamwork and spirit. Spirituality and faith in democracy are the cornerstones of our country. Today, we're all patriots and the Patriots are world champions."

And so the spectacle of the Super Bowl provided a striking panorama of US nationalism. Other media spectacles, however, were producing rising anti-US sentiment. The treatment of bound, gagged, and sedated al-Qaeda and Taliban prisoners being held in Guantanamo Bay, Cuba, was creating an uproar in world diplomatic circles and in the human rights community, as the United States refused to recognize its "unlawful combat" detainees as prisoners of war and thus denied them the protection of the Geneva Convention. When George W. Bush proclaimed that the United States was out to destroy an "axis of evil" in his late January 2002 State of the Union address, there was extreme anger and worry in both the Middle East and the Arab world. Moreover, the United States' European and other allies feared that it was going to take the Terror War to dangerous and unprecedented levels.

Indeed, as the Winter Olympics opened in Salt Lake City on February 8, it featured more troops and police than were stationed in Afghanistan. Security was at an all-time high, with some 50,000 law enforcement forces deployed, domestic flights over the site of the Olympics grounded, and Black Hawk helicopters patrolling the area. After some debate, the United States was allowed to unfurl a US flag saved from the ruins of the World Trade Center in the opening ceremonies (later lost or stolen in transit). Members of the International Olympic Committee initially thought that such a patriotic symbol might conflict with the internationalist flavor of the Olympics, and others had said that the flag should go to the Smithsonian, or another suitable venue, and not be subject to the vicissitudes of weather. The ceremonies opened, however, with the usual hoopla and another major spectacle was under way as an estimated 3.5 billion people worldwide watched the festivities, which were broadcast to 160 nations.

In the opening ceremonies, as always, the identity of the final torch-bearer was a closely guarded secret, and the crowd was ecstatic to see Mike Eruzione and the 1980 US Olympic ice hockey team that had upset the favored Soviet Union during the last hot phase of the Cold War. George W. Bush emerged to deliver a political speech, breaking with a tradition that excluded nationalist proclamations, stating: "On behalf of a proud, determined, and grateful nation, I declare open the Games of Salt Lake City!" Bush then surrounded himself with the heroes of the US 1980 hockey team for a spectacular photo opportunity that combined patriotism, power, and US victory in the Cold War.

Forgotten was the corruption whereby US Olympic organizers had bribed the International Olympic Committee with over $1 million to swing their votes Salt Lake City's way. Likewise, there was little mention of the criminal investigations, fifteen counts of bribery, fraud, and conspiracy in a US Justice Department indictment still pending, and the resignation of ten members of the US Olympic committee. No one had the bad taste to mention the Olympic scandal and connect it with the Bush administration and Enron scandals, which will provide media spectacles for the coming years and forthcoming books, films, and TV movies. Instead, there was pomp and pageantry, fireworks, and an orgy of patriotism, as the Winter Olympic Games opened and the parades and competition began. Bring on the games and let media spectacle rule!

The games, as it turned out, were a spectacle of scandal, nationalism, and controversy. In what seemed to most observers to be an injustice, a Russian figure-skating pair was awarded a gold medal over the Canadian pair that most people agreed had offered a superior performance. A French judge broke down and confessed in a meeting that she had been pressured by a French Olympic group to award the medal to the Russians! Soon after, a committee decided to award a dual gold medal to stem the controversy that was flaming through the global press; some days later the French judge said that it was really the Canadians who had been pressuring her! The Russians, in turn, protested that their athletes had been "humiliated," were "greatly unappreciated," and were robbed of medals by officials' decisions, threatening to boycott the closing ceremonies and perhaps future games. But, in July 2002, it was alleged that a Russian Mafia figure had helped manipulate a victory for the Russians in one category and for French skaters in another! When a Korean speed skater lost his gold medal to an American after being accused of a foul, tens of thousands of angry Koreans bombarded the Olympic committee with e-mail. And Canada went wild in a patriotic orgy of enthusiasm when its team upset the US ice hockey team to claim an Olympic victory, while the Germans enthusiastically celebrated winning the most gold medals. Hence, nationalism and patriotism trumped the internationalism of the games and media spectacle triumphed once again.

For the film community and its fans, the annual Oscar awards is the major spectacle of the year, and the 2002 awards were particularly controversial and noteworthy. The 74th Oscar awards took place in Hollywood for the first time since 1960. Under the tightest security ever, entire blocks of Hollywood were closed to traffic, all shops were closed, and even the local subway station was shut down. Leading up to the awards, fierce Oscar campaigns were waged, with unprecedented attacks on *A Beautiful Mind*. This film dealt with the life of mathematician John Forbes Nash's battle with schizophrenia, and a whispering campaign demeaned the film for leaving out the rough edges of Nash's life, such as rumors of bisexuality, adultery, fathering a child out of wedlock, and anti-Semitism. Meanwhile another smear campaign unfolded against the film's star Russell Crowe, who was up for an Oscar for best actor. Crowe was systematically bad-mouthed for his womanizing and lashing out at a director at a UK awards ceremony who had cut off his poetry reading; footage was also released of a rowdy Crowe in a fight in the parking lot of a bar.

The spectacle was as outrageous as ever, with star-studded Hollywood royalty prancing along the fabled red carpet, wearing designer clothes and jewelry. Accessories included a borrowed million-dollar diamond brooch, a $3 million "pumpkin diamond" ring for Halle Berry, a $4 million 24-carat raw-diamond Bulgari necklace for Nicole Kidman, and a $27 million diamond necklace and $1 million diamond-studded shoes for Laura Harring. Cameras during the Oscar ceremonies focused on the young and the beautiful of Hollywood's aristocracy, attempting to capture, as always, intimate glimpses of the major players' responses to winning and losing. While fashion critics raved over the most spectacular clothes and accessories, fashion mavens mocked some of the stylists and couture, such as Gwyneth Paltrow's see-through dress, Cameron Diaz's messy hair, which gave the impression that she had just got out of bed, Jennifer Lopez's overlaid and trussed-up hair, or Russell Crowe's silly frock coat, which made the bad boy look like a nineteenth-century preacher.

Oscar 2002 was ultimately a spectacle of race as African Americans won both major acting awards for the first time. Halle Berry was awarded best actress and appeared to have had an anxiety attack before she overcame her sobbing and thanked every black actress who had preceded her and all those who had helped her. These included "my lawyer who cut that deal" (to pay off the victim of a hit-and-run accident, preventing a trial that might have had Halle incarcerated, rudely ending her budding career). Denzel Washington gained best actor award, just after presenting the iconic Sidney Poitier with a lifetime achievement award. The Oscar's TV hostess, Whoopie Goldberg, provided a set of race jokes, interspersed with snide comments lampooning the celebrity stars who were up for the awards.

There was also a serious side to the spectacle, as Tom Cruise opened with an evocation of the horrors of the September 11 terrorist attacks and an assurance for Hollywood that it was all the more important that it continue in its film-making efforts to provide necessary entertainment and inspiration for the public. Woody Allen made his first Academy Awards appearance to make a pitch for film making in New York. And Kevin Spacey made an emotional appeal for a moment's silence to commemorate the victims of the terrorist attacks, as the Academy remembered those members of the film industry who had passed on the previous year.

But first and foremost the Oscar awards are a spectacle of Hollywood itself and of its importance in the production and reproduction of a culture of the spectacle, one that is now global in import. Combining television performance, musical numbers, film clips, and other forms of entertainment, the evening provides an opportunity for the spectacle to celebrate itself and promote its myriad forms, values, and significance. The Academy Awards are also a celebration of victory, the primal US and global capitalist passion play. Indeed, the prize-garnering films make millions more in revenue from the prestige and position of being Oscar winners, which allows the winning studios and players to make a big score in the next deal. This is, after all, what media spectacle is all about.

❖ ❖ ❖

Thus, the new millennium is marked by a diversity of spectacles in the field of politics, culture, entertainment, and every realm of social life. In this context, it is important to develop a critical theory of the spectacle to provide students and citizens with the tools to unpack, interpret, and analyze what the spectacles of the contemporary era signify and tell us about the present and the future. This project requires the connection of cultural studies with diagnostic critique.

Cultural studies as diagnostic critique

Cultural studies as a diagnostic critique is concerned with in what media spectacle tells us about contemporary society and culture, in developing readings that illuminate the present age, and in decoding "signs of the times" that allow us to grasp better the defining characteristics, novelties, and conflicts of the contemporary era. Media spectacle provides a fertile ground for interpreting and understanding contemporary culture and society because the major spectacles provide articulations of salient hopes and fears, fantasies and obsessions, and experiences of the present. Media spectacles also put on display the politics of representation, encoding current problematics of gender, race, and class. A diagnostic critique thus attempts to discern how media culture articulates dominant discourses and circulates opposing political positions around class, race, gender, sexuality, politics, and other crucial concerns of the present.[20]

I am making use in my studies of concepts developed by Stuart Hall and British cultural studies of the distinction between encoding and decoding, the concept of articulation, and the importance of engaging the politics of representation of gender, race, class, and so on. Yet, cultural studies as a diagnostic critique not only engages in ideological appraisal of the texts and spectacles of media culture, but analyzes how they put on display social content, such as hopes and fears, circulate ideological discourses and political positions, and allow a diagnosis of contemporary pathologies, anxieties, political contestation, and ambiguities. For diagnostic critique, media culture also puts on display dreams and yearnings for a better world that provide utopian content that can be used for social critique and to mobilize political opposition (see Kellner and Ryan 1988; Kellner 1995). Diagnostic critique engages social pathologies but also envisions healing and desires for a better world and social transformation.

The media spectacles of the contemporary era are especially important for diagnostic critique. They are the products of culture industries in many different media such as film, television, advertising, journalism, the Internet, and new multimedia, and they are the result of heavy investment, research, creative activity, and experimentation and development. The major media spectacles of the culture encapsulate the most significant concerns of the era, which is why they are popular and arouse the interest, and even obsession, of contemporary audiences.

Like Roland Barthes' mythologies (1983), the media spectacles that I interrogate are key cultural phenomena that naturalize and idealize the given social system. McDonald's provides a mythology for the fast-food corporation that renders McDonald's' golden arches a mythological site of fun and good food, while the Big Mac becomes a mythology of American goodness. Michael Jordan provided a mythology of the "man who flies," "Air Jordan," and the ideal basketball player and role model for youth. Barthes studied a range of phenomena from wrestling to soap ads, while dissecting their social functions and ideological meanings. The mythologies Barthes analyzed functioned to naturalize and eternalize the historically contingent forms of French bourgeois culture. In his famous reading of a picture of a Black African soldier saluting the French flag, for example, Barthes claimed that the image erased the horrors of French imperialism, presenting a sanitized portrait of a French soldier that made it appear natural that an African should salute the French flag and exhibit the proper signs of military behavior.

Barthes constructed methods of analyzing figures and rhetorical strategies of media culture, taking apart the mythologies that colonize social life and helping produce a critical consciousness on behalf of the reader. Diagnostic critique also takes apart the mythologies of celebrity, sports, media culture, and politics, showing how they are socially constructed, infused with ideological meaning, and function to cover over social struggle, negative aspects such as excessive commercialism or exploitation, or the promotion of social justice. Driven by a demythologizing ethos, critical cultural studies wants to raise critical consciousness and to promote the construction of an alternative society.

Furthermore, to paraphrase Paulo Freire (1972; 1998), I am engaged in reading the culture and the media in order to read the world. A diagnostic critique uses critical social theory and cultural studies in order to teach students and citizens how to read their culture, how to see what media culture and spectacle reveals about the world, and how culture functions to shape desire, behavior, and identity. Diagnostic critique discerns how media culture and spectacle are worldly and perform in the world, how they relate to major social and political issues, and how they have significant effects and potentially productive uses. As I have argued before, it is important to overcome the dichotomy between seeing media culture as an all-powerful force of manipulation and as a mere popular entertainment that audiences can deploy for their own purposes (Kellner 1995). Rather, one needs to see the intersection of media texts and spectacles with the public, to mediate between the power of the media and audiences, to see how the texts and spectacles of media culture encode significant social issues and material, and to discern how the public can use and decode media in more critical and self-empowering manners.

Thus, my project combines media critique with media pedagogy, aimed at teaching how to read, analyze, and learn how the media both present a version of reality and also can be used to learn about social reality (Kellner 1995). On this view, the texts of media culture help provide material for a diagnostic critique of the contemporary era whereby critical readings of popular artifacts and spectacles are interrogated to provide knowledge of the contemporary era. In the following studies, I provide detailed examples of cultural studies as a diagnostic critique, critically interrogating media spectacles such as McDonald's, Michael Jordan and the Nike spectacle, the O. J. Simpson trial, *The X-Files*, and presidential politics in the United States in order to illuminate defining features and novelties of contemporary society, economy, politics, and everyday life.

In *Media Spectacle*, I will accordingly engage in some close and detailed readings, contextualization, and analysis of the broad effects of major cultural texts and events deploying the methods of cultural studies, as well as use critical social theory to interrogate what the texts tell us about contemporary reality. While some critics talk incessantly about cultural studies as a historical phenomenon, or endlessly debate the method and concepts of cultural studies, I do cultural studies through dissection of the production of texts, textual analysis of its meanings, and study of their effects and resonance, deploying a multiperspectivist approach.[21] And while some close readings stay ensconced in the textures and surfaces of texts, I want to go beyond the texts to the contexts in which they are produced, consumed, and used, using media spectacles to illuminate their historical and cultural situations.

The conception of cultural studies as a diagnostic critique thus combines using social theory to interpret and contextualize phenomena of media culture with developing close readings and situating of cultural texts to elucidate contemporary culture and society. A diagnostic critique exposes hopes and fears, and problems and conflicts of the existing society, as well as the nature of the contending corporate, political, and social groups in the contested terrain of existing society and culture. Seeing culture and society as a field of contestation with forces of domination and resistance, repression and struggle, co-optation and upheaval, provides a more dynamic model than that of certain forms of Marxism or feminism that primarily see the dominant culture as one of domination and oppression, or of populist cultural studies that excessively valorizes resistance, overlooking the moments of domination. By contrast, envisioning society and culture as contested terrains articulates the openings and possibilities for social transformation, and the potentials for resistance and struggle, as well as providing a critique of ideology and domination.

Hence, my conception of cultural studies combines a critique of domination with valorization of the forces of resistance and struggle. While the politics of representation are engaged with criticizing racism, sexism, classism, homophobia, and other forms of oppression, I also attempt to discern more liberating representations and social forces struggling against domination. Criticizing domination and arguing for a more egalitarian and just social order envisages progressive social transformation. This involves, in part, educating individuals to resist cultural manipulation and to become media literate. Thus, I am also interested in the promotion of media literacy, the pedagogy of learning how to read cultural texts critically and politically, and the use of culture to understand and democratically transform the world. I would therefore identify my project with that of Brazilian educator Paulo Freire (1972; 1978) who wants to develop literacy to teach people to read the word and through reading the word to read and transform the world.

Consequently, a diagnostic critique uses culture to analyze the conditions of contemporary culture and society and to provide instruments of social change. It combines theory with practice, uniting doing cultural studies with reflecting on the society and culture under analysis. It seeks to reconstruct disciplinary practice, drawing on a wealth of disciplines from textual analysis to political economy. And it seeks to transform society, providing a critique of domination and subordination and valorization of forces struggling for social justice and a more democratic and egalitarian society. Seeing cultural studies as a diagnostic critique and transformative practice thus seeks those phenomena that best illuminate contemporary society and that provide either obstacles or forces of social progress.

Notes

1 Debord's *The Society of the Spectacle* (1967) was published in translation in a pirate edition by Black and Red (Detroit) in 1970 and reprinted many times; another edition appeared in 1983 and a new translation in 1994. Thus, in the following discussion, I cite references to the numbered paragraphs of Debord's text to make it easier for those with different editions to follow my reading. The key texts of the Situationists and many interesting commentaries are found on various websites, producing a curious afterlife for Situationist ideas and practices. For further discussion of the Situationists, see Best and Kellner (1997: Chapter 3); see also the discussions of spectacle culture in Best and Kellner (2001), upon which I draw in these studies.

2 Wolf's book is a detailed and useful celebration of the "entertainment economy," although he is a shill for the firms and tycoons that he works for and celebrates them in his book. Moreover, while entertainment is certainly an important component of the infotainment economy, it is an exaggeration to say that it drives it and is actually propelling it, as Wolf repeatedly claims. Wolf also downplays the negative aspects of the entertainment economy, such as growing consumer debt and the ups and downs of the infotainment stock market and vicissitudes of the global economy.

3 Another source notes that "the average American household spent $1,813 in 1997 on entertainment – books, TV, movies, theater, toys – almost as much as the $1,841 spent on health care per family, according to a survey by the US Labor Department." Moreover, "the price we pay to amuse ourselves has, in some cases, risen at a rate triple that of inflation over the past five years" (*USA Today*, April 2, 1999: E1). The NPD Group provided a survey that indicated that the amount of time spent on entertainment outside the home – such as going to the movies or a sporting event – was up 8 percent

from the early to the late 1990s and the amount of time spent on home entertainment, such as watching television or surfing the Internet, went up 2 percent. Reports indicate that in a typical US household, people with broadband Internet connections spend 22 percent more time on all-electronic media and entertainment than the average household without broadband. See "Study: broadband in homes changes media habits" (pcworld.com, October 11, 2000).

4　Gabler's book is a synthesis of Daniel Boorstin, Dwight Macdonald, Neil Poster, Marshall McLuhan, and various trendy theorists of media culture, but without the brilliance of a Baudrillard, the incisive criticism of an Adorno, or the understanding of the deeper utopian attraction of media culture of a Bloch or a Jameson. Likewise, Gabler does not, à la cultural studies, engage the politics of representation, or its ideologies and political economy. He thus ignores mergers in the culture industries, new technologies, the restructuring of capitalism, globalization, and shifts in the economy that are driving the impetus toward entertainment. Gabler also does not address how new technologies are creating new spheres of entertainment and forms of experience and in general describes rather than theorizes the trends he is engaging.

5　The project was designed and sold to the public in part through the efforts of the then floundering son of a former president, George W. Bush. Young Bush was bailed out of heavy losses in the Texas oil industry in the 1980s by his father's friends and used his capital gains, gleaned from what some say was illicit insider trading, to purchase part-ownership of a baseball team (the Texas Rangers). The soon-to-be Governor of Texas, and future President of the United States, sold the new stadium to local taxpayers, getting them to agree to a higher sales tax to build the stadium, which would then become the property of Bush and his partners. This deal allowed Bush to generate a healthy profit when he sold his interest in the Texas Rangers franchise to buy his Texas ranch, paid for by Texas taxpayers (for sources on the life of George W. Bush and his surprising success in politics, see Kellner (2001) and the discussion on Bush Jr. in Chapter 6).

6　See Nicholai Ouroussoff, "Art for architecture's sake," *Los Angeles Times*, March 31, 2002.

7　See Chuck Philips, "New spin on collapse of Jackson's charity project," *Los Angeles Times*, July 13, 2002.

8　There is little doubt but that the emergent technologies of virtual reality, holograms, and computer implants of sensory experience (if such exotica emerge) will be heavily invested in the reproduction of sex. In a webpost by Richard Johnson, "Virtual sex is here" (www.ThePosition.com, January 4, 2001), British Professor Kevin Warwick's latest experiment is described, which involves the implanting of a computer chip, which, if successful, will make possible the communication of a wide range of sensory experience and new types of sexual stimulation. The 1995 film *Strange Days* portrayed a futuristic culture, with addictive virtual reality devices, in which spectators become hooked on videos of extreme sex and violence. *The 13th Floor* (1999) portrayed a virtual reality gadget whereby players are transported to recreations of other times, places, and identities, experiencing full bodily fears and pleasures.

9　For a critique of Debord, see Best and Kellner 1997: 118ff.

10　The analyses in this book are primarily cultural studies, and I explore in more detail elsewhere the consequences for social theory of the phenomena explored here. Theoretical grounding, in turn, for the investigations is found in past works, such as Kellner and Ryan (1988), Kellner (1989a, b), Best and Kellner (1991; 1997; 2001), Kellner (1995).

11　On the various stages of development of the Frankfurt School and for an earlier introduction of the concept of technocapitalism, see Kellner (1989b). For more recent reflections on the roles of new technologies in the current stage of capitalist development, see Best and Kellner (2001) and Kellner (2000a).

12　It is striking how many theories of globalization neglect the role of information technology, often falling prey to economic determinism, while many theories of information technology fail to theorize their embeddedness in the global economy, thus falling prey to technological determinism. See Kellner (2000b) and Best and Kellner (2001).

13 Frank Webster (1995: 5, *passim*) wants to draw a line between "those who endorse the idea of an information society" and "writers who place emphasis on continuities." Although he puts me in the camp of those who emphasize continuities (p. 188), I would argue that we need to grasp both continuities and discontinuities in the current societal transformation we are undergoing and that we deploy a both/and logic in this case and not an either/or logic. In other words, we need to theorize both the novelties and differences in the current social restructuring and the continuities with the previous mode of societal organization. Such a dialectical optic is, I believe, consistent with the mode of vision of Marx and neo-Marxists such as those in the Frankfurt School.

14 See the chart in *The Nation* (January 7, 2002) and the accompanying article by Mark Crispin Miller, "What's wrong with this picture?" as well as the analysis of the impact of "media unlimited" in Gitlin (2002), who discusses oversaturation, intensifying speed, and an increasingly media-mediated existence in the contemporary era.

15 See Adorno (1991; 1994) and Benjamin (1969); on the strengths and limitations of the critical theory approach to cultural studies, see Kellner (1989a); and for various readings of Adorno, see Gibson and Rubin (2002).

16 See Brian Lowry, "Big Brother's watchers see everything but privacy" (*Los Angeles Times*, February 12, 2000:A1, A50) and "The electronic fishbowl" (*New York Times*, May 21, 2000). The new reality shows exhibit the confluence of television and Internet entertainment; the Dutch show *Big Brother* featured a live website with four video streams that one could check out, gaining 52 million hits, and the CBS series deployed roughly the same setup, although it charged viewers to subscribe to its website for the 2001 and 2002 seasons. It is interesting from the perspective of globalization that recent hit TV formats have come from Europe to the United States. The 1999–2001 ABC TV sensation *Do You Want to Be a Millionaire?* was closely based on a hit UK TV series, as was a 2001 follow-up, *The Weakest Link*. Reality TV hits *Survivor* and *Big Brother* were also derived from European models. It appears in these cases that it is precisely the crassest and most commercial aspects of global culture that crosses borders the most easily. The *Big Brother* series continued to be a popular popcult phenomenon into 2002; see the collection of studies in *Television and New Media*, Vol. 3, no. 3 (August 2002).

17 This popular, and then reviled, program featured a supposed millionaire (who turned out to be a sleazy hustler) who chose a wife from female contestants, the winner sharing a million-dollar reward with her new husband. As it turned out, the bride could not stand being with the man, quickly left him, proclaimed her virtue, and tried to exploit her fifteen minutes of fame, eventually posing nude in a men's magazine. The tabloids uncovered the unsavory pasts of both the husband and the wife, and Rupert Murdoch's Fox Network suffered some slight embarrassment, although it is unlikely that the Fox people suffer much in the way of shame or humiliation.

18 German television found that the White House translation of bin Laden's video was not only inaccurate but also "manipulative" (see dc.indymedia.org/front.php3?article_id=16389&group=webcast). For a full study of Bush, bin Laden, and Terror War see Kellner (forthcoming).

19 I am indebted to Richard Kahn for sharing his Super Bowl notes. For a now classic analysis of the Super Bowl spectacle, see Reel (1977). Reel (1977: 93) timed the actual football action, from quarterback snap to whistle ending the play, and found that the four-hour spectacle contained a mere seven minutes of actual football action!

20 On encoding and decoding, see Stuart Hall's classic study with this title (collected in Durham and Kellner 2001); on articulation, see Hall (1986), and for specific developments and uses of these concepts, as well as the concepts of diagnostic critique, see Kellner and Ryan (1988) and Kellner (1995).

21 On the concept of a multiperspectivist cultural studies, see Kellner (1995). By this, I mean cultural studies that analyze the circuits of production, textuality, and reception, deploying a dialectic of text and context to provide critical readings of media texts and that use the texts to illuminate the contemporary era. A multiperspectivist approach also deploys a multiplicity of theories and methods of interpretation to provide more many-sided readings and critiques.

2 Commodity spectacle

McDonald's as global culture

McDonald's fast-food company has emerged as a major icon of global capitalism and Americanization, as well as a highly contested symbol of all that many detest about Americanized corporate globalization. McDonald's is undoubtedly a corporation of tremendous magnitude, with outlets in over 30,000 sites in 121 countries, serving over 35 million customers a day and earning profits of over $2 billion annually. It is a sociological phenomenon of utmost significance that exemplifies the processes of modernization, rationalization, efficiency, and cultural homogeneity throughout the globe. It is also an important form of cultural pedagogy that educates people into standardized fast-food consumption and ideological conformity. McDonald's is thus a cultural ambassador for Americanization and global capitalism, promoting the commodity spectacle and its consumer culture throughout the world.

In this chapter, I read McDonald's as a commodity spectacle incorporating cultural hegemony and resistance, dynamics of the global and the local, a mode of fast-food production and consumption, and a form of cultural pedagogy and ideological hegemony. McDonald's is at once a global economic, social, political, and cultural phenomenon that circulates spectacles of Western modernization and Americanization as it traverses the boundaries between the modern and the postmodern, combining modern forms of production and consumption with postmodern ones. It is increasingly resisted and presents a spectacle of political contestation and opposition to globalization, as well as projecting an icon of global mass culture. My study will draw on the resources of cultural studies, critical social theory, and a vast array of empirical studies to capture the multidimensionality and significance of the McDonald's spectacle, using it to provide a diagnostic critique of global capitalism and commodification in the contemporary era.

McDonald's and McDonaldization

Capitalist society presents itself to consumers as a collection of commodities. The commodity spectacle promotes corporate commodity goods and services through a multiplicity of media and sites. McDonald's, for instance, is ubiquitous through its distinctive architecture, its products, its imagery, and its role in individual fantasy lives. McDonald's signs and images circulate through its "golden arches," billboards, movies, TV and print ads and, more recently, the Internet. The McDonald's spectacle plays out when a Midwestern father announces to his family that "we're going to McDonald's tonight" and the kids break out with joy. The spectacle unfolds in Beijing when a couple's only child announces to the family that they will eat out at McDonald's and proceeds to consume a bagful of Big Macs. In Korea, a family celebrates its child's birthday by taking his friends out for a Big Mac party, while a homeless boy in Mexico City spends the money he has begged to buy a McDonald's burger and fries. The spectacle is reproduced any time that someone in the world follows the McDonald's script, thinking that they will get some fast food, good times, and fair value – and then proceeds to McDonald's golden arches to consume its food.

McDonald's success was largely a result of articulation of its product and services with changing social and cultural conditions in the United States and then a global economy that enabled the fast-food industry to thrive and made McDonald's triumph possible. An accelerating car culture following the post-World War II development of a national highway system, the exodus to the suburbs, and the rise of a youth culture all contributed to McDonald's success. Increased mobility, social fragmentation, and a situation in which young people had discretionary income helped generate an inviting environment for fast-food joints in the United States. Young people sought their own spaces and could hang out in hamburger havens.

In turn, mothers were freed from the necessity of cooking meals at home every night, as more and more women worked and as the ethos of the service economy spread from class to class and region to region. McDonald's packaged itself both as a fun place for kids and as a site for family togetherness. Families who might feel guilt in not cooking healthy food for their kids had it assuaged through the pleasure gained by their kids wanting to go to McDonald's to eat and enjoying the experience. And parents could rationalize the activity on the grounds that they were saving money and getting a good deal.

The McDonald's era was sociologically the time of the rise of service industries and mass society and culture. McDonald's came to represent the major trends and values of mass society in the United States in the 1950s, including conformity, uniformity, standardization, efficiency, instrumental rationality, and technology. It was part of a process of social transformation that substituted commodified products and pleasures for traditional goods and practices. Whereas previously people raised and cooked their own food, as advanced industrial societies evolved activities such as food production and consumption were themselves mechanized and rationalized. And whereas food was once a largely regional phenomenon, in a massified society, millions consumed the same modes of fast foods, just as they consumed the same TV programs and read the same magazines.

McDonald emerged, as well, during a time of processed food, in which science, technology, and industry entered into the food production process. Artificial foods appeared with chemicals to promote flavorsome tastes, substances to make the food last longer before spoilage, and additives to accelerate the production process and substitute cheaper processed material for more natural foodstuffs. McDonald's helped acclimatize the consumer nation to an artificial culture and environment, involving individuals in novel culinary practices and products, whereby processed and artificial food replaced traditional fare.

McDonald's thus accompanied the rise of a service economy, the growth of women in the labor market, the modern propensity to let machines or service industries do domesticated labor, and a standardized mass society and culture. These processes allowed families to renounce food production and to go and consume dinners in fast-food emporia. It was a period of transformation of the traditional family in which mothers were not expected to cook dinners from fresh produce every night and members of the family could go out dining alone or in combinations. It was an era of an increased pace of life in which pressures from work and multiple leisure activities cut into long-established activities such as dining, which could be speeded up to correspond with a quickened pace of life and the multiplication of the activities of everyday life.

The rise and expansion of McDonald's also marked an era in which techniques of mass factory production were applied to service industries such as restaurants and food production. McDonald's paved the way for the industrialization and rationalization of a wide number of traditional industries that had been on a smaller scale, traditional, and family owned and run. McDonald's exhibited a wholly rationalized method of food production, with its division of labor and functions, assembly-line organization, and highly disciplined, fragmented, and alienating work environment, exemplifying developments in the capitalist system of labor and its effects on the workers described by Harry Braverman (1974).

In his book *Labor and Monopoly Capitalism*, Braverman describes the fragmentation of the labor process produced by an ever-expanding division of labor, the deskilling and standardization of labor, and the decline of workers' wages and union protection. During the twentieth century, in Braverman's interpretation, work became more homogenized, labor was replaced by machines, and corporations moved their factories to regions in which they could pay lower wages while facing less government regulation, taxation, and union control.

Providing a look at conditions of contemporary labor by examining the various forms of work that go into manufacturing McDonald's products, Eric Schlosser, in *Fast Food Nation* (2001), undertakes a muckraking exposé of McDonald's labor practices and mode of production. His studies range from examination of the growing of crops to feed cattle and other animals slaughtered to make burgers and other foodstuffs, to the alienating, dangerous and unsanitary conditions in animal slaughterhouses, to the production of the artificial substances that go into McDonald's products, to reporting on the deadening working conditions in McDonald's restaurants today. The result is similar to Upton Sinclair's 1906 classic novel *The Jungle,* which explored the horrifying conditions of meat production. McDonald's young restaurant workers are overworked, underpaid, and subjected to incredible stress and discipline. The factory farms that produce potatoes and meat are industrial units that utilize pesticides and other chemicals that are highly polluting. The slaughterhouses and meat production plants are extremely unhygienic, with bones, feces, chemicals, additives, and dangerous pathogens entering into the food, just as in Sinclair's *The Jungle*, while animals face inhumane living conditions and butchering.

In *The McDonaldization of Society,* George Ritzer (1993; 1996) interprets the

McDonald's phenomenon as a process of societal rationalization that serves as a model for what the author calls the "McDonaldization of society." McDonaldization is defined by increased efficiency, calculability, predictability, and control through substitution of technology for human labor power, all of which constitute a quantitative, and to some alarming, growth of instrumental rationalization.[1] Ritzer privileges Max Weber's conception of rationalization to theorize the phenomenon of McDonaldization, which he sees as "coming to dominate more and more sectors of American society as well as of the rest of the world" (1996: 1). Ritzer extends Weber's analysis to a wealth of phenomena, demonstrating that the principles of McDonaldization are restructuring a vast array of fields, ranging from the food, media, education, and healthcare industries, encompassing fundamental life processes from birth to death (ibid.: 161ff.). The strength of the analysis is the light that such focused perspectives shed on general social dynamics and the mapping of the macrostructures of contemporary social organization. The limitation is that the Weberian-inspired analyses often generate a one-sided and limited optic that needs to be supplemented, corrected, and expanded by further critical perspectives.

One might, for instance, deploy a Marx–Weber synthesis to theorize McDonaldization as a combination of instrumental rationalization of production and consumption with a sustained corporate attempt to increase profit through exploiting labor and consumers.[2] Indeed, McDonaldization seems equally to involve commodification and rationalization, to commodify food production and to rationalize its production and consumption to increase profitability. While Ritzer applies the McDonaldization model to production and consumption, he largely emphasizes consumption and thus downplays the ways in which McDonaldization has revolutionized production – despite some references to Taylorism and Fordism (Ritzer 1996: 24–7, *passim*). Likewise, although Ritzer stresses the role of profit in driving McDonaldization (1996: 44, 62f., 87f., *passim*), one could contextualize the phenomenon within the framework of globalization and a restructuring of capitalism, noting how McDonald's at once aims to increase both productivity and profit through rationalization of production and consumption. For, in addition to being a model for societal rationalization processes, McDonaldization is a key component of an expanding global technocapitalism in which world markets are being rationalized and reorganized to maximize capital accumulation.

In this study, I distinguish between "McDonald's" as a fast-food corporation with global reach and "McDonaldization" as a specific mode of economic production and organization that McDonald's introduced and which has had massive influence on other industries, as Ritzer has demonstrated. McDonald's is typically presented as a US corporate success story (Kroc 1977; Love 1986). In his early days of developing McDonald's franchises, its founder, Ray Kroc, reportedly drove around the country to detect where McDonald's might be placed to take advantage of traffic flows and lack of competing restaurants. Later, McDonald's executives flew over the terrain they were searching for investment and applied computer simulation models to calculate where they might best construct a restaurant, according to customer and traffic flows and proximity to local economic development plans and competing restaurants. There are also stories of McDonald's purposely putting competing family restaurants out of business by placing its fast-food emporia adjacent to established businesses vulnerable to loss, much as Starbucks, Borders, and other corporate chains would do later in order to eliminate independent coffee houses and book stores. In this context, McDonald's is part of a project of predatory corporate capital set upon eliminating alternatives and establishing the market dominance and power of corporate models that eliminate independent businesses.

After conquering the United States, McDonald's set out on a process of global conquest. As *The Economist* (June 29, 1996: 61) noted:

> The scale of the global Mac attack is impressive. The company, which has 18,700 McDonald's outlets serving 33m. [million] people every day, will open up to 3,200 new restaurants both this year and next, compared with 2,430 in 1995 and 1,787 in 1994. About two-thirds of them will be outside America. By 2000, predicts James Cantalupo, president of McDonald's International, more than half of all the firm's restaurants will be abroad.

By 1985, some 22 percent of units were located overseas, accounting for $2.2 billion (20 percent of total) sales and 18 percent of operating profit; by 1996 overseas sales had reached $14 billion, constituting 47 percent of total sales and 54 percent of its $2.6 billion operating profit: "Overseas, then, is where burgers have become most bankable" (ibid.). Hence, by 2000 over half of McDonald's sales were to the foreign market, whereas a decade earlier only about one-third of its sales went to non-US sites.

Yet, as a global phenomenon, McDonald's often articulates with local cultures and traditions.[3] Combining mass production and consumption with hybridized cultural forms and processes, it produces a new kind of niche food production and specialization. Moreover, McDonald's embodies a form of cultural pedagogy and promotes a certain form of cultural hegemony that has been strongly contested in recent years, opening up the McDonald's spectacle as a contested terrain. Illuminating this terrain should help us to understand the accelerating role of the commodity spectacle in globalization and the ways in which certain forms of commodification and culture are being resisted. This requires analysis of the contradictions of the McDonald's spectacle and development of a standpoint of critique from which to evaluate McDonald's and McDonaldization and to propose forms of resistance and alternatives to its mode of food production and consumption and cultural hegemony. Accordingly, I develop a multiperspectivist approach to capture the complexity of McDonald's and McDonaldization in order to critically evaluate its multifarious aspects and effects and to present alternatives to McDonald's food, cultural pedagogy, and culinary practices.[4]

Theorizing McDonald's: a multiperspectivist approach

Few artifacts and institutions of the contemporary world are as well known and ubiquitous as McDonald's, with its Big Macs, golden arches, Ronald McDonald, promotional tie-ins with popular films and toys, its charities, saturation advertising, and, more recently, the worldwide protests against it. McDonald's mobilizes advertising campaigns and promotional stunts to create an experience of fun, of family togetherness, and of Americanization itself, which is associated with the McDonald's experience. Thus, when one bites into a Big Mac one is consuming the sign values of good times, communal experience, consumer value and efficiency, as well as the (dubious) pleasures of the product. The McDonald's spectacle is not just the selling and consuming of fast food, but it is a family adventure of eating out together, intergenerational bonding, and a communal experience, as its advertising campaigns reiterate in various ways. Purchasing and ingesting a specific food product is only one part of this experience, which includes the consumption of sign values, such as inexpensive food, a family outing, Americana, or modernity (see Goldman 1992: 85ff.; Kincheloe 1997: 249ff.; 2002; Watson *et al*. 1997).

Although on the global scale McDonald's signifies a mode of homogenization, massification, and standardization, reducing the McDonald's spectacle to this dimension neglects the variety and diversity of consumer practices in different regions and parts of the world and the various uses to which consumers can put McDonald's, using its products and practices to serve their own needs. British cultural studies have stressed the importance of analyzing the ways in which audiences or consumers create their own meaningful experiences. The McDonald's fast-food chains generate a variety of specific pleasures, meanings, and effects that a microanalysis of particular forms and experiences of McDonald's can interrogate. As I suggest below, people in diverse countries no doubt experience both McDonald's and McDonaldization in a variety of ways, and there are wide-ranging gender, race, class, and regional variations in the consumption of fast food and responses to societal rationalization. Hence, there are subjective aspects of the McDonald's spectacle and a diversity of ways in which various individuals and groups deploy McDonald's to serve their own needs and interests.[5]

McDonald's between the global and the local

As McDonald's becomes a global phenomenon, it teaches non-Western and non-US audiences new forms of producing and consuming food, while initiating some cultures into modernization and modernity itself. Studies of the introduction of McDonald's into Asia, for instance, stress how McDonald's teaches consumers to queue up and wait in line and enter rationalized processes of food consumption. It provides an experience of cultural otherness that enables non-Westerners to participate in the ethos of Western modernity. It teaches non-Western workers speed and efficiency, as well as food hygiene and customer service (see Watson *et al*. 1997). It is thus part and parcel of the process of globalization that is producing novel forms of culture, social practices, and ways of life.

McDonaldization is thus a cultural pedagogy and an ideology as well as a set of social practices. It is a cultural construct with its own myths, semiotic codes, discourses, and set of transformative practices. Domestically, in the United States, McDonald's promotes an ideology of the nation as a melting pot in which all citizens participate equally in its democratic pleasures, regardless of race, class, gender, and age. It furnishes a model of the United States as a land of consumer innovation and technical rationality, which produces inexpensive and desirable goods for all, serving its customer's needs and providing a product perceived to be a good deal. McDonald's associates itself with traditions such as the family, national holidays, patriotism, Christian charity, and the icons of media culture such as Coke and Disney. Going to McDonald's, for denizens of the United States, is thus joining US consumer society, participating in the national culture, and validating common values.

In a globalized world, the McDonald's spectacle will have diverse meanings and effects in assorted cultures. For global citizens, McDonald's represents the charisma of the golden arches, Ronald McDonald and McDonaldland, the tie-ins and promotions, and the ubiquitous advertising, aimed at a variety of genders, races, classes, and national subject-positions, which attempt to incorporate more and more cultures and sets of consumers into its McWorld.[6] Upping the theoretical ante on Ritzer, Benjamin Barber has depicted the rise of McWorld (Barber 1996), based on universalizing markets, and constructing a homogenized set of social practices, cultural forms, and products that McDonald's exemplifies. For Barber, antagonistic forces of jihad oppose McWorld, with both subversive of democracy and liberal values.

But McDonald's functions in a complex way in a global McWorld, both transmitting forms of US-centric cultural imperialism and circulating novel and alternative forms that produce cultural hybridity and novelty in non-Western cultures. Several critics have noted how McDonald's molds its products, architecture, and atmosphere to local conditions, and generates a multiplicity of experiences, social functions, and significance in diverse local conditions. Studies collected in James Watson's edited text *Golden Arches East: McDonald's in East Asia* (1997), for example, provide ethnographic studies of the ways in which McDonald's is experienced by customers in China, Taiwan, Japan, Hong Kong, and other East Asian sites. Watson points out in a later study how young people regularly hang out in McDonald's in Taiwan after school and during the evening, while older people inhabit the site during the day (Watson 2000).

I experienced the varied dynamics of McDonald's spatiality and cultural scene myself one night in Taichung, Taiwan, during the mid-1990s, as I sought a restroom in the middle of the city. While wandering through the site of the local McDonald's – a three-story building within a densely populated urban region – I noticed that the place was packed with students studying, young people talking, and couples courting. My host said that, in a crowded city, McDonald's was a good place for study and socializing, and the Taichung inhabitants were taking advantage of this. Obviously, the social purposes and functions were quite different in Taiwan than in the US, which neither encourages nor, in some cases, even allows hanging out and using the site as a study den, or courtship space. The point is that McDonald's, or any global artifact, has diverse meanings, functions, and consequences in various regions and parts of the world. Thus, a concrete analysis should interrogate the local conditions in which consumers provide their own narratives of their site-specific and particular experiences to capture the variety and diversity of the McDonald's effect.

My Taiwanese host told me that it was especially young children who sought the McDonald's eating experience, demanding of their parents to take them to McDonald's for special treats or celebrations. Watson (1997) notes how, in China, McDonald's introduced the practice of holding children's birthday parties in its restaurants. Yunxiang Yan points out how McDonald's in Beijing gave the Chinese the experience of participating in cosmopolitan modernity, being part of the Western world, seeing and experiencing new modes of food production and consumption, and being seen as part of modern life. McDonald's popularity, he concludes, indicates that "consumers are interested in the spectacle, the show, that this new form of eating permits" (Yan in Watson 1997: 48).

Thus, for people in non-Western societies, the McDonald's spectacle signifies Western modernity and offers alternatives to their traditional culture in terms of cuisine and social experience. Yet, no doubt it is also advertising and promotion that helps produce these meanings, providing a phantasmagoric consumer experience for the denizens of the many corners of the globe who consume Western modernity when they ingest a Big Mac. Moreover, McDonald's adapts to local cultures and cuisines, serving noodle dishes in Asian countries along with the Big Macs, and allows regional owners to vary the menu according to local tastes. In Watson's summary, variations on the original Americanized menu included: "Chilled yogurt drinks (*ayran*) in Turkey, espresso and cold pasta in Italy, teriyaki burgers in Japan (also in Taiwan and Hong Kong), vegetarian burgers in the Netherlands, McSpaghetti in the Philippines, McLaks (grilled salmon sandwiches) in Norway, frankfurters and beer in Germany, McHuevo (poached egg hamburger) in Uruguay" (Watson 1997: 24).

So, while on one level McDonald's helps to standardize and homogenize a global consumer culture, on another level it brings variety, diversity, and novelty to many parts of the world, thus contributing to the creation of a hybridized postmodern global popular culture. Consequently, Ritzer's privileging of the category of rationalization in characterizing McDonald's practices and effects is too objectivistic and fails to articulate the subjective and cultural complex of the McDonald's spectacle, while Barber's notion of McWorld also overly generalizes. Further, I would argue that Weber's metaphor of the "iron cage" which Ritzer priviledged is not the best way to interrogate the McDonald's phenomenon. In the case of McDonald's – and many other fast-food emporia, sites of mass entertainment and consumption, and media culture – perhaps something like "the plastic fun house" is more appropriate. Whereas societal rationalization accurately describes aspects of the socioeconomic roots of McDonaldization, there is a more hedonistic and fun-oriented cultural side that metaphors of a "cage" do not adequately capture.

It is, for example, unlikely that many McDonald's customers see themselves as trapped in a cage, although no doubt scores of its workers feel enclosed and encaged in their constrictive labor conditions, as evidenced by their especially high turnover rates (see below). On the cultural side, McDonaldization hides the conditions of rationalization with a colorful environment, often decorated with images from current films and icons of popular entertainment, to provide a funhouse experience and to entertain the customers as well as to fill their stomachs. Beneath the glitzy and kitschy appearance, to be sure, inexorable conditions of rationalization (and attempts to maximize profits) work behind the backs of the customers, masked by the façade of the promised experience of McDonald's restaurants as providing fun and pleasurable eating for a fast-paced consumer society.

McDonald's between the modern and the postmodern

On the one hand, McDonald's and McDonaldization are symptomatic examples of rationalization, homogenization, standardization, and mass production and consumption that many equate with modernity itself. Clearly, the rationalization or industrialization of food production constitutes a break with traditional life.[7] As theorists of modernity have argued, increased rationalization of everyday life involves ruptures with tradition and the substitution of new "modern" forms, thus creating tensions between the modern and the premodern.

Yet, from another perspective, the globalization of McDonald's throughout the world, the cultural forms and semiotics that promote it, and the way that it is experienced and lived by many people suggest that McDonald's also exemplifies a postmodern logic. As a mode of global production, McDonald's is coming to exemplify postFordism, hybridized forms of culture and identities, and a new realm of simulation and hyperreality that supersedes "the real" and the modern.[8] Postmodern theorists such as Baudrillard (1983a–c; 1993) and Kroker and Cook (1986) claim that we are now leaving modernity behind for a new postmodernity. Various thinkers claim, as I note below, that McDonald's embodies new postmodern forms, conditions, and experiences.

Against extreme binary either/or positions which would hold that we are still within modernity or have entered a new postmodernity and left modernity behind, I would argue that we are currently between the modern and the postmodern, in a liminal space between two cultural and social paradigms (Kellner 1995; Best and Kellner 1997; 2001). Further, I will show that there are identifiable features of both the modern and the postmodern involved in the McDonald's spectacle. In particular, McDonaldization as a rationalization of production and consumption is clearly modern in inspiration and form, whereas the proliferation of sign values in the McDonald's experience, through advertising and publicity stunts, has postmodern ramifications, as its consumers enter a quasi-mythical hyperreal world of Americana, family fun, and good times.[9]

The concept of "hyperreality" developed by Umberto Eco (1986) and Jean Baudrillard (1983a; 1983b; 1983c) signifies a world that is realer-than-real, as when Disneyland presents a model vision of Americana, more American (and white middle class) than a complex social reality could ever be. McDonald's ads project this hyperreal United States (or modernity for its global consumers), and its architecture attempts to set its space off in a world of golden arches in which one can retreat from the real and consume mythologized food and cultural space.

The McDonald's spectacle thus represents a postmodern hyperreal experience that carries customers into a model and fun house of present-day life. Moreover, a globalized McDonald's represents postFordism and postmodern cultural hybridization. Modern corporations, like McDonald's in the United States during its now classic period from the 1950s into the 1990s, were highly centralized and top-down and hierarchical in their corporate structure. The modern corporation engaged in mass production and consumption, marked by standardization and homogeneity in a mode now described as Fordism.[10] Today, however, a globalized McDonald's is less centralized, more local in orientation, and more diverse in its cultural practices, thus exemplifying what Harvey (1989) and others have described as "postFordism." In its global expansion, McDonald's attempts to rely on local food suppliers, local managers and workers, and local cultural and architectural forms, while at the same time promoting standard McDonald's products such as Big Macs, shakes, and fries *and* introducing phenomena such as McDonald's birthday parties to the Chinese.

Joe Kincheloe (2002: 190ff.) argues that the shift in the corporate hierarchy and structure of McDonald's is evident in the ascendancy of Jack Greenberg as CEO in 1997. In Kincheloe's analysis, new McDonald's products such as the Arch Deluxe and the Fish Fillet Deluxe were pitched to more upscale consumers, while the Lean Deluxe was offered to more weight- and diet-conscious consumers, representing diversification and appeal to niche markets. Moreover, Jack Greenberg represented a move to more postmodern corporate practices:

> Where [Ray] Kroc [McDonald's founder and first CEO] said, "Keep it simple, stupid" … Greenberg pushes innovation to the point of complexity. Literally before he was officially appointed CEO, Greenberg was already pushing the development of eight new products to the top of the corporation's priority list. Viewing his mission as the *reinvention of McDonald's*, Greenberg has promoted the Big Xtra (a whopper-like burger with lettuce and tomato), Chicken Selects (fried slices of chicken breast more reminiscent of real chicken than the 'fused' McNuggets), a selection of breakfast bagel sandwiches, the McFlurry (a soft ice cream and topping concoction), the Lobster Sandwich, the Western Breakfast Omelet, the Mexican Burger (garnished with salsa and Mexican cheese) and other innovative products. As in other postFordist multinationals, Greenberg plans to learn and borrow innovations from the firm's international division. Understanding the benefits of management decentralization as demonstrated by the success of the fast-growing international division, Greenberg is working to apply such strategies in U.S. operations … In this context the notion of McDonald's exerting a homogenizing effect on the world becomes even more remote. The hegemony of the twenty-first century is even more locally informed and decentralized than what occurred in the last few decades of the twentieth century.
>
> (ibid.: 208–9)

While Kincheloe nicely describes shifts to a more postmodern ideology and corporate practices, I would argue that McDonald's continues to be articulated with modern modes of production and consumption as well. Increasingly, the McDonald's commodity spectacle is articulated with myriad forms of global capital and reproduces itself through a variety of sites and media. Although in the 1950s Disney refused to enter into a strategic alliance with McDonald's, by the 1990s the two were tightly intertwined, with Disney featuring McDonald's at its theme parks and McDonald's giving away toys that promoted Disney films. McDonald's was also allied with Coca Cola, another major symbol of US McCulture, and engaged in tie-in promotions with these global giants, producing synergy between the McDonald's spectacle and the spectacle of Disney and Coke.

McDonald's thus articulates its cultural hegemony with Disney, Coca Cola, athletic events, and spectacles such as the 2002 Winter Olympics, which prominently displayed Ronald McDonald, ads for its products, and corporate sponsorship of the games. Hence, whereas initially McDonald's was pre-eminently an expression of modernity in its mass production and consumption of food, it crossed the postmodern divide through its phantasmagoric advertising and commodity spectacle, drawing its customers into a world of simulation, hyperreality, and the implosion of boundaries, especially as it became globalized and part of the postmodern hybridization that synthesizes the signs and products of modernity with local traditions and culture.

In its global attempts to articulate McDonald's with local forms of various cultures, the corporation calls Ronald McDonald "Uncle" in China and also has an "Aunt" figure, drawing on Chinese respect for elders and relatives. In Japan, where the "r" sound is rarely pronounced, Ronald McDonald is known as Donald McDonald. And in France, a 2001 campaign drew on the popular figure of Asterix, a figure of resistance to the Roman empire, in ad campaigns and displays. (Who said that the French have no sense of humor?!)

Consequently, it is a mistake to insist that McDonaldization is primarily an expression either of modernity or of postmodernity, for it is arguably both. Indeed, McDonald's and McDonaldization not only relate to Weber's analysis of rationalization and Marx's theory of commodification, but also articulate with postmodern conceptions such as hyperreality, simulation, postFordist globalization, and the hybridization of identity, all of which can usefully be deployed to interpret the McDonald's spectacle.

As noted, the McDonald's consumer, especially in the non-Western world, enters a hyperreal domain of Americanized food production and consumption, partaking of a cultural experience as well as cuisine. For Baudrillard (1983a; 1993), the hyperreal also describes the model body, as projected in fashion images and the entertainment industry, or the model home, as described by magazines or projected in media images. McDonald's products thus constitute a technological model of fast-food production and consumption reconstituting food itself, using food technologies to produce synthetic substances, tastes, and materials, and anticipating the artificial technofoods of the future. Further, the McDonald's model of fast-food consumption replaces the traditional model of home-prepared food with commodified food. The fast-food model, then, becomes a new norm for food production, replicated through frozen and prepared food and the spin-off of countless other chains of fast-food restaurant businesses and synthetic food production.

Interpreted from a Baudrillardian postmodern perspective, McDonald's cuisine can also be seen as a simulation of food, since its artificial products, tastes, and pleasures simulate such familiar items as burgers, fries, and shakes. The foodstuffs themselves are heavily dependent on chemical additives and artificial substances for their flavor, texture, and materiality, and can thus serve as examples of artificially produced cuisine. McDonald's food is a processed product for an artificial and processed world.

Consequently, McDonald's provides a new model of what food and eating are, mediated by its food technologies and organization of food production and consumption. As suggested earlier, McDonald's customers are also made to feel that they are especially virtuous and smart to take their family or to treat themselves or their friends to a fast, inexpensive, and ready-made meal. And the advertising and promotion enables the McDonald's customer to participate in the hyperreal ideologies of Americana, family togetherness, and social bonding. McDonald's also implodes boundaries between tradition and the contemporary, coding its ads with traditional images of Americana and family ideology, as it undermines family eating practices and redefines diet and culinary value, familial togetherness, and communal experience.

As we will see in the next section, McDonald's fortunes have ebbed, but it is still an icon of an Americanized global commodity spectacle. Yet, in stressing the post-modern aspects of McDonald's and McDonaldization, I do not want to downplay or cover over the modern aspects such as standardization and homogenization of production and consumption, forms that are often highly dehumanizing and degrad-ing to workers and consumers. The McDonald's spectacle thus encompasses, in my analysis, both the forces of instrumental rationality and efficiency *and* a postmodern realm of hyperreality, simulation, hybridity, and global postFordism. Consequently, it requires a multiperspectivist social theory to provide a more contextual and multidimensional paradigm for analyzing the multiplicity of economic, sociopoliti-cal, and cultural aspects of the McDonald's spectacle. This requires mobilizing the resources of both modern and postmodern theory, as well as the tools of cultural studies and a critical ethnography, to theorize the full range of the phenomenon of the global hybridization of McDonaldization, its cultural and ideological construction, and its complex effects. The McDonald's spectacle is a many-sided phenomenon, and the more perspectives that one can bring to its analysis and critique, the better the grasp of the phenomenon that one will have, and the better one will be able to develop alternative readings and generate oppositional practices.

Criticizing/resisting the McDonald's spectacle

Detractors of McDonald's have tended to make arguments similar to those of the Frankfurt School critique of mass society, which attack homogenization, standard-ization, commodification, and instrumental rationality for precipitating a decline of individuality, freedom, and, in Habermas's terminology, a colonization of the life-world by the social system.[11] These critical perspectives on modernity and rationalization articulate people's fears of increased conformity, loss of freedom and diversity, and domination by external societal forces bound up with the evolution of modern societies. McDonald's encapsulates, in a provocative way, these concerns and thus itself can serve as a target for those discontented with modernity and its problematical aspects.

George Ritzer's study of McDonaldization raises the question of from what standpoint one can offer a critique of a popular phenomenon such as McDonald's and how one can justify one's critique without falling prey to charges of elitism. Ritzer is to be commended for taking on a popular part of US and now global culture, such as McDonald's, and generating a critical discussion. Ritzer's critics often accuse him of elitism (Parker 1998; Rinehart 1998; Taylor *et al.* 1998), but his critics themselves often fall prey to an uncritical populism (Watson *et al.* 1997; Parker 1998; Taylor *et al.* 1998). The also often fail to offer adequate critical perspectives, or to articulate how one resists fast-food restaurants or social processes such as McDonaldization.

Many of the opponents of McDonald's critique thus produce apologies and a celebration of mass culture and consumption. Such uncritical optics replicate a position, increasingly widespread in cultural studies, that puts all the weight of production of meaning and practice on the side of the subject, thus effectively erasing the problems of domination, manipulation, and oppression from critical social theory (see the critique of this position in Kellner 1995). Promoting the primacy of the subject promotes, however, a naive subjectivity that fails to appreciate that the "subject" itself is not "natural," but is, at least partly, socially constructed. The uncritical populist cultural studies also exaggerates the importance of consumption over production. Cultural populism tends to put a positive gloss on McDonald's, media culture, or consumerism in general, in which moments of resistance and the construction of meaning are highlighted, as if these phenomena merely furnished resources to empower individuals and to resist dominant meanings or practices.

In general, it is a mistake to be overly subjective and one-sided in relation to complex phenomena such as McDonald's and McDonaldization, or, for that matter, such things as media culture, consumerism, or the consumer society itself. Contemporary positions are often skewed into partial optics that primarily celebrate or denigrate the phenomenon under scrutiny, rather than providing a more contextual and dialectical approach that evaluates specific phenomena, articulates negative and/or positive dimensions, and then makes nuanced judgments. Perhaps McDonald's critics do not adequately appreciate or valorize the positive features of McDonaldization, but often McDonald's apologists do not acknowledge the negative side, and are all too eager to defend mass culture, consumption, or McDonaldization against criticism.[12]

To begin critical interrogation of the McDonald's spectacle, we need to distinguish between evaluating McDonald's as a fast-food corporation and the broader sociological phenomenon of McDonaldization. Failure to make this distinction often skews normative judgments and evaluations of the two phenomena. In other words, one should differentiate between specific aspects of the McDonald's spectacle, such as the McDonald's corporation and its food, and the more general societal dynamics associated with rationalization and the application of instrumental rationality to social phenomena, relations, and institutions, which Ritzer has labeled McDonaldization.

Interestingly, McDonald's seemed beyond criticism in the popular media until the 1990s. It was taken as a US, and then global, corporate success story and managed to get incredibly positive media coverage, perhaps in part because of effective public relations campaigns, but probably also because of its multimillion-dollar advertising budget. In addition, McDonald's, like Disney, was highly litigious and would send threatening lawyer's letters to media that criticized them, or to anyone who allegedly infringed their copyrighted images, making satire or criticism potentially expensive.[13]

Consequently, from its founding in the 1950s into the 1990s, positive images of McDonald's radiated through the society of the spectacle. On the whole, the media tended to present largely favorable representations of a corporation that contributed so much to its advertising budgets, as well as to charities. It seemed as if every time a new McDonald's opened there would be positive coverage, especially when it penetrated markets in Russia, China, and other parts of the former communist bloc. McDonald's quickly became a global success story as well as a US business legend, and the popular and business press was full of its praises.

Suddenly, however, McDonald's became the target of choice in protests against globalization and the poster child for what was wrong with Americanized and globalized consumer culture. The worldwide protests began getting global media attention when McDonald's sued members of the London branch of Greenpeace in 1990 on libel charges for distributing a pamphlet entitled "What's wrong with McDonald's?" The libel trial began in 1994 and became the longest and most publicized trial in UK history. A website emerged in the mid-1990s, which is still up and running, that contained anti-McDonald's material, distributing to a global audience a fantastic amount of critical material (see www.mcspotlight.com). Thereafter, it seemed that every anti-globalization demonstration featured the trashing of a local McDonald's and a wide range of groups began protesting and organizing against McDonald's, making it one of the most contested corporations and media spectacles of the present moment. In the following discussion, I will lay out the Greenpeace and other anti-McDonald's critique, with which I largely agree, and will then suggest that the phenomenon of McDonaldization with which Ritzer engages is more complex and requires dialectical analysis of its costs and benefits. But, first, let us examine some critiques of the McDonald's corporation.

The case against McDonald's

I want to mobilize a variety of perspectives in this section to criticize the McDonald's corporation and its products. This process is facilitated by the existence of a well-documented book by award-winning *Guardian* reporter John Vidal (1997) on the libel trial pitting McDonald's against two British activists, as well as an extremely impressive website that furnishes a vast amount of information about McDonald's and offers ample material for a substantive critique.[14] The McSpotlight site was developed by the supporters of two British activists, Helen Steel and Dave Morris, who were sued by McDonald's for distributing leaflets denouncing the corporation's low wages, false advertising to children, involvement in deforestation, harvesting of animals, and promotion of junk food and an unhealthy diet. The activists counter-attacked and, with help from supporters, organized a McLibel campaign, produced the McSpotlight website, and assembled expert witnesses to testify and confirm their criticisms. The three-year civil trial, the United Kingdom's longest ever, ended ambiguously on June 19, 1997, with Justice Rodger Bell, the judge in the McLibel case, defending some of McDonald's claims against the activists while substantiating some of the activists criticisms (Vidal 1997: 299–315).

The legal spectacle created unprecedented bad publicity for McDonald's, and material critical of the corporation was circulated throughout the world via Internet websites, mailing lists, and discussion groups. The McLibel/McSpotlight group claims that its website was accessed over 15 million times during the trial and was visited over two million times in the month of the verdict alone (ibid.: 326).[15] Building on material assembled in the libel trial, one can construct a very strong case against McDonald's. To begin, from a nutritional point of view, as Ritzer notes (1996: 126ff. and 179f.), McDonald's food is overly saturated with salt, sugar, and fats, rendering it high in cholesterol and dubious in nutritional content. It is standardized and homogenized fare, providing predictably bland and artificial tastes. As Joel Kovel remarks, the label "junk food" is perfectly appropriate:

> [I]n the light of the fact that nutritional experts almost universally agree that the kind of food sold by McDonald's is bad for you. With 28 grams fat, 12.6 of which is saturated, in a Big Mac, and another 22 grams in an order of french fries, along with fifty-two additives being used in its various food products, it is scarcely surprising that an internal company memorandum would state: "[W]e can't really address or defend nutrition. We don't sell nutrition and people don't come to McDonald's for nutrition." When the company's cancer expert, Dr Sydney Arnott, was asked his opinion of the statement that "a diet high in fat, sugar, animal products and salt and low in fibre, vitamins and minerals is linked with cancer of the breast and bowel and heart disease," he replied: "If it is being directed to the public then I would say it is a very reasonable thing to say."
>
> Kovel (1997: 28)

Although the McDonald's corporation defends its products as forming part of an overall "balanced diet," Professor Michael Crawford, a consultant to the World Health Organization, testified at a public hearing: "Not only are McDonald's encouraging the use of a style of food which is closely associated with risk of cancer and heart disease, whilst health professionals are trying to reduce the risks to Western populations, but they are actively promoting it in the same cultures where at present these diseases are not a problem" (McLibel Support Campaign 1994). In addition, in relation to the challenge of more health-conscious parents seeking better diets for their children, McDonald's is now heavily targeting advertising at children. They aggressively use tie-ins with popular films and pop culture artifacts, their Ronald McDonald clowns, and saturation advertising aimed at children in order to attract younger customers, who presumably will persuade their parents to take them to eat at McDonald's. Justice Bell, however, ruled in the McLibel trial, that McDonald's advertising practice "exploits children by using them, as more susceptible subjects of advertising, to pressurize their parents into going to McDonald's" and that advertising that "pretended to a positive nutritional benefit … did not match" (Vidal 1997: 306–7).

The consequences of McDonald's' targeting of children to eat its food were made clear in a 2001 *Frontline* documentary entitled "Fat." It pointed out that one in four American children suffers from obesity and that the amount of obesity in children is growing throughout the world. It also claimed that one in ten children in Beijing now suffers from obesity and that the alarming rise in weight in Chinese children can, in part, be correlated with the dramatic spread of McDonald's in China and the propensity of parents to please their "Little Princes," as single offspring are referred to in China. The Little Princes respond to advertising and demand to go to McDonald's, and soon become Little Blimps. A segment showing grotesquely overweight Chinese boys in exercise class dramatically made the point.[16]

There are also dangers from the *E. coli* bacterium and other health problems associated with McDonald's and other fast food. In 1982, dozens of children fell sick after eating hamburgers contaminated with *E. coli* at McDonald's in Oregon and Michigan, and there was a rash of other health scares.[17] These problems include outbreaks of mad cow disease (Creutzfeldt–Jakob disease or CJD) in the United Kingdom in 1996 and 2001, discovery of dioxin-polluted chicken in Belgium in 1999, an outbreak of mad cow disease in a slaughterhouse in Italy that supplies McDonald's in 2001, and eruption of *E. coli* food poisoning in the United States in summer 2002. These events caused a precipitous decline in McDonald's profits in the new millennium and imperiled its future.

Moreover, reading Schlosser's (2001) account of the unsanitary conditions in the slaughterhouses and meat-packing premises that produce McDonald's raw materials should give one pause for thought before one ingests a McDonald's burger. Such health concerns are responsible, in large part, for the decline of McDonald's sales globally, especially in regions with growing health consciousness. McDonald's Big Worry, in fact, is the long-term viability of its hamburger-based cuisine. As more and more individuals become health conscious and as protests against McDonald's food grow in intensity and scope, the age of the burger may be coming to an end and future generations may be astonished that such mediocre fare as McDonald's assumed the status of the globally popular in the twentieth century.

Further, from the perspective of culinary taste, one could argue that McDonald's cuisine is regressive, even in terms of hamburgers and fast food. I remember going to my first drive-in burger stand in Virginia in the 1950s and discovering the pleasures of a juicy cheeseburger with all the trimmings, a thick milk shake, and crunchy french fries. I remember the introduction of McDonald's from this same era and how bland and boring its fare was in comparison with the rich and succulent burgers and shakes from the local hamburger joint. From my current perspective of concern with health and nutrition, I would not eat any fatty burger without guilt, but I would argue that even within the range of possible burgers McDonald's is among the most mediocre. And from the perspective of choosing from the possible range of health and gourmet foods open to us, I would say that from the standpoints of culinary taste and nutrition, McDonald's offers an obviously inferior option.

Ritzer uses Weber's theory of rationalization and argues that, even from the standpoint of economic rationality, McDonald's does not provide the value that it promises. He suggests that there is a tremendous mark-up for profit in the fries, drinks, burgers and other products sold (1996: 60f.). Its multibillion-dollar profit margin every year would suggest that consumers are not getting good value from the product but are enriching the corporation at their expense. This argument is convincing, and McDonald's decline in sales after 1996–97 may be due in part to consumers recognizing that they were being ripped off, that McDonald's did not give good food value. Subsequent efforts to offer new products, such as the Arch Deluxe, the Fish Fillet Deluxe, and the Lean Deluxe, flopped and, as its market share and profits continue to decline, McDonald's has not offered any really new and innovative successful products in years.[18]

In addition, the McDonald's experience in eating is an example of assembly-line consumption that is hardly conducive to conversation and social interaction, and is thus rarely a good-quality family social experience or communal eating experience. The McDonald's goal is to guarantee a ten-minute eating experience (Love 1986), and the production and consumption operation is geared to getting customers in and out of the restaurant as quickly as possible, with some McDonald's franchises telling customers to leave as soon as they finish their meal. As a reflection of the corporation, McDonald's ads, which celebrate traditional and family values, as well as good economic value, are highly misleading, and as Ritzer points out, its practices often contradict the imperatives of value, efficiency, and wholesomeness that its ads and corporate propaganda proclaim (1996: 121ff.).

From the standpoint of the production and consumption of food, McDonaldization articulates the tendencies toward conformity and massification noted by social theorists of the 1950s. The whole McDonald's experience forces one into the mold of preformed sameness and homogenization; one orders from a small range of choices and one must fit one's taste to the corporate experience. Whereas standard multipage menus address consumers as individual subjects, with their own complex likes and tastes, and allow them privately to contemplate the range of choices, the McDonald's marquee illustrates the product in a public space, fitting the individual into the slot of homogenized consumer subject. McDonaldization in this sense is essentially a phenomenon of rationalized modernization, part and parcel of the mass society, with its frenzied pace and standardized consumption and production.

However, McDonald's homogenization of food consumption has gone so far that it appears now as a caricature, a joke, the ultimate in kitschness and junk food. From a postmodern perspective that valorizes difference, otherness, and variety, McDonald's is the paradigm of mass homogeneity, sameness, and standardization, which erases individuality, specificity, and difference. In this sense, McDonald's is profoundly out of synch with the postmodern turn and, if it survives, it is because of the weight of nostalgia, tradition, and habit that will drive those former consumers back to the site of earlier pleasant memories. McDonald's ads indeed stress the continuity, stability, and tradition guaranteed by the corporation. One ad pictures a man returning to his town after many years away and finding that everything has changed, that much has disappeared, except for the good, old McDonald's, still serving the same fare in the same place after all these years.[19]

Curiously enough, those who defend McDonald's, who are still attached to it, are nostalgic for those very institutions of modernity that destroyed tradition. Indeed, the paradox of McDonald's longevity is that an institution that undermined tradition (i.e. home cooking, individualized family restaurants, a balanced and healthy diet) has itself become a tradition that accrues nostalgia and the aura of Americana – in part the result of McDonald's advertising campaigns. Yet nostalgia for McDonald's, and continuing loyalty to its product and institution, is, to a degree, the result of its longevity. For McDonald's by now has accumulated billions of consumers who can return to the site of pleasant remembrances of when one was younger.

Architecturally, the McDonald's environment is a sterile and dehumanizing site of standardized and banalized design and structure, signifying sameness, corporate homogeneity, and artificial, standardized space. As for its workers and conditions of labor, the McDonald's production mechanism is a conspicuous example of high-pressure, repetitive, and poorly paid labor, offering "minimum wage from cradle to grave" and generating extremely high turnover rates. Ray Kroc's sexism was legendary. For the first 10 years, Kroc resisted hiring women executives, even choosing to have male secretaries, and McDonald's management was reportedly blind to gender issues such as sexual harassment well into the 1980s (Kincheloe 2002: 96–7). McDonald's is also notorious for resisting unionization and firing workers who try to create a union. In the UK McLibel trial, Justice Bell ruled that McDonald's wages were extremely low and that many of its labor practices were unacceptable (see Vidal 1997: 213–35 and 309–10). Moreover, as the Workers' Solidarity Network reported, McDonald's is especially rapacious in exploiting labor in developing countries:

Seventeen year old women are forced to work 9 to 10 hours a day, seven days a week, earning as little as six cents an hour in the Keyhinge factory in Vietnam making the popular giveaway promotional toys, many of which are Disney characters, for McDonald's Happy Meals.[20]

After working a 70 hour week, some of the teenage women take home a salary of only $4.20! In February, 200 workers fell ill, 25 collapsed and three were hospitalized as a result of chemical exposure.

Included in the Happy Meals sold at McDonald's are small toys based on characters from Disney films. According to McDonald's senior vice-president Brad Ball, the Happy Meals characters from the "101 Dalmatians" movie were the most successful in McDonald's history.

Ball adds, "As we embark on our new global alliance, we anticipate ten great years of unbeatable family fun as customers enjoy 'the magic of Disney' only at McDonald's." (PR Newswire Associates, March 19, 1997)

Located in Da Nang City, Vietnam, the Keyhinge Toys Co. factory employs approximately 1,000 people. Ninety percent of them are young women 17 to 20 years old. Overtime is mandatory: shifts of 9 to 10 hours a day, seven days a week. Wage rates average between six cents and eight cents an hour – well below subsistence levels.

Overcome by fatigue and poor ventilation in late February, 200 women fell ill, 25 collapsed and three were hospitalized as a result of exposure to acetone. Acute or prolonged exposure to acetone, a chemical solvent, can cause dizziness, unconsciousness, damage to the liver and kidneys and chronic eye, nose, throat, and skin irritation.

All appeals from local human and labour rights groups continue to be rejected by Keyhinge management, which refuses to improve the ventilation system in the factory or remedy other unsafe working conditions.

Along with demanding forced overtime, Keyhinge management has not made legally required payments for health insurance coverage for its employees, who now receive no compensation for injury or sickness.

Many of the young women at the Keyhinge factory making McDonald's/ Disney toys earn just 60 cents after a 10 hour shift. The most basic meal in Vietnam – rice, vegetables, and tofu – costs 70 cents. Three meals would cost $2.10. Wages do not even cover 20 per cent of the daily food and travel costs for a single worker, let alone her family.

(flag.blackened.net/revolt/ws/ws51_vietnam.html)

Although McDonald's and Disney got a lot of bad publicity from the exposure of their Vietnam sweatshops, they continued using child labor in sweatshop conditions to produce toys for their outlets. Hence, in September 2000, McDonald's was accused of employing underage Chinese workers in sweatshops to make Snoopy, Winnie the Pooh, and Hello Kitty toys found in McDonald's Happy Meals. According to *Ad Age Global* (October 1, 2000: 25), "children as young as 14 worked 16 hours a day for 18 cents an hour, well below the minimum wage and the minimum employment age of 16." Hong Kong activists accordingly picketed local McDonald's, calling for boycotts, while halfway across the world protestors in Prague at an IMF/World Bank meeting protested against the corporation's labor practices and attacked McDonald's franchises.

Interestingly, McDonald's is using its toy promotions as a weapon to overcome what is perceived as a "gender gap." According to a report in the *Wall Street Journal* (April 11, 2002), McDonald's is offering at a high discount "the most expensive toy in the Happy Meal's 25-year history: the Madame Alexander Doll." According to the *WSJ* article by Shirley Leung:

[A]s girls grow older, they lose interest in dining at McDonald's more quickly than boys do, some research data suggest. According to Children's Market Services Inc.'s Kid Trends survey, 45 percent of six- to eight-year-old girls say McDonald's is their favorite restaurant; only 22 percent of nine- to 11-year-old girls choose the chain. Boys, in comparison, are more steadfast: 47 percent of six-to eight-year-old boys favor McDonald's, compared with 37 percent of nine- to 11-year-olds.

At around 11 or 12, girls and boys begin to exhibit very different eating habits, dietitian Tammy Baker says. Boys develop voracious appetites and don't think twice about downing burgers, fries and milkshakes. Meanwhile, girls at that age start to become aware of their looks. Many gain weight during puberty and start to diet. They begin to gravitate to salads and yogurt. According to Vegetarian Resource Group, a Baltimore education group, girls are twice as likely as boys to grow up to become vegetarians.

Boys and girls also have different role models, Ms Baker says. "Boys start looking at sports heroes," she says. Girls "are influenced by the models and movie stars who are underweight."

Thus, McDonald's traditionally used Barbie doll promotions to attract girls to their restaurants, and are now using more upscale dolls and promotions. This practice calls attention to the ways in which McDonald's attempts to manipulate children toward its unhealthy diets. And, as noted above, since these promotion items are often produced by near-slave labor, McDonald's exploits those that produce its goods at the same time as it manipulates its potential customers.

In addition, from an environmentalist perspective, McDonald's products are ecologically degrading and contribute to depreciation of the soil, rainforests, rivers, grasslands, and other resources that are used to make its beef and dairy products. The production of beef, in particular, uses territory and resources that could produce more nutritious food and contributes to environmental pollution from the excessive waste products involved in intensive cattle raising. Cattle require an awesome amount of resources to produce a single beefsteak, necessitating up to 1,200 gallons of water and up to 16 pounds of soybeans and grain to produce 1 pound of meat; moreover, cow manure is a major source of pollution (see Rifkin 1992).

Whereas McDonald's initially denied that it imported beef from rainforest areas, such as Costa Rica and Brazil, that were threatened by excessive deforestation, subsequent legal procedures revealed that McDonald's did receive supplies of meat from these areas (see Vidal 1997 and www.mcspotlight.org). Thus, while McDonald's has made concessions to environmental concerns – under intense public pressure – by substituting more biodegradable products for their previously non-biodegradable styrofoam cups and other packaging materials, on the whole its products and practices have been environmentally harmful.[21]

In August 1999, a French farmer and activist, José Bové, and a group of fellow sheep farmers symbolically attacked a McDonald's under construction outside the French village of Millau, painting some slogans on the construction site and taking off some roof tiles. A local judge in France, angered after a summer of anti-GM crop protests in the region, ordered Bové and six others to be arrested and detained at unusually high bail and charges. From his incarceration and during the subsequent trial, Bové became a major celebrity, protesting against GM food and *malbouffe* (bad food and eating), while defending natural food and good French cuisine. Bové was hailed as a national hero in France and has since appeared throughout the world in protests against McDonald's and the negative aspects of globalization.[22]

Thus, McDonald's is a highly contested institution and symbol that is increasingly criticized and contested. Many groups and individuals have called for a boycott of McDonald's in the interests of good health, good-quality eating experiences, fair labor practices, environmental concerns, and sociopolitical concerns with McDonald's corporate policies. To critics who argue that such condemnation negates the popular pleasures of members of socioeconomic groups other than one's own, I would argue that there are a variety of objective reasons, revolving around health, environment, economics, and politics, that would justify criticism of McDonald's and resistance to its products.

Indeed, many groups and individuals have been protesting against McDonald's in recent years. Ritzer notes that, following the opening of a McDonald's in Jerusalem, a kosher restaurant inspector commented that: "McDonald's is contaminating all of

Israel and all of the Jewish people" (Ritzer 1998: 18). Further, a Prague Jewish group was able to stop the erection of a McDonald's restaurant that would send "foul air" into its synagogue. A prominent Roman Catholic group in Italy wrote an editorial in a church publication arguing that McDonald's hamburgers and french fries lacked "the communitarian aspect of sharing," that McDonald's "has completely forgotten the holiness of food," and that Catholics should seek out "other alternatives for their meals."[23] As noted, McDonald's has been attacked in almost every major anti-globalization movement demonstration, including protests in Seattle, Prague, Washington, Davos, Toronto, and Ottawa. When the United States bombed Kosovo in the offensive against Serbia in 1999, McDonald's branches were destroyed in Kosovo and elsewhere in Serbia in retaliation. In Schlosser's summary:

> In 1995, a crowd of four hundred Danish anarchists looted a McDonald's in downtown Copenhagen, made a bonfire of its furniture in the street, and burned the restaurant to the ground. In 1996, Indian farmers ransacked a Kentucky Fried Chicken restaurant in Bangalore, convinced that the chain threatened their traditional agricultural practices. In 1997, a McDonald's in the Columbian city of Cali was destroyed by a bomb. In 1998, bombs destroyed a McDonald's in St Petersburg, Russia, two McDonald's in suburban Athens, a McDonald's in the heart of Rio de Janeiro, and a Planet Hollywood in Cape Town, South Africa. In 1999, Belgian vegetarians set fire to a McDonald's in Antwerp, and a year later, May Day protestors tore the sign off a McDonald's in London's Trafalgar Square, destroyed the restaurant, and handed out free hamburgers to the crowd. Fearing more violence, McDonald's temporarily closed all fifty of its London restaurants.
>
> (Schlosser 2001: 244)

McDonald's suffered another scandal in 2001 when it was reported that eight employees were involved in a scheme that fraudulently netted them more than $13 million worth of McDonald's game prizes. Part of the McDonald's spectacle involves promotional games such as "McDonald's Monopoly," or "Who Wants to Be a Millionaire?", and the FBI charged McDonald's employees with illicitly "winning" $13 million from grand prizes in a scheme that had been going on for years."[24]

In yet another 2001 public relations debacle, it was revealed that McDonald's' assertion that its french fries were prepared in vegetable oil, and were thus appropriate for vegetarians, was bogus. Although the corporation had maintained since 1990 that its fries were cooked in pure vegetable oil, it admitted in response to a threatened lawsuit by vegetarians and Hindus that it used a beef extract, described as a "natural flavor" in its ingredient list, to season the fries. Upon hearing the confession that McDonald's used beef flavoring in its fries, a Hindu group vandalized the Bombay McDonald's restaurant, since the Hindu religion prohibits the eating of beef products. There were also protests and lawsuits elsewhere, generating a wave of bad press throughout the world.[25]

In the aftermath of the September 11 terrorist attacks, violent assaults on McDonald's have intensified, with a McDonald's in Turkey bombed by protesters and one in Pakistan vandalized by a crowd angry at the United States bombing in Afghanistan. Joe Kincheloe reported that a US McDonald's corporate executive admitted to him that on the day of the terrorist attacks all McDonald's' regional offices were evacuated and closed. Further, an internal memo was sent out stating that, since the United States was under attack, McDonald's was vulnerable and should prepare for the worst (Kincheloe 2002: 4). In December 2001, a McDonald's was bombed in China and two people were killed. In January 2002, a McDonald's restaurant in Canberra, Australia, was firebombed and more than thirty McDonald's franchises received packages containing white powder, similar to that used in the anthrax attacks and scares following September 11, causing some to close. In Argentina, when the peso lost 42 percent of its value in January 2002, protestors ransacked US-owned banks and a McDonald's. In the Ukraine, when thousands turned out to protest at the construction of a franchise in the city's central square, local authorities decided to prohibit the building of the restaurant. And as I write in summer 2002, there are ongoing struggles in Voronezh, in the Russian Federation, against a similar McDonald's to be built on the site of the only park in the city center, and in Toronto to block the building of a McDonald's in the city's Humewood area. Indeed, in response to a question at the January 2002 World Economic Forum, McDonald's CEO Jack Greenberg conceded that "McDonald's is oftentimes the poster child for anti-globalization sentiment."

Evaluating McDonaldization

McDonald's has thus become a major target of the anti-globalization movement and a highly contested phenomenon. Moreover, its sales have declined in recent years for a variety of reasons. In addition to the McDonald's scandals and the many-sided protests against it that I mentioned above, McDonald's in Europe suffered a particularly bad year in 2001 because of a mad cow disease scare that led consumers to question meat products. On a global level, McDonald's' profits fell for five straight quarters in 2000–1 and its lower earning estimate for 2002 caused a 6 percent fall in stock prices. Analysts say that McDonald's' declining fortunes are due to growing concern about diet and nutrition, complaints about poor service, and the targeting of McDonald's by anti-globalization protestors. McDonald's has also faced complaints from franchise managers that it has been introducing too many new franchises, cutting back on the profits of existing ones.[26]

The phenomenon of McDonaldization, however, interpreted as a set of processes geared toward increasing efficiency, calculability, predictability, and control, is more complex and ambiguous. There are times when one wants what Ritzer (1993; 1996; 1998) calls McDonaldization, when efficiency and various modes of instrumental rationality are particularly beneficial and when one desires to avoid their opposite. Rationalization/McDonaldization of labor might serve to deskill labor and oppress the workforce, as Braverman (1974) and Schlosser (2001) remind us, but this same procedure might free workers from dehumanizing and alienating labor that is better done by machines and automation. Likewise, there are some products and services that one wants to be as rationalized, predictable, and instrumental as possible, such as safe and efficient air travel and habitable hotels. Ritzer's celebration of such things as bed-and-breakfast establishments or the older forms of non-franchised motels could be the site of unpleasant surprises, as well as quirky and pleasing novelty and more customized service. When traveling, seeking food or shelter in unfamiliar environments, or utilizing machines and products, one often wants rationalized and predictable forms of goods and services, while other times one goes for the more novel and unpredictable experience.

The same dialectical perspective can be applied to Weber's analysis of bureaucracy and rationalization, as Gouldner (1976) and others argue. Whereas bureaucracies can be insensitive to individual differences and oppressive of particularity, highly rational and legally articulated rules and regulations can protect individuals against the excessive power of potentially oppressive institutions. Although within universities, all students and teachers have suffered from the oppressive force of bureaucracy, it is often useful to have codified, calculable, efficient, and controllable bureaucratic rules, procedures, and practices. Thus, rationalization can promote the forces of domination and hierarchy, but it can also empower individuals against institutions via appeal to standardized rules and regulations.

In terms of resisting McDonaldization as societal rationalization, one needs to organize oppositional practices and subcultures that provide alternatives to more rationalized corporate forms of social and economic organization. Food co-ops, health food or ethnic restaurants, and growing and preparing one's own food generate alternatives to the sort of massified and standardized food that McDonald's offers. In terms of healthcare, travel, and a variety of other everyday practices, one can often seek or devise alternatives to the corporate mainstream. In each case, it is a question of whether corporate rationalization does or does not serve individual and social needs in a socially responsible manner, provide a useful product or service at a fair price, and proffer a reasonable commodity or service in comparison with other alternatives – and whether, in specific cases, one enjoys the luxury of choice.

On the whole, one might choose to pursue alternatives to corporate rationalization and mass-produced goods and services and to avoid McDonaldization at all costs. On the other hand, one is sometimes forced to utilize services or products from large, McDonaldized corporations if there are no reasonable alternatives. Ritzer's analysis, however, in some ways replicates the critique of mass society and culture produced by both the left and the right. Such critique bemoans the increase in the contemporary world of standardized sameness and homogenization and the decline of individuality, diversity, and tradition. The mass culture critic also seems to assume that McDonaldization is inexorably and relentlessly homogenizing the world, obliterating individuality and variety. While there are undeniably tendencies toward homogenization, massification, and standardization taking place on a global scale, for which the rubric McDonaldization provides a useful optic, there is also a proliferation of diversity and heterogeneity, as some forms of postmodern theory suggests. And while globalization often produces the homogenizing of local culture and differences, it also involves proliferation of difference, hybridization, and the expansion of consumer and lifestyle choices – at least for some privileged groups and individuals (see Watson *et al.* 1997).

The personal and the political

Ultimately, choosing one's attitude toward McDonald's and McDonaldization is a question both of one's politics and of one's personal identity, of who you are and want to be. As the German philosopher Feuerbach noted, "you are what you eat," and thus it is important to make wise and intelligent choices concerning what you put into your body, as well as your mind. McDonald's, by contrast, encourages a certain mindlessness, and not by accident was founder Ray Kroc contemptuous of intellectuals (Kincheloe 2002: 144). No reflective person thinking about what sort of food they should eat for health and nutrition should choose McDonald's. Indeed, when reflecting on where one might eat, one should ask whether one wants to constitute oneself as a junk-food consumer or a mindless Big Mac chomper. Questions of ethics as well as culinary choice should be raised, and individuals should consider whether they want to accept or protest McDonald's labor practices, its environmental proliferation of waste, its fast-food experience, and its animal-, fat-, and chemical-based food.

When contemplating going to a McDonald's or standing in line waiting to purchase its fast food one should pose to oneself the following questions: What am I doing eating fast food? Is this the kind of diet and body I want? Do I identify with eating junk food, with killing animals, with a conservative, multinational corporation? Do I care that rainforests are being destroyed and cropland that could feed people is being used to raise the cattle that are cooked up in the McDonald's products?

Choosing or resisting McDonald's is not just an issue of individual choice, but it is also a social, ethical, and political issue. Many groups are devising collective responses to the McDonald's spectacle and, as I have stressed, McDonald's is an increasingly contested terrain. The McDonald's spectacle at present includes actions undertaken by oppositional groups and social movements (see Vidal 1997; Kincheloe 2002). In concluding his study of the fast-food industry, Schlosser (2001: 262ff.) stresses the need for regulating advertising of unhealthy foods to children, stronger government regulation of food production, more rigorous monitoring and stricter labor laws to protect workers in food production and distribution, and generally stronger regulation of food safety to protect the public against disease. But Schlosser recognizes that the incredible political power of the highly monopolistic food conglomerates makes it unlikely that there will be stronger legislation, at least in the United States, in the foreseeable future. Yet he notes that significant boycotts and protests have in the past forced McDonald's to change its food packaging and make concessions to environmental concerns, as well as to pay lip-service to health and safety issues. Thus, it is an important political issue of the present era to inform and organize the public concerning food and health issues and to organize protests and boycotts against objectionable products and practices.[27]

Contesting the McDonald's spectacle challenges us to consider precisely what form of society, values, and practices we desire. While McDonaldization is here to stay as a mode of social production, we need to question how social rationalization can serve individual and social needs *and* what sort of activities, such as education, sports, or creative endeavors, should not be McDonaldized. As for McDonald's the junk-food producer, we need to ask what sorts of alternatives are preferable to McDonald's fast food. I have suggested that we should simply refuse McDonald's (and other junk-food sites) as a form of culinary practice, that we should exercise Herbert Marcuse's "great refusal" (1964) and refuse to have anything to do with this highly objectionable form of unhealthy, assembly-line food.

Finally, the McDonald's spectacle provides insight into the current terrain of global capitalism. Although unimpeded globalization and neo-liberal economics permeated the 1990s, a movement against capitalist globalization is now contesting forces of global capitalism such as McDonald's. McDonald's thus provides an exemplary case of a certain kind of global corporation that demonstrates what is wrong with aspects of global capitalism. The global movement against McDonald's and the excesses of capitalism, however, show that globalization itself spawns resistance, as well as forms of domination and hegemony. The worldwide campaign against globalization shows contradictions within globalization itself, which represent at once the relentless march of global capitalism, and its products and spectacle, *and* global movements of resistance and struggle. Without the Internet to circulate anti-McDonald's information, the McLibel struggle would probably have failed to attract attention and significant support.

Hence, globalization itself is highly contradictory and contains openings for struggle, resistance and democratization, as well as capitalist hegemony. The McDonald's spectacle thus provides privileged access to the very dynamics of globalization in the contemporary era. Interrogating McDonald's critically can therefore help us to understand better the current form of contemporary society and to attempt to conceive of and create a better one.

Notes

1 Ritzer's (1993) book generated an unprecedented number of sales and amount of scholarly interest, as demonstrated by highly impressive sales figures, new editions of the book (1996), and the growing critical literature dedicated to the phenomenon (Alfino *et al.* 1998; Smart 1998; Ritzer 1998; 2002). I contributed an introduction to the first of these four works and a commentary to the second, and I draw on these studies in the current text, which fleshes out my own perspectives on McDonald's as a global commodity spectacle. Ritzer combines the use of Weber's sociological theory to generalize about McDonald's with a wealth of empirical data to illustrate and flesh out his argument. Ritzer's research method follows what Alvin Gouldner (1976) called "newspaper sociology," assembling information and news on McDonald's through gathering and citing newspaper articles to illustrate his arguments. My own approach to studying McDonald's is multiperspectivist, drawing on Internet sources, critical social theory, historical sociology, ethnography, phenomenology, cultural studies, and a wealth of other theoretical perspectives.

I might add parenthetically that computer databases and the World Wide Web supersede the sort of newspaper sociology that had been widespread earlier and which Ritzer put to good use in his study of McDonaldization. It used to be that one way to gather sociological data was through compiling newspaper articles on one's topic of inquiry. This was a highly specialized and time-consuming mode of research – which I myself engaged in for years – requiring access to a large number of newspapers, the ability to find material in periodic reader's guides, and the patience to search out the articles in question. Computer databases simplified this process and I was able to publish my book on the Gulf War the year after the event itself (Kellner 1992), thanks to the use of Nexus–Lexis databases, as well as PeaceNet and alternative sources. This mode of research was even more costly and specialized, unless one had access to a free university account – as I did. But now the World Wide Web makes accessible a tremendous amount of information, including collections of newspaper articles, scholarly studies, and a wealth of other material. These resources, of course, generate their own problems as well (reliability of information, information overload, learning how to access the most productive sites, and so on). Yet the Internet revolutionizes research and makes it relatively easy to track the fortunes and vicissitudes of a corporation such as McDonald's. Such research is, of course, aided when activist groups create resources such as the McSpotlight website, which contains a tremendous amount of constantly updated information, and their list-serve, which sends new material to one's e-mail account.

2 For examples of the Marx–Weber dialogue and the issues involved, see Antonio and Glassman (1985), which contains my own take on the connections between Marx, Weber, and critical theory (Kellner 1985).

3 See the studies in Cvetovitch and Kellner (1997) for examples of the dialectic between the global and the local.

4 On the concept of a multiperspectivist cultural studies, see Kellner (1995). Following this model throughout my studies, I critically interrogate the McDonald's production process, the circulation of its goods, their effects and use, and the way in which the corporation embodies certain processes of capitalist rationalization. I combine Marx, Weber, a variety of sociological studies, postmodern theory, and other perspectives to try to get at the many sides and contradictory effects of the McDonald's spectacle.

5 For ethnographic accounts of McDonald's, which draw on personal experience to analyze the menu, the line, the order, and the dining, see Shelton (1995) and Kincheloe (1997; 2002). The last study interrogates the author's own personal experiences with McDonald's and years of investigation of McDonald's' customers and products. Goldman (1992) and Kincheloe (2002) dissect the ideological and cultural meanings of McDonald's, while there are several histories containing a wealth of stories, anecdotes, and lore concerning the origins, history, and dynamics of McDonald's as a corporate organization and product of individuals (e.g. Kroc 1977; Love 1986). These last two books are largely promotional celebrations of the McDonald's success story and are thus exercises in corporate mythology that should be decoded as such.

6 McDonald's has expanded its target audiences in the United States over the years, moving from family-oriented ads to targeting urban minorities and even GenXers (see Goldman 1992: 89; Goldman and Papson 1996: 11f. and 237f.). On a global scale, McDonald's has tried to incorporate the whole world as its customers and devotees (see Barber 1996; Watson *et al.* 1997).

7 For earlier analyses of the mechanization of agriculture, food, labor, housework, the objects of everyday life, and death, see Giedion (1969).

8 On Fordism, see note 10. On postFordism, see Harvey (1989), and on postmodernism, see Baudrillard (1983b,c; 1993), and my interpretation of the latter's postmodern turn in Kellner (1989b). I will describe below how McDonald's incorporates postFordist and postmodern tendencies.

9 Ritzer emphasizes the modern aspects of McDonaldization but neglects the semiotic and cultural aspects of the McDonald's experience, in which consumption of sign values is as fundamental as actually consuming the products in the act of eating. In

other words, the McDonald's customer is not only chomping a burger, but gaining identity as a McDonald's consumer, participating in the communal experience of family fun or social belonging promised by the McDonald's ads and promotions. Non-Western customers consume the experience of Western modernity in eating McDonald's food and gain new hybridized identities as they combine tradition and novel McDonald's' products and practices.

10 The term "Fordism" derives from Italian Marxist Antonio Gramsci (1971) and became widely circulated in contemporary social theory when Harvey (1989) and others began comparing the current regime of postmodern production and globalization with the earlier model of Fordism.

11 For my take on the Frankfurt School's critical theory, see Kellner (1989a). For Habermas's interpretation of the dialectic of system and lifeworld, which he relates to Weber's theory, see Habermas (1984; 1987).

12 Ritzer's (1993) book is valuable for provoking a theoretical and practical debate concerning the key novel and defining features of our contemporary world that McDonaldization embodies, thus forcing individuals to define their response to crucial aspects of everyday life. Although many of Ritzer's critics chide him for being too pessimistic and negative, this dose of critical negativity is salutary in an age of positive thinking only too eager to embrace and celebrate the joys of consumer culture. Ritzer's analysis of McDonaldization is thus valuable for articulating discontents of critical individuals with relentless rationalization and accordant standardization, homogenization, and massification of experience. Ritzer himself claims in the revised edition that "I bear no particular animus toward McDonald's" (1996: xix). I will argue, however, that *McDonald's* deserves a negative animus from many possible perspectives, while *McDonaldization* itself is more complex and must be judged in its particular manifestations in specific contexts in order to appraise its effects adequately, as I will do in the following pages.

13 Schlosser points out that McDonald's sued at least eighty British publications and organizations in the 1980s alone, making critics wary of questioning its products or practices (Schlosser 2001: 246). Like Disney, McDonald's is also eager to copyright its concepts and images and sue anyone who infringes them. In "Serving up the McDictionary," Kate Silver lists the concepts copyrighted by McDonald's (*Las Vegas Weekly*, May 22, 2001). These include: "1-800-MC1-STCK; Always Quality. Always Fun; America's Favorite Fries; Arch Deluxe; Automac; Big Mac; Big N' Tasty; Big Xtra!; Birdie, the Early Bird and design; Bolshoi Mac; Boston Market; Cajita Feliz; Changing The Face of The World; Chicken McGrill; Chicken McNuggets; Chipolte Mexican Grill; Cuarto De Libra; Did Somebody Say; Donatos Pizza; emac digital; Egg McMuffin; Extra Value Meal; Filet-O-Fish; French Fry box design; Gep Op Mac; Golden Arches; Golden Arches logo; Good Jobs For Good People; Good Times. Great Taste; Gospelfest; Great Breaks; Grimace and design; Groenteburger; HACER; Hamburglar and design; Hamburger University; Happy Meal and Happy Meal box design; Have You Had Your Break Today?; Helping Hands logo; Hey, It Could Happen!; I am Hungry and design; Immunize for Healthy Lives; Lifting Kids To A Better Tomorrow; Mac Attack; McBaby; McBacon; McBurger; McBus; McCafe; McChicken; McDia Feliz; MCDirect Shares; McDonaldland; McDonald's; McDonald's Earth Effort and logo; McDonald's Express and logo; McDonald's Means Opportunity; McDonald's Is Your Kind of Place; McDonald's Racing Team design; McDouble; McDrive; McExpress; McFamily; McFlurry; McFranchise; McGrilled Chicken; McHappy Day; McHero; McJobs; McKids; McKroket; McMaco; McMemories; McMenu; McMusic; McNifica; McNuggets; McNuggets Kip; McOz; McPlane; McPollo; McPrep; McRecycle USA; McRib; McRoyal; McScholar; McScholar of the Year; McSwing; Mac Tonight and design; McWorld; Made For You; Mighty Wings; Millennium Dreamers; Morning Mac; Quarter Pounder; Ronald McDonald and design; Ronald McDonald House and logo; Ronald McDonald House

charities and logo; Ronald Scholars; Sausage McMuffin; Single Arch logo; Speedee logo; Super Size; The House That Love Built and design; twoallbeefpattiesspecialsauc elettucecheesepicklesoniononasesameseedbun; We Love to See You Smile; What's On Your Place; When the US Wins You Win; World Famous Fries; You Deserve a Break Today."

14 For a more detailed account of the McLibel campaign, see Kovel (1997: 26ff.; Vidal 1997).

15 The UK *Guardian* reported that the McSpotlight website "claimed to be the most comprehensive source of information on a multinational corporation ever assembled" and was part of one of the more successful anti-corporate campaigns (February 22, 1996; the website is at www.mcspotlight.org).

16 On obesity and fast food, see Schlosser (2001: 240f.), who notes that the United States has the highest obesity rate of any industrialized nation in the world, with more than half of all American adults and about one-quarter of American children suffering from obesity. The rate of obesity in the United States is double what it was in the early 1960s, and obesity is now spreading throughout the world, due in part to the circulation and spread of junk food such as McDonald's. A 2002 report by the US Surgeon General stated that 61 percent of adults in the United States are overweight or obese, and the number of obese children has tripled in the last 20 years. The cost of healthcare and lost wages from obesity-related illnesses was estimated to be over $117 billion! See the discussion in Megan McArdie, "Can we sue our own fat asses off?" (*Salon*, May 24, 2002), and Amanda Spake, "A fat nation" (*USA News and World Report*, August 19, 2002).

17 Journalist and food-pathogen expert Nicols Fox, in her book *Spoiled: Why Our Food is Making Us Sick and What We can Do About It* (1998), claims that McDonald's was the culprit in the outbreaks of *E. coli* illnesses, but that the company denied responsibility and the media did not look into the issue, a point that Schlosser (2001) confirms.

18 See CNN, "Inside business world" (June 7, 1997) and *Los Angeles Times* (November 11, 1997: D16) on McDonald's' declining sales and consumer dissatisfaction with its products during 1996–97. The downward trend has continued and, as I note in the text, over the four quarters of 2001 and the first quarter of 2002 profits sunk steadily in McDonald's greatest period of decline in its history. See note 26 below.

19 See the detailed analysis in Goldman (1992: 97f.)

20 On the importance of alliances between Disney, McDonald's and Coca-Cola, see "The science of alliance" (*The Economist*, April 4, 1998: 69).

21 The McSpotlight campaign documented that, despite paying lip service to environmental concerns, the actual impact of McDonald's on the environment is extremely harmful. As Kovel (1997: 30) notes: "Professor Graham Ashworth (director-general of the Tidy Britain Group, sponsored by McDonald's) had to testify that McDonald's was in the 'top 1 or 2 percent' of all companies whose products end up as litter, it being estimated that on a given day in the UK, the company disgorges 7.9 million items as takeout that end up on the street … When multiplied by the number of stores in the world, the in-house garbage is equivalent to over 1 billion pounds of waste every year." And Schlosser (2001: 268–9) points out that, although McDonald's stopped using polystyrene boxes in the United States and switched to paper ones, it continues to use the plastic boxes in many overseas countries.

22 For his own version of the story, see Bové and Dufour (2001); for an excellent contextualization and analysis of how the protests of Bové and his colleagues shifted the debate over genetically modified organisms in France, from one of risk assessment by experts to a more general public debate over globalization, see Heller (2002). Bové was jailed for 40 days in summer 2002, undergoing a hunger strike to protest his incarceration and adding prisoners' rights to his anti-globalization issues. See "José Bové released from jail (*Associated Press*, August 1, 2002).

23 "Roman Catholic group urges the faithful not to eat Big Macs," *Euromarketing via*

E-mail, November 24, 2000. Watson (1997: 23) notes how in South Asia McDonald's attempts to modify its menu to accord with local religious practices, although he fails to note the protests from religious figures and groups against McDonald's fare, which violates the food laws of several major world religions.

24 See "FBI arrests 8 in McDonald's prize scheme" (*Associated Press*, August 21, 2001).

25 Eli Sanders, "Fast-food lawsuit extracts a fry fact" (*Seattle Times*, May 3, 2001) and "McDonald's vandalized by Hindu group" (*Associated Press*, May 4, 2001). To settle the lawsuits, McDonald's eventually offered to pay $4,000 to those who sued it for fraudulent advertising and to donate $10 million to charity; see Ameet Sachde, "McDonald's nears settling vegetarians' lawsuit" (*Chicago Tribune*, April 26, 2002).

26 See Yahoo, October 29, 2001, and Daryl Lindsey, "Will mad cows kill the Big Mac?" (*Salon*, March 26, 2001). McDonald's announced in November 2001 at its annual presentation to business analysts in Oak Park, Illinois, that it would cut back the number of new restaurant openings in 2002, eliminate hundreds of jobs, and shut down nearly half of its regional offices as part of a restructuring aimed at reducing costs and improving profits. See "McDonald's warns on 2002 profits" (*Associated Press*, November 29, 2001). In a startling announcement in mid-September 2002 of dramatic declines in earnings in the US and Europe during the year, following an earlier announcement of 81 percent declines in Japan, McDonald's stock fell 11 percent over two days to a seven year low. See "McDonald's warns on profits" (*Reuters*, September 17, 2002).

27 A new strategy to mobilize publics against junk foods is to sue fast-food corporations such as McDonald's for false advertising, promoting an unhealthy diet, or other issues. See Peg Tyre, "Fighting 'big fat'" (*Newsweek*, August 5, 2002), and McArdie, "Can we sue?," cited in note 16 above. In September 2002, McDonald's announced a plan to use a new cooking oil for its french fries that will halve the trans fatty acid levels while increasing the amount of the more beneficial polyunsaturated fat. Such changes are obviously a response to criticism of McDonald's products and an attempt to win back consumers, showing both that McDonald's is vulnerable to denigration and that it responds to criticism and boycotts. See "McDonald's tries to reduce fat in french fries" (*Associated Press*, September 3, 2002).

3   The sports spectacle, Michael Jordan, and Nike*

Michael Jordan is widely acclaimed as the greatest athlete who ever lived, named "Athlete of the Century" by the TV network ESPN. Yet he is also a major media spectacle on a global scale, combining his athletic prowess with skill as an endorser of global commodities and as a self-promoter, which has enabled him to become a commodity superstar and celebrity of the first rank. In Michael Jordan, globalization, commodification, sports, entertainment, and media come together to produce a figure who serves as an emblematic totem of athletic achievement, business success, and celebrity in the contemporary era. His sensational basketball prowess has made him one of the most successful African American sports figures and businessmen, combining spectacles of race, sports glory, and business success. Yet Jordan's participation in a series of scandals and periods of bad press, mixed with his usually laudatory media presentation, captures the contradictions of spectacle culture, illustrating that those who live by media spectacle can also be brought down by its cruel omnipresent power and eye of surveillance.

As the millennium came to a close, Jordan reigned as one of the most popular and widely known sports icons throughout the world. The announcement of his retirement from basketball in January 1999 after leading the Chicago Bulls to six NBA championships unleashed unparalleled hyperbole describing his superlative athletic accomplishments. In China, the Beijing *Morning Post* ran a front-page story entitled "Flying Man Jordan is Coming Back to Earth," and in Bosnia Jordan's statement declaring his retirement was the lead story on the evening TV news, pushing aside the war in Kosovo.[1] An icon of global popularity, Jordan is "a kind of new world prince," in the words of Pulitzer prize-winning author David Halberstam, who has published a biography of the basketball legend (1999): "You hear time and again about people being in Borneo or somewhere and coming across a kid in a tattered Michael Jordan T-shirt. He's the most famous American in the world."[2]

*Earlier versions of my Michael Jordan study have appeared as "Sports, media culture, and race – some reflections on Michael Jordan," *Sociology of Sports Journal*, 13 (1996): 458–67, and "The sports spectacle, Michael Jordan and Nike: Unholy alliance?" in Andrews, D. (ed.), *Michael Jordan, Inc. Corporate Sport, Media Culture, and Late Modern America*, Albany, NY: State University of New York Press, 2001, pp. 37–64. Thanks to David Andrews for providing material and comments that have helped with the production of this study, as well as to Richard Kahn for helpful critical comments and suggestions.

Not only has Jordan been acclaimed as a global superstar, he is also frequently characterized in terms of deity. The Boston Celtics great Larry Bird marveled that he had encountered "God disguised as Michael Jordan" after Jordan scored sixty-three points against the Celtics in a 1986 playoff game. Jason Williams of the New Jersey Nets sanctified him as "Jesus in tennis shoes" and many referred to him as a "Black Jesus." At a 1992 Olympic press conference, Jordan was embarrassed to be asked if he were a "god" (LeFeber 1999: 15) and *France Soir* headlined: "Michael Jordan in France. That's better than the Pope. It's God in person." (cited in Halberstam 1999: 4).

Jordan's acclaim and popularity results in part because he is a perfect embodiment of the sports spectacle in which media culture uses hi-tech wizardry to magically transform sports into a media extravaganza of the highest order. Images of Jordan's windmill dunking, blazing baseline heroics, and flying through the air to net key shots thrilled sports spectators throughout the world, as did his controlled fade-away jump shooting and uncanny ability often to bag the decisive game-winning shot in his best years. Moreover, Jordan provides the spectacle of intense competition and the thrills of winning, perhaps *the* US passion play, leading the Chicago Bulls to the NBA Championships during six of his eight seasons in the 1990s (the two seasons that the Bulls failed to win were during Jordan's quixotic retirement in 1993–95, in which he tried to become a baseball star). Jordan thus embodies the success ethic and the quintessential capitalist ideal of competition and winning.

In addition to being perhaps the greatest basketball player of all time, Jordan is one of the most successfully managed idols and icons of media culture. Parlaying his athletic triumphs into commercial product endorsements, Jordan became the highest paid celebrity advertising figure ever, endorsing a multitude of products for multi-million-dollar fees, promoting his own line of athletic shoes, cologne, and clothing. Jordan also participated in film spectacle, starring with Bugs Bunny in the movie *Space Jam* (1996) and serving as the subject of a popular Imax film, *Michael Jordan to the Max* (2000), as well as a series of documentaries, now available in a 2002 DVD *Ultimate Jordan*.

Michael Jordan is thus an icon of media spectacle, combining extraordinary athletic achievement, an unrivaled record of success and winning, high entertainment value, and an ability to exploit his image into highly impressive business success. In a commercial culture that blends celebrity, product, and image, it is only natural that the sports shoe transnational Nike – as well as many other corporations – would purchase Jordan's star power to promote its products. Accordingly, I argue that the Michael Jordan/Nike connection calls attention to the extent to which media culture is transforming sports into a spectacle that sells the values, products, celebrities, and institutions of the media and consumer society. The Jordan–Nike nexus calls attention to the *sports entertainment colossus* that has become a major feature of media culture in the new millennium. The Nike–Jordan alliance discloses the extent to which contemporary global culture is constituted by image and spectacle and mediated by the institutions of the media, advertising, public relations, and image management. In this chapter I will show how Jordan embodies the increasing commercialization of the sports spectacle as well as its contradictions and problems. The following study will thus use the Nike–Jordan sports spectacle to uncover the central dynamics of contemporary media and consumer culture and the implosion between sports, entertainment, celebrity, and commerce in contemporary global culture.

The sports spectacle

Professional sports are one of the major spectacles of media culture. From the original Olympics in Ancient Greece and the chariot races and gladiator fights in Ancient Rome, sports have long been a major site of entertainment and spectacle. Yet contemporary sports are a largely untheorized and neglected aspect of the society of the spectacle whereby sports celebrate and reproduce dominant societal values, products, and corporations in an unholy alliance between sports, commercialism, and media spectacle. Moreover, in the current era, sports articulate spectacles of race and nationalism, celebrity and star power, and transgression and scandal, elevating its icons to godlike status, and then sometimes bringing them down into the depths of scandal and disgrace.

Today, sports are a major part of the consumer society whereby individuals learn the values and behavior of a competitive and success-driven society. Sports heroes are among the best paid and wealthiest denizens of the consumer society and thus serve as embodiments of fantasy aspirations to the good life. Sports fans also learn the art of consumption of sports spectacle and inserting themselves into fandom and celebration of sports virtue and achievement. Whereas the activity of participating in sports involves an active engagement in creative practice, spectator sports involve passive consumption of images of the sports spectacle, which mobilizes spectator energies into deification of players and teams and the celebration of the values of competition and winning. Yet there is also an active dimension in fandom, in which sports consumers learn tremendous amounts of folklore, become experts and critics, and actively participate in sports communities.

One of the characteristic features of contemporary postindustrial societies is the extent to which sports have become commercialized and transformed into a spectacle. During the industrial era, actually playing sports was an adjunct to labor and production. Sports helped create strong and skillful bodies for industrial labor and taught individuals both how to play as part of a collective, to fit into a team, and how to display initiative and distinguish themselves. Sports players were thus taught to gain recognition and success by hard work and individual skill *and* to be good team players, thus training workers for productive industrial labor.

Crucially, sports celebrated the values of competition and success, and were thus part of the reproduction of the capitalist ethic. Sports helped successive generations of immigrants in the United States to assimilate into US life, teaching them distinctly US values and providing access to success. In the early twentieth century, immigrants took to basketball, football, and baseball, helping to make them increasingly important pastimes. Later, sports became a major field of integration and cultural assimilation of people of color into mainstream US society and the glories of the American dream – for those who played by the rules and distinguished themselves within the system.

Modern sports were organized around the principles of the division of labor and professionalism, celebrating the capitalist values of competition and winning. Sports in the modern era replicated the structure of the workplace, in which both individual initiative and teamwork were necessary, and sports celebrated at once both competing values. Sports became an increasingly important social concern and realm with its own professional ethic, carefully regulated rules, and highly organized corporate structure. Postindustrial sports, by contrast, merge sports into media spectacle, collapse boundaries between professional achievement and commercialization, and attest to the commodification of all aspects of life in the media and consumer society.

Although sports were an important mode of participation in, and assimilation into, modern societies, during the postindustrial era spectator sports have emerged as the correlative to a society that is replacing manual labor with automation and machines, and requires consumption and appropriation of spectacles to reproduce the consumer society. The present-day era also sees the expansion of a service sector and highly differentiated entertainment industry, of which sports are a key part. Thus, significant resources are currently devoted to the augmentation and promotion of the sports spectacle. Athletes such as Michael Jordan accordingly have the potential to amass high salaries from the profits generated by the sports/entertainment colossus, while spectators are taught to idolize icons like Jordan, making them the deities of everyday life.

There are many ways in which contemporary sports are subject to the laws of the spectacle and are becoming totally commercialized, serving to help reproduce the consumer society. For starters, sports are ever more subject to market logic and commodification, with professional athletes making millions of dollars. Furthermore, sports events such as basketball games are hypercommodified, with the "Bud player of the game," "Miller Lite genuine moments," the "Reebok half-time report," the "AT&T Time Out," and "Dutch Boy in the Paint," along with ads featuring the star players promoting merchandise. TV networks bid astronomical sums for the rights to broadcast live professional sports events, and major spectacles, such as the Super Bowl and NBA Championship games, command some of the highest advertising rates in television.

Recent years have exhibited a dramatic implosion of the sports spectacle, commerce, and entertainment, with massive salaries and marketing contracts for the superstar players/celebrities. The major media conglomerates are becoming increasingly interested in sports channels and franchises, and the most marketable athletes earn enormous multimillion-dollar salaries. Moreover, sports stars are able to secure even more lucrative marketing deals to endorse products, star in films or TV programs, and even, in the case of Michael Jordan, to promote their own product lines.

Competing with baseball and football as the US sports of choice in the contemporary era, professional basketball has emerged during the Jordan era as the game that best symbolizes the contemporary sports/entertainment colossus. To some extent, the three major US sports encapsulate different periods of socioeconomic development. Baseball represents the challenge to a highly individualist country of uniting individual aspirations and talents with teamwork and spirit. Emerging in the nineteenth century, baseball disciplined individuals to fit into teams, but still rewarded individual accomplishments during a highly entrepreneurial and competitive era of capitalist development, which celebrated individual achievement, distinction, and success.

Football is organized on a mass-production industrial model, which was appropriate to the era of factory production, and which reached its highest stage of development in the first half of the twentieth century. Football is a team sport that exemplifies arduous collective physical labor mated with individual achievement. Although the star running backs, quarterbacks, and touchdown scorers often get the credit and headlines, it is disciplined collective labor that provides the infrastructure for football accomplishments and victory. Without a strong defense and well-co-ordinated offense, even the most spectacular players cannot function adequately and their team cannot win consistently.

NBA basketball, by contrast, has increasingly featured superstar feats of individual brilliance, especially during the heyday of the Michael Jordan spectacle. Professional basketball is the ideal TV sport, fast paced, full of action, and resplendent with spectacle. Hard-charging full-court action, balletic shots, and ubiquitous instant replays make basketball the right sport for the era of MTV and ESPN. NBA commissioner David Stern remarked in a 2000 Museum of Broadcasting lecture that sports are "the most important programming on television" because they are original, exciting, dramatic, entertaining, and highly compelling. Sports present a primal form of live television with immediacy, action, and drama built into the event. Sports, Stern argued, drove cable penetration, creating the demand for the new technology that allowed it to succeed brilliantly, and in time sports became the United States' major export, the cultural ambassador of choice for US games, heroes, values, and products.

In 1989, the ESPN network began broadcasting sports full-time on cable and soon became a powerhouse. ESPN originally signified Entertainment Sports Programming Network, an instructive abbreviation that called attention to the nexus between sports and entertainment in the age of television. "ESPN" also signaled the way that the sports/entertainment colossus was programming the nation to become one of sports addicts and to idolize its celebrities, values, and dramas, so as to become networked into a sports/entertainment/consumer society.[3] By the 1980s, ESPN began applying MTV-type techniques to sports events and broadcasting celebrity sports shows, which helped to elevate athletic stars such as Jordan to super-icon status. Initially aimed at a male audience, the network targeted female viewers by adding more entertainment features and women commentators. It also cultivated audiences of color, adding black sportscasters such as Stuart Scott, who combined ethnic street talk and attitude with cutting-edge flashy suits and an idiosyncratic style, as with his signature "Boo-ya!" salutation, which itself became part of the contemporary sports idiom, signaling especially spectacular moves and plays.

Basketball is a high-speed game that moves rapidly down the court, and television made a spectacle of velocity, totally appropriate for an ever faster-paced society, intensifying motion and action with quick cuts, close-ups, and zooms. Helping to speed up the game for television, the NBA instituted a twenty-four-second "shot clock," forcing teams to accelerate the pace of the game. In addition, playbacks highlighted the mechanics of brilliant plays, while the intimacy of television caught the sweat and concentration, anger and exultation, and other moments of physical and emotional intensity. Furthermore, basketball is sexy, showing glistening and well-honed male bodies in a state of semi-undress, clad in skimpy jerseys and shorts. Compared with the gladiator-like body armor of football players and the nineteenth-century full-body attire of baseball, basketball presents a mode of male beefcake, especially with TV close-ups capturing the hard and agile bodies of NBA hunks.

Thus, NBA basketball became a powerful media spectacle, and television helped the sport to gain popularity and importance in the 1980s by broadcasting more games and heavily promoting basketball as it became ever more fashionable and attracted a greater and greater following. Completely embodying the fragmentary postmodern aesthetics, razzle-dazzle technical effects, and accelerating pace of today's television, basketball has emerged as a major arena of the spectacle, the ultimate game for the sports/entertainment society. Once a primarily US game, by the 1990s it had become globally popular.

Consequently, although the NBA was once the ne'er-do-well stepchild of the more successful professional baseball and football franchises, in recent years it has become one of the most popular of the US sports industries on a global scale (Andrews 1997; 2002; LeFeber 1999). Whereas the NBA fed only thirty-five weekly telecasts to foreign companies in the mid-1980s at the beginning of Jordan's basketball career, by 1996 the roster had swelled to 175 foreign broadcasts in forty languages to 600 million households. By 2000, the NBA was broadcasting to 205 countries in forty-two languages with a total worldwide audience of over 750 million fans.

By 2000, NBA basketball was big business as well as megaspectacle. The average player's salary was over $2.5 million, cumulative NBA player salaries were over $1 billion, and Michael Jordan had made over $40 million in 1999 and cumulatively had collected more than $150 million from Nike over the course of his career (Halberstam 1999: 410, 412).

Many credit Michael Jordan with being one of the chief figures in promoting NBA basketball to become globally popular, recognized and beloved throughout the world. Certainly, Jordan emerged as global basketball's premiere superstar, immediately identifiable everywhere. David Halberstam described him as "the first great athlete of the wired world" (in Coplon 1996: 35), and "arguably the most famous American in the world, more famous in many distant parts of the globe than the President of the United States or any movie or rock star" (Halberstam 1999: 7).

In his book *Michael Jordan and the New Global Capitalism* (1999), Walter LeFeber describes the process whereby Jordan, NBA basketball, and US global corporations such as Nike all attained a global reach, transnationalizing US sports, products, and idols. The globalization of Michael Jordan and Nike was made possible by a global network of cable and satellite television that broadcasts US media, sports, and advertising throughout the world, and a global economy that distributes its products, services, sports, and images. The Internet, too, contributed to the globalization of sports and culture and, as we will see later, played an ambiguous role in Michael Jordan's own personal saga.

Sports have previously often promoted nationalism, and the intensification of global sports events through omnipresent media continues to do so, although a phenomenon such as Michael Jordan and the Chicago Bulls helps produce a transnational popular sports culture. Whereas global events like the World Cup or Olympics (which I examined in Chapter 1) clearly generate nationalism and national identities and passions, in the US the major sports of baseball, football, and basketball generally engender competition between cities, and thus more communal identities. While Michael Jordan and the Bulls have given a tremendous boost on the national scale to Chicago pride and identity, and helped promote NBA basketball as a major national sport, on the global level Michael Jordan has more of a universalizing iconic effect as a global popular who represents a fusion of sports culture and starpower, commodity culture, and an Americanized globalization. That is, the Jordan effect and his deification as a global popular makes him an iconic figure of Americana, as do the global circulation of Nike shoes, Chicago Bulls hats or T-shirts, and the proliferation of NBA basketball to different countries.

The dramatic evolution of the sports spectacle thus has a global dimension, with the major players now becoming international figures, marketed in global sports extravaganzas, advertising campaigns, product promotions, films, websites, and other venue of media culture. As Michael Jordan's highly successful and respected agent, David Falk, puts it: "Michael has transcended sport. He's an international icon" (in Hirschberg 1996: 46).[4] Indeed, in 1996–97, Falk put together deals that netted Jordan a record-breaking $30 million contract for the next season. Moreover, Falk's deals continued the lucrative connections with Nike and other corporations to promote their products to the estimated tune of $40 million. Jordan was also able to introduce his own cologne, Eau de Michael Jordan, and negotiated a contract to star in a hi-tech film, *Space Jam*, which paired him with other NBA superstars, Bugs Bunny, and assorted cartoon characters. Including accompanying product lines, estimates circulated that Jordan could conceivably earn $20 million from his commercial projects (*USA Today*, October 14, 1996: 6B), pointing to a growing convergence between the sports spectacle, entertainment, and business.

Moreover, the sports spectacle is at the center of an almost religious fetishism in which sports become a surrogate religion and its stars demigods. For many, sports are the object of ultimate concern (Paul Tillich's definition of religion), providing transcendence from the banality and suffering of everyday life. Sports stars constitute its saints and deities, while sports events often have a religious aura of ritual. Sports fans are like a congregation and their cheers and boos are a form of liturgy. In sports events, fans become part of something greater than themselves, the participation provides meaning and significance, and a higher communal self, fused with the multitudes of believers and the spirit of joy in triumph and suffering in tribulation. Sports are a break from average everydayness, providing participation in ritual, mystery, and spiritual aura (although, as my discussion is suggesting, sports also celebrate dominant social values such as individuality, winning, teamwork, and, increasingly, commercialism). In the pantheon of sports deity, Michael Jordan is one of the reigning gods, and in the next section I will accordingly engage his iconography and celebrity.

The spectacle of Michael Jordan

Among the spectacles of media culture, Michael Jordan is a pre-eminent figure. As an NBA superstar, Jordan is the very picture of grace, co-ordination, virtuosity, and all-round skill – adeptly marketed to earn a record salary and endorsements. Jordan received $30 million to play for the Chicago Bulls in 1997 (*Time*, July 29, 1996: 61) and $33 million in 1998. He earned over $40 million in endorsements and promotions in 1995, making him the highest paid athlete in the world (*Guardian*, June 11, 1996: 6), and reaped over $45 million in endorsements in 1996, maintaining his position as the world's highest paid athlete. In June 1998, *Fortune* magazine estimated that Jordan had generated over $10 billion during his spectacular professional career, in terms of increased ticket sales, television advertising revenue, increased profits from products endorsed, the exploitation of his name by basketball merchandising, and his own films, businesses, and product lines. Jordan *is* big business and has accelerated the trend toward the implosion of business, entertainment, and sports.

"His Airness," along with "Air Jordan," a popular nickname for "the man that flies," thus epitomizes the postmodern sports spectacle both on the playing field and in advertisements and media spectacles. The Michael Jordan spectacle implodes athletic achievement with commercialization, merging his sports image with corporate products and celebrity superstardom, making Jordan one of the highest paid and most fecund generators of social meaning and capital in the history of media culture. He is the iconic exemplar of the media/sports spectacle, obsession with winning and success, and quest for unimaginable wealth and popularity, which are defining cultural features of the last two decades of the twentieth century into the present.

Jordan first appeared as a rookie with the Chicago Bulls in 1984 and, although he was not yet a fully fledged superstar, his agent signed him to what turned out to be an incredibly influential and lucrative contract with the Nike Corporation. Nike is the Greek personification of victory, represented as a figure with wings who could run and fly at great speed – a mythological image made to order for a shoe company and Michael Jordan. A constant companion of Athena, Nike was also connected in Greek mythology with intelligence. Curiously, the US military had earlier, in the 1950s, appropriated the Nike symbol for a guided missile system, and the World Wide Web is full of pages celebrating the missile system, shut down by the SALT Treaties, as well as Nike shoe pages.

The Nike figure's connotations thus combine spirituality, speed, intelligence, and power in a potent figure. Initially, the Nike Corporation assimilated the Nike winged victory symbol from Greek mythology with images of a basketball flanked with wings, presenting an almost angelic symbol of sports mixed with divinity. Eventually, the Nike symbol mutated into its famous "swoosh," and presented a more abstract image of the wing, a distinctive corporate logo that became instantly associated with the Nike brand. In an era of branding, in which name and image are all-important, Nike thus possessed an extremely resonant media image, and bringing in Michael Jordan and other superstar athletes to enrich the symbolism of the Nike spectacle and to attract audiences to its products was a winning combination in the commodity spectacle and the competition to sell shoes and athletic ware.

Hence, the Michael Jordan mythology was articulated with a Nike figure that connoted speed, intelligence, and victory, as well as the military symbolism of the guided missile system, an apt metaphor for Jordan's basketball heroics. With Jordan and a new marketing agency, Weiden & Kennedy, the Air Jordan product line and Nike's "swoosh" symbol became icons of US and then global culture. At the same time, Michael Jordan became an authentic American hero, generally acknowledged as one of the greatest basketball players of all time, one of the most popular and well-known celebrities of media culture, and, since 1988, the sports celebrity most desired to market corporate products. During the era of Nike–Jordan's ascendancy, cable and satellite television and the aggressive promotion of the NBA by its commissioner, David Stern, increased tremendously the visibility and popularity of professional basketball. The Jordan–Nike era had arrived.

There seemed to be nothing that Jordan could not do on the basketball court. His slam-dunk is legendary and he seems to defy gravity as he flies through the air toward the Holy Grail of the basket. His "hang-time" is fabled and as C.H. Cole (1996) points out, designations such as "Rare Air" "render him extraordinary. .. and even godlike," a figure of transcendence. Nike developed a product line of Air Jordan sports shoes around the flying mythology, and a 1989 NBA Entertainment documentary entitled *Michael Jordan. Come Fly with Me* describes the player as "the man who was truly destined to fly," and celebrates him as the very embodiment of professional excellence, morality, and US values. The published collection of photographs of Michael Jordan as sports icon, media celebrity, and down-home good guy, entitled *Rare Air*, highlights the efficacy of the Michael Jordan publicity machine in fine-tuning his image as a transcendent figure, a god of media culture.

Sports writers, too, participate in the canonization of Michael Jordan, regularly describing him as "the best player ever," "the greatest basketball player who has ever lived," and even the "greatest athlete of all time." The phrase "there is nothing he cannot do" is recurrently used to inscribe Jordan's sign value as superstar sports deity, and in Nike ads that star Jordan the corporate logo "Just Do It" signifies that you, too, can be like Michael and do what you want to do. The Gatorade "Be Like Mike" commercial also highlights Jordan's status as a role model and embodiment of iconic values and high aspiration.

Not surprisingly, McDonald's hired Jordan to promote its wares and named a McJordan burger after him. Once, after an NBA Championship game, a McDonald's advertising crew was on hand to film a commercial. A voice-over said, "Michael, you've just won your third straight NBA Championship. Are you hungry for a fourth?" The sweating and smiling Jordan answered, "I'm hungry for a Big Mac" (cited in LeFeber 1999: 117–18). Film footage from the game was added and McDonald's had an ad ready to circulate on the cable and satellite networks within 24 hours.

There have been, to be sure, some glitches in the Michael Jordan success story. After dropping out of professional basketball to pursue a baseball career,[5] Jordan returned to the Chicago Bulls in 1995 and led the team to three straight NBA Championships. In the process, he reinvented himself as a superstar player, moving from his patented flying air shots to become one of the great jump shot scorers of all time. In the words of one analyst:

> At 33, Jordan is a half-step slower than he once was. He is more beholden to gravity, less nuclear in his liftoff. He can still take wing and be *Air* when he needs to, still shift into turbo and batter the rim, but he chooses his spots now, waits for clear paths. He no longer hurls himself into walls of elbows and forearms, giving the other side's behemoths free shots at his kidneys. He has traded risk for feel, nerve for guile, spectacle for efficiency … and because he is Jordan, even his efficiency can seem spectacular.
>
> (Coplon 1996: 37).

During the 1996–98 seasons, the Bulls emerged as a media culture spectacle of the highest order, setting records for attendance and winning regular season games and three straight NBA Championships (Halberstam 1999). With Jordan, bad guy extraordinary Dennis Rodman, all-round star Scottie Pippen, and Zen-inspired coach Phil Jackson, the Bulls earned unparalleled media attention and adulation. The Jordan spectacle helped make NBA basketball globally popular and Michael Jordan a superstar of extraordinary resonance. Jordan henceforth was identified with ardent competition and winning, embodying the values of hard drive, success, and coming out on top; his shots repeatedly won key games and he became fabled for the magnitude of his competitiveness and drive to win.

Thus, Michael Jordan is both a great player and represents a highly successful marketing phenomenon, which draws attention to the construction of the media/sports spectacle by corporations, public relations, and the techniques of advertising. Just as Jordan marketed Nike, Wheaties, and other products, so did these corporations help produce the Jordan image and spectacle. Likewise, Jordan was used to market the NBA and in turn its publicity machine and success helped promote Jordan.

In the sports/entertainment colossus, a vast marketing apparatus of television, radio, magazines, and other media help to promote and manufacture the stars of sports and entertainment, attesting to an implosion between media and sports culture, and thus sports and commerce. Indeed, Jordan himself is an entire sports franchise with special pitches geared toward kids [i.e. an 800 (free) phone number for ordering Nikes that Jordan gives them "permission" to call], toward urban teens, and targeting young adults, in this case with his fragrance products. And as Cole (1996) has documented, Jordan was part of a Nike PLAY program ("Participate in the Lives of America's Youth"), designed to present a positive corporate image and promote its products to a youth audience. Then, in 1999, he began his own Jordan Fundamentals Grant Program, to provide funds to schools with outstanding youth programs.

Michael Jordan is thus a dazzling sports spectacle, who promotes both commercial sports and the products of the corporations that sell their goods to sports audiences. His distinctive image is often noted, and Jordan's look and style are truly striking. His shaved head, extremely long shorts, and short socks are often cited as defining features, which are highlighted in a Spike Lee Nike ad that, in a brilliant effort to get the Nike message across, repeatedly insists, "*It's gotta be the shoes!*" (i.e. that make Jordan the greatest). In addition, his wrist band, jersey number 23, and tongue wagging and hanging as he concentrates on a play are all distinctive of the Jordan trademark image. In fact, Jordan is so handsome that he has often been employed as a model, and his good looks and superstar status have won him count- less advertising endorsements for products such as Nike, McDonald's, Gatorade, Coca Cola, Wheaties, Haines shorts, and numerous others. A Gatorade ad tells the audience to "Be like Mike," establishing Jordan as a role model, as the very icon of excellence and aspiration. In anti-drug ads, Jordan tells the nation to, "Just say no," to avoid drugs, to do the right thing, and to be all you can be, mobilizing the very stereotypes of the conservative postindustrial United States in one figure. Michael Jordan is also the paradigmatic figure of the "hard body" (Jeffords 1994), which was the ideal male image of the Reaganite 1980s, a model of the powerful bodies needed to resurrect US power after the flabbiness of the 1960s and 1970s.

Jordan is a fashion spectacle as well, nattily dressed in expensive clothes, drenched in his own cologne, and exhibiting the trademark well-oiled and shiny bald head. He is a connoisseur of fine wine and gourmet food and an upscale lifestyle. He is also willing to promote almost anything from sporting gear to underwear. As such, he was the perfect sports icon to market Nike shoes, combining tremendous athletic ability with a well-honed fashion image. Thus unfolded the fateful mar- riage of Michael Jordan and Nike, which I will interrogate after an analysis of the contradictory nexus between Jordan, race, and the sports spectacle.

Michael Jordan and the sports/race spectacle

Initially, Jordan was perceived as both black and not black, as a superior athlete and an all-American clean-cut young man who transcended race and yet was obviously an African American. Throughout his career, there were attempts by image managers and commentators to present Jordan as a quasi-deity who transcended racial markers, and yet at other times his color and race were part of the spectacle. It is generally acknowl- edged that he was one of the first African American athletes to break advertising's color barrier, helping to pave the way for lucrative contracts for the next generation of black athletes.[6] During his difficult transitional year of 1993, when Jordan was under intense critical scrutiny by the media and NBA because of his alleged gambling problems and the unsolved murder of his father, whose death many speculated was related to gambling debts, he became for the first time recipient of the sort of negative press visited upon such African American sports luminaries as Muhammad Ali, Mike Tyson, and his one-time Chicago Bulls team-mate Dennis Rodman.

The Jordan publicity machine has recurrently taken the line that Jordan "transcends race," and commentators have claimed that Jordan is "trans-racial."[7] Jordan himself usually plays it both ways in interviews, admitting that he recognizes he is black, while calling upon people to see him as a human being (for example in an interview with

Larry King on CNN in 1996). Yet, as a cultural signifier, as the "universal singular" who represents more general social significance (Denzin 1998, reprinted in Andrews 2001: 3–14), Jordan is a highly polysemic signifier who encodes conflicting meanings and values. Michael Jordan is an example both of what Berlant (1994) calls the "national symbolic" (see the discussion in Cole 1996) and of the "global popular" (see the discussion in Kellner 1995 and Andrews *et al.* 1996). Jordan embodies national values of hard work, competitiveness, ambition, and success. As a black superstar, he presents the fantasy that anyone can make it in the society of competition and status, that one can climb the class ladder and overcome the limitations of race and class. As a national and global superstar, he represents different things to different people in different countries (see the studies by Andrews *et al.* 1996). Indeed, as Wilson and Sparks (1996) remind us, various individuals and audiences are going to receive and appropriate the text of Michael Jordan in different ways according to their own race, gender, class, region, and other subject positions.

As a polysemic signifier, Jordan thus presents a figure that mobilizes many fantasies (i.e. athletic greatness, wealth, success, and upward mobility) for the national and global imaginary, providing a spectacle who embodies many desirable national and global features and aspirations. Yet Jordan is extremely black and his race is a definite signifier of his spectacle, though his blackness too has conflicting connotations. On the one hand, as noted, he is a privileged role model for black youth ("Be like Mike"), he reportedly helps mentor young athletes, and he is a symbol of the African American who has transcended race and who is integrated into US society, representing the dream of assimilation, wealth, and success. But as Andrews (1996) has demonstrated, Jordan's blackness is overdetermined and has also served to signify black transgressions, as when his gambling behavior became a subject of negative media presentation and when his father's murder led to speculation on connections with organized crime. In these images, Jordan is presented as the threatening black figure, as the negative fantasy figure of black deviance from white normality. Jordan's physique, power, and dominance might also feed into the fear of black bodies, as Giroux (1994) suggests in his analysis of how contemporary media culture is characterized by a simultaneous fascination with the accomplishments of the black male body and fear of the threat it poses.

Yet Jordan also lends his personality to anti-drug ads and campaigns, represents constructive ideals of hard work and discipline, and is regularly presented as a positive role model. However, Jordan's "Just say no!" conflicts with his "Just do it!" creating an ambiguous figure, who at once represents restraint and control, and misbehavior and excess. "Just say no" implies morality and constraint, whereas "Just do it!" signifies indulgence and immoderation, as well as determination and grit. Indeed, Nike's self-proclaimed corporate philosophy of "Just do it!" is itself self-contradictory, connoting both the indulgence and thrust toward gratification that makes a consumer society work (i.e. just go out and buy the shoes!), with an evocation of the commitment and hard work needed to succeed in sports or business. Jordan combines both of these impulses, but linking the "Just do it!" philosophy with his well-known interest in gambling and self-gratification could condone behavior coded as immoral by a traditional morality.

The Jordan mythology wants it all ways at once, to combine individualism and morality, but these ideologies can come into conflict, as has Jordan himself occasionally come into conflict with conventional morality in his own life. On the whole, Jordan became positioned in media culture as the "good black," especially against the aggressiveness and visual transgressions of one-time Chicago Bulls team-mate Dennis Rodman. Rodman seemed to cultivate and revel in the bad-boy image, with his bleached and undisciplined hair, ear and nose rings, fancy clothes, and frequent rebellious behavior, coming to represent the "bad" black figure, as opposed to Jordan's "good" one. Jordan is also a privileged figure of the corporate black, renowned for his business acumen as well as his athletic skill. He is the role model who incarnates basic American values and who fashioned his image into a highly beloved celebrity. Indeed, Jordan was deemed the most popular person alive between 1987 and 1993, tying with God in an *Associated Press* survey as the person whom black children most admired, and in a poll of Chinese students he ran neck and neck with Zhou Enlai (Coplon 1996: 37). who?

Thus, for the most part, the Michael Jordan spectacle serves as an icon of positive representations of African Americans. Jordan's concentration is often remarked upon, and his awesome skills are obviously mediated by intelligence. His "air-driven bullets" seem to be guided by a highly effective mental radar system and his trademark "aerial ballets" represent grace and spiritual transcendence as well as brute force. Todd Boyd sees Jordan's talents as exemplary of a black aesthetic and compares him to great black musical performers, writing: "You can't watch Michael Jordan and not be moved in the way one has been moved, at an earlier time, listening to a John Coltrane solo" (Boyd 1997a: 49).[8]

Jordan combined grace and cool, style and skill, drive and polish, energy and aptitude. Like the great American jazz musicians, he merged formal mastery of the instrument and its rules with great improvisational panache. Moreover, as remarked earlier, Jordan seems to embody central American values and to serve as a role model for American youth and as the white fantasy of the good African American. Thus, while it appears wrong to claim, as is often done, that Michael Jordan transcends race, the Jordan spectacle projects unusually positive representations of African Americans, undercutting racist stereotypes and denigration.

The extent to which the spectacles of sports have promoted the interests of African Americans and people of color has not yet been adequately appreciated. As recently as the 1940s, professional sports were segregated and athletes of color were forced to toil in "colored" leagues, condemned, in effect, to the minor leagues. With the breaking of the color-line in professional baseball in the 1940s by Jackie Robinson, African American athletes could be part of professional sports and eventually icons of the sports spectacle. Indeed, during the 1950s and 1960s prominent African American baseball players such as Willie Mays, Larry Doby, and Hank Aaron were acknowledged as superstars of the spectacle.

Black and brown athletes succeeded in equally spectacular ways in professional football, boxing, and basketball. Sports thus became an important route for people of color to grab their share of the American dream and cut of the great spectacle of "professional" (read commercial) sports. On the positive side, the US fascination with sports promoted racial equality, acceptance of racial difference, and multicultural-ism. When black athletes began to participate in professional sports, they entered mainstream media culture as icons of the spectacle, as role models for youth, and as promoters (often unaware) of racial equality and integration.

Sports aided the cause of women's rights as well. Women played basketball shortly after its invention in 1891 and in the early 1970s the US government passed Title IX, which required equal facilities for men's and women's sports at institutions which received federal funding. The result was the expansion of women's basketball programs in college from a couple of hundred in the mid-1970s to thousands by the 1980s. The Women's National Basketball Association (WNBA) emerged in the the 1970s and, over the past decade, the WNBA has become increasingly popular and powerful, with televised games, devoted fans, who often sell out the stadiums, media attention, and an active official website. Women's basketball is now one of the most popular high-school and college games, and more and more women are participating in the sport and getting recognized for their achievements.

Indeed, women's sports are now popular in several fields, and the September 11, 2000 covers of both *Time* and *Newsweek* featured superstar African American track icon Marion Jones. Consequently, sports, once a white male preserve, are becoming open to women and players of color, thus spearheading the development of a multicultural society. In fact, I would argue that the prowess of black sports heroes and the rhythms of rock music have done much to promote racial equality and the rights of African Americans and people of color.[9] The postindustrial United States has become more and more of a media culture, and professional sports and entertainment have become key features of media spectacle. Once African Americans were allowed to sparkle and shine in media culture they were able to enter the mainstream – or at least major figures of the spectacle, such as O. J. Simpson, Hank Aaron, and Michael Jordan, were so empowered. In Spike Lee's *Do the Right Thing* (1989), Mookie, a pizza delivery man played by Spike Lee, confronts Pino, the racist Italian son of the owner of the pizzeria, about his racist, but contradictory, attitudes toward African Americans.

Mookie: Pino, who's your favorite basketball player?
Pino: Magic Johnson
Mookie: Who's your favorite movie star?
Pino: Eddie Murphy
Mookie: Who's your favorite rock star? Prince, you're a Prince fan.
Pino: Bruce!
Mookie: Prince!
Pino: Bruce!
Mookie: Pino, all you ever talk about is "nigger this" and "nigger that," and all your favorite people are so-called "niggers."
Pino: It's different. Magic, Eddie, Prince, are not niggers. I mean they're not black. I mean … Let me explain myself. They're not really black, I mean, they're black but they're not really black, they're more than black. It's different.
Mookie: It's different?
Pino: Yeah, to me it's different.

Nike has often presented African American athletes as "different" in their ads, as part and parcel of the American dream, thus helping to promote them to superstar celebrity status. Nike also helped to promote the NBA and professional basketball to global iconic status, enabled black athletes such as Michael Jordan to attain world-class superstar status, and addressed the situation of African Americans. Yet one could argue that these appropriations of the black sports spectacle were geared to sell shoes and other commercial products. Thus, the commodity transformation offered to the consumer with the Nike shoe is arguably a false transcendence. Such commodity transformation does not produce a new superself, but simply exploits its customer's pocketbook, forcing the unwary purchaser to buy a product much more expensive than many of its competitors, simply because of its sign value and prestige. And while one can affirm Nike's emphasis on activity and exercise over passivity and boredom, it is not clear that the sort of activity that Nike is promoting is really going to advance the interests of minority youth. Gangs versus sports is not the only dichotomy of contemporary urban life, and one might argue that education, technical skills, and career choice and motivation are more important for contemporary youth than running down a basketball court and shooting hoops.

Moreover, the elevation to cultural icons of black athletes such as Michael Jordan is itself a double-edged sword. On the one hand, Jordan is a spectacle of color who elevates difference to sublimity and who raises blackness to dignity and respect. An icon of the sports spectacle, Michael Jordan is *the* black superstar, and his prominence in sports has made him a figure that corporate America can use to sell its products and values. Yet, such are the negative representations and connotations of blackness in US culture, and such is the power of the media to define and redefine images, that even the greatest African American icons and spectacles can be denigrated to embody negative connotations. As Michael Jackson, O. J. Simpson, and Mike Tyson have discovered, those who live by the media can die by the media, and overnight their positive representations and significance can become negative.

Media culture is only too ready to use black figures to represent transgressive behavior and to project society's sins on to African Americans. Indeed, despite an endemic national and global problem of sexual harassment, Clarence Thomas became the representative figure for this transgression in the 1990s. Despite the troubling problem of child molestation cutting across every race and class, Michael Jackson was the media figure who came to represent this iniquity (until 2002 when Catholic priests became the poster people for sexual child abuse).[10] Further, despite an epidemic of violence against women, O. J. Simpson became the ultimate wife abuser (see Chapter 4), and although date rape is a deplorable, frequent, and well-documented phenomenon across races, classes, and regions, it was Mike Tyson who emerged as "poster boy" for this offense. Indeed, Tyson became the whipping guy in 1997–98 for all of the ills of professional boxing after his behavior in a title fight, his violence against seniors in a driving accident, for which he was sentenced to a year in jail, and his generally aberrant behavior.[11]

Hence, such is the racism of US culture that African Americans are the figures of choice to represent social transgressions and tabooed behavior. Michael Jordan has had his bouts with negative media representations, though on the whole his representations have been largely positive and his figure has been used to represent an ideal of blackness that US society as a whole can live with. Indeed, for many, Jordan presents an image of the transcendence of race that many celebrate as a positive ideal. Yet despite his adulation, it would be a mistake to make Michael Jordan *the* role model for African Americans or the youth of the world. Comparing Jordan with baseball star Jackie Robinson, who broke the major league color barrier in 1947, Jack White describes Robinson's speaking out against racial injustice, his actions with Martin Luther King, and his consistent upholding of his political principles:

> You can hardly imagine contemporary black sports superstars taking an equally brave stand on a divisive moral issue. Most are far too concerned with raking in endorsement dollars to risk any controversy. In 1990 Michael Jordan, who occupies the psychological spot that Robinson pioneered as the dominant black athlete of his time, declined to endorse his fellow black North Carolinian Harvey Gantt over troglodyte racist Jesse Helms in a close contest for the US Senate on the grounds that "Republicans buy shoes too." More recently, Jordan brushed off questions about whether Nike, which pays him $20 million a year in endorsement fees, was violating standards of decency by paying Indonesian workers only 30 cents per day. His curt comment: "My job with Nike is to endorse the product. Their job is to be up on that." On the baseball field or off it, when Robinson came up to the plate, he took his best shot and knocked it out of the park. The superstar athletes who have taken his place, sadly, often strike out.
>
> (White 1997: 90)

When asked what he thought about the LA uprisings after the police who beat Rodney King were declared not guilty in May 1992, Jordan replied, in Todd Boyd's paraphrase, "I'm more concerned with my jump shot." Boyd comments: "Nobody's asking you to be Malcolm X, but when an opportunity arises, don't run from it" (Boyd 1997a: 49). But Michael Jordan, like many athletes corrupted by the sports spectacle and commercial culture, has abrogated his basic political and social responsibilities in favor of expensive clothes, commodities, and a mega stock portfolio. Nike has played a key role in promoting these values and is a major cultural force, a powerful instrument of socialization, and an arbiter of cultural and social values, as well as a shoe company. Consequently, the Nike–Jordan nexus is worthy of critical reflection as the contradictions of Michael Jordan's persona come to the fore in a striking way in his intimate connection with the Nike Corporation.

Michael Jordan, Nike, and the commodity spectacle

Media culture is notorious for destroying precisely the icons it has built up, especially if they are black. Jordan eventually received his share of bad, as well as adulatory, press. During the 1990s, Jordan was regularly criticized when Nike was sharply attacked in the media for its labor policies. Put on the defensive, Jordan was frequently asked to comment on Nike's labor practices. As first he refused to answer questions about Nike's corporate practices, and then, in a carefully prepared public relations response, Jordan countered that it was up to Nike "to do what they can to make sure everything is correctly done. I don't know the complete situation. Why should I? I'm trying to do my job. Hopefully, Nike will do the right thing" (cited in Herbert 1996: 19A). Yet the media continued to pester him, and he was often portrayed in images during the summer of 1996 turning away from interviewers with a curt "No comment," when asked what he thought of Nike's exploitation of Third World workers, especially women, at extremely low wages.

Nike and Michael Jordan are thus intricately connected. As noted, Nike signed the relatively untested young basketball player to a contract in 1984 and evolved one of the most successful marketing campaigns in history. There have been seventeen annual editions of Nike's Air Jordan shoes as of 2002, and Jordan has helped make Nike's corporate logo and swoosh sign one of the most familiar icons of corporate culture, as well known as McDonald's' golden arches and the Coca Cola bottle. From the beginning, Nike deployed the spectacle of Michael Jordan and produced ads that celebrated its products in a commodity spectacle that connected Jordan's prowess and image with its product.

After its move back to the Weiden & Kennedy advertising agency in 1987, Nike devised some of the most spectacular advertising campaigns in history, with many featuring Michael Jordan.[12] One of the distinctive features of the Nike campaigns was the merging of advertising, entertainment, and sports in its ads. Nike hired Spike Lee, who deployed the Mars Blackmon character, played by himself, featured in his first commercial film *She's Gotta Have It* (1986). Nike ad copy-writer Jim Riswold and producer Bill Davenport first thought of using the Spike Lee character:

> … when they noticed that Mars didn't take off his Jordans even to do the nasty. Light bulbs went off in their heads. Was it tough to sell Spike the idea of doing an ad with Jordan? "I think he would've done the commercial free, just to meet Michael," says Riswold.
>
> (Reilly 1991: 77)

Lee accordingly produced the first Michael Jordan Nike ad, "Hang Time," using the black and white photography of his first commercial film to show Mars hanging on a basketball rim while Jordan dunks him. Lee used the character schticks from the film, having Mars calling out to Jordan, "Money! Why you wanna leave me hangin'?" and, in an ad shot in Mars' bedroom, shouting, "Shuddup down there! We're trying to make a commercial!" Thus, the ads blended humor and entertainment with the advertising pitch and helped to circulate the star/celebrity image of both Lee and Jordan, just as O. J. Simpson's ads for the Hertz car rental company made him a familiar icon of media culture.

In another ad drawing on *She's Gotta Have It*, Jordan is standing with his arm around the film's star, Nola Darling, as Mars tries to find out why she prefers Jordan to him, finally concluding, "Its gotta be the shoes, *the shoes!*" Lee tired of the Mars persona, and in an innovative series of ads in the mid-1990s, Nike disposed of the shoe presentation altogether, drawing on familiarity with the corporate logo and swoosh sign, as well as celebrities such as Jordan, to market its product. In one set of Nike ads, urban blacks discuss the pleasure of playing basketball, equating participating in sports and wearing Nike shoes with uplifting their race. And the 1994 Nike-financed PLAY campaign featured urban youth in crisis, facing the alternatives between bored passivity and (Nike-powered) activity, and ultimately between sports and gangs.[13]

Behind the Nike spectacle, there is, of course, the unedifying reality of underpaid workers, toiling at sub-subsistence wages under terrible working conditions to produce highly overpriced shoes for youth, many of whom cannot afford and do not need such luxury items. Nike was one of the first major corporations to shift to a mode of production labeled "postFordism" and "flexible accumulation" (Harvey 1989). Shifting production of its shoes from the United States to Asia in the early 1980s, Nike first set up factories in Japan, Taiwan, and South Korea. The last two countries had at the time military dictatorships, low wages, and disciplined workforces. They frequently subcontracted work to local companies, which would then be responsible for such things as wages, working conditions, and safety. While there were no established unions, the mainly women workers in South Korea began organizing themselves in response to poor working conditions, humiliating treatment by bosses, and low wages. At the same time, a democracy movement began in South Korea and when mounting labor unrest was apparent:

> [F]actory managers called in government riot police to break up employees' meetings. Troops sexually assaulted women workers, stripping them, and raping them "as a control mechanism for suppressing women's engagement in the labor movement," reported Jeong-Lim Nam of Hyosung Women's University in Taegu. It did not work. It did not work because the feminist activists in groups, such as the Korean Women Workers' Association (KWWA), helped women to understand and deal with the assaults. The KWWA held consciousness-raising sessions in which notions of feminine duty and respectability were tackled along with wages and benefits. They organized themselves independently of the male-led labor unions to ensure that their issues would be taken seriously, in labor negotiations and in the pro-democracy movement as a whole.
>
> (Enloe 1995: 12)

Conditions and wages improved for Korean women workers, but Nike was already in the process of moving production to countries with lower wages and more control of labor, such as China and Indonesia. From the 1980s to the present, Nike's shoes have been produced mostly in Asia, where the average wage paid to its workers is often below the subsistence level. There was much publicity over Nike's Indonesian sweatshops, in which women would be paid approximately $1.20 per day to produce shoes in the early 1990s. In 1992, 6,500 workers in the Sung Hwa Dunia factory in Serang, Indonesia, went on strike and wages were raised to $1.80 a day and eventually to $2.20 a day (Kirshenbaum 1996: 23). Under intense pressure from the Clinton administration to improve working conditions and labor rights in order not to lose its privileged trading status, the Indonesian government raised the minimum wage to (a still pitiful) $1.80 an hour and promised that the military would no longer harass and brutalize workers. But, as Greider reports, the concessions were largely a charade because:

> despite the official decrees, the military kept on intervening in labor disputes, showing up at the plant gates and arresting strike activists, herding the women back into the factories. This occurred 22 times within the first month following the supposed reform.
>
> (Greider 1994: 43)

In addition, the companies often refused to pay the workers even the legal minimum wage. The response of the Indonesian workers was a series of wild-cat strikes, international campaigns to publicize their plight, and continued efforts to organize themselves. Accordingly, Nike sought other sites of production, increasing its number of factories in China and then moving to Vietnam, where the minimum wage is $30 per month and they could return to the one-dollar-plus-change a day wages of an earlier era. Basing his figures on an analysis by Thuyen Nguyen, a US businessman who studied the conditions of Nike workers in Vietnam, Bob Herbert wrote in a *New York Times* editorial piece, "Nike's boot camps," that "Nike workers in Vietnam are paid $1.60 a day while three meager meals cost $2.10 a day, renting a room costs $6 a month. Nike's workers are paid subsistant wages and work in conditions described as 'military boot camps' with widespread corporal punishment, molestation of women workers, and deteriorating health of the workers." (Herbert 1997: A16).

There was so much negative publicity concerning working conditions in sweatshops producing Nike gear that the corporation hired Andrew Young, the former mayor of Atlanta and a highly respected African American politician, to review its labor practices and working conditions (*New York Times*, March 25, 1997). When Young returned some weeks later with a report that whitewashed Nike, it took out full-page ads to trumpet the results, though generally there was skepticism concerning Young's account and his inadequate inspection of the Asian worker's plight.[14]

Thus, Nike shifts production from country to country to gain ever lower labor costs. NAFTA and GATT trading standards treaties have made it even easier for Nike and other global corporations to move production across the US border. Consequently, Nike is able to shift around its manufacture at will, searching for the lowest labor costs and most easily exploitable working conditions. Meanwhile, its CEO Phil Knight earns millions per year, his stock is worth an incredible $4.5 *billion*, and Jordan, Andre Agassi, and Spike Lee are paid staggering sums for their endorsements and advertisements (Herbert 1996). Nike's profit margins have been enormous: Enloe (1995: 13) estimated that for a $70 pair of Nike Pegasus shoes, $1.66 goes for labor; $1.19 to the subcontractor; $9.18 goes for materials; $2.82 for administration and overheads; and Nike thus pockets $22.95 while the retailer takes in $32.20.

During the late 1990s' Asian financial crisis, the situation of Nike workers became even more dire:

The *Village Voice* reported that Jeff Ballinger, director of the workers' rights group Press for Change "… would like to see Jordan make good on his pledge to visit factories in Southeast Asia where Michael-endorsed products are manufactured. In a cover story for *ESPN. The Magazine* last April, Jordan said, 'I want to go to Southeast Asia to see the Nike plants for myself … when basketball is done.' … Ballinger says that a Jordan visit would highlight the plight of Nike workers in countries such as Vietnam and Indonesia that have been hit by the Asian financial crisis. He estimates that: "Nike factory wages in Indonesia have dropped to the equivalent of about $1 a day since the currency crash – while the plummeting value of the rupea has translated into about $40 million in labor-cost savings for Nike."

(*Jockbeat*, January 20–26, 1999)

Indeed, Nike engages in superexploitation of both its Third World workers and global consumers. Its products are not more intrinsically valuable than other shoes but have a certain distinctive sign value that gives them prestige value,[15] which gives its wearers a mark of social status, and so it can charge $130–140 per pair of shoes, thus earning tremendous profit margins. Nike provides a spectacle of social differentiation that establishes its wearer as cool, with it, and part of the Nike–superstar spectacle nexus. Nike promises transcendence, a new self, to be like Mike, to fly, to gain respect. It enables the customer to participate in the Nike–Jordan magic by purchasing the shoes he sells. As the Spike Lee/Michael Jordan ad insists, "It's the shoes!", and those who buy the shoes buy into a lifestyle, an image, and a commodity spectacle. But a *New York Times* writer raised the question: "Does being Mike entail any responsibilities beyond doing your best on the court?" And then answered:

> Let's ask Inge Hanson, who runs Harlem RBI, a youth baseball and mentoring program. She was mugged earlier this year by a 14-year-old and his 10-year-old henchboys. After they knocked her down and took about $60, a mugger kicked her in the face. The next day, the bruise that had welled up on her left cheek bore the imprint of a Nike swoosh. It lasted for three weeks and she felt sad thinking she was probably robbed to finance a fancier pair of Nikes.
>
> "But I can't honestly answer your question," she said. "How could Michael Jordan possibly know that by endorsing sneakers – sneakers! – he was involved in a crime? And yet, one does wonder if he has any responsibility to his audience beyond just saying, "Just do it!"

(cited in Lipsyte 1996)

While Michael Jordan tries to present himself as the embodiment of all good and wholesome values, he is clearly tainted by his corporate involvements with Nike in the unholy alliance of commerce, sports spectacle, and celebrity. His symbiosis with Nike is so tight, they are so intertwined with each other, that if Nike is tarnished, so too is Jordan (and vice versa – similarly, Hertz moved quickly to sever its ties with O. J. Simpson after the discovery of the murder of his former wife, Nicole, and her friend Ron Goldman; see Chapter 4). The fate of Nike and Michael Jordan is inextricably intertwined, with Nike taking on Jordan to endorse its products early in his career and helping to make him a superstar known to everyone, while the Air Jordan product line helped to reverse Nike's declining sales and make it an icon of the corporate United States with a global reach that made Nike products part of the global popular (Andrews 1997). Thus, whereas Jordan was no doubt embarrassed by all the bad publicity that Nike received in the 1990s, his involvement with the corporation was obviously too deep to "just say no" and sever himself from this prime example of a greedy and exploitative corporation.

Third coming, sex scandals, and the contradictions of the spectacle

About a year after he had announced his retirement in January 1999, Michael Jordan revealed on January 12, 2000 that he was returning to basketball as president of operations and part-owner of the Washington Wizards, at the time one of the least successful basketball teams in the NBA. The Baltimore Bullets franchise had moved to Washington in 1973, and in 1997 the name was changed to Wizards, allegedly to send out messages of non-violence and anti-gangs to the community, and this semantic shift helped to create an image that Michael Jordan could amalgamate himself with.

It appeared that Jordan had new aspirations, to become a successful CEO and major player in the corporate world, which he had long admired. Before his retirement, Nike had opened a new high-end shoes and clothing line called Brand Jordan and appointed Jordan as CEO. But Jordan had even higher corporate ambitions and, as Sam Walker (2001) tells the story, a meeting in October 1999 with former AOL marketing genius Ted Leonsis pointed to the direction of Jordan's aspirations. Leonsis had purchased part-ownership of the Washington Wizards and majority ownership of the Washington Capitals NHL hockey team, and obviously had ambitions of a sports empire and wanted Jordan aboard. Jordan, in turn, dreamed Internet dot.com fantasies and craved connection with the Internet mogul Ted Leonsis of AOL fame.

Indeed, Jordan had already begun efforts to build his own Internet empire, and in January 2000 announced the formation of an Internet sporting goods site MVP.com, along with his partners, retired athletics stars John Elway and Wayne Gretzky. In February, Jordan added sports.com to his Internet portfolio, a joint venture with Tiger Woods, Shaquille O'Neil, and various venture capitalists. Jordan was also approached to associate himself with an Internet company run by a Chicago software entrepreneur called Divine Interventures, which would help organize, run, and produce stock offerings for Internet companies. Jordan announced that when his current string of endorsements expired he would not renew them, and thus it appeared that he was on the way to a new career and success as a corporate player and rising Internet business star.

Unfortunately for Jordan, the dot.com boom was coming to a close and, although his Internet ventures raised money and got publicity, they failed to yield the golden goose of capital accumulation and Jordan's CEO dreams appeared to be going bust. Jordan broke his promise not to sign any more endorsement contracts to promote a new Palm Pilot, but this venture was not a big success either. On top of this, the Washington Wizards performed poorly during Jordan's first year as president, and he was criticized for not being hands-on and on site in Washington with his team.

Hence, around the time of the September 11, 2001 terrorist attacks, rumors were flying that Jordan was planning to return to the court, making his second major comeback and what could be called a "third coming." On September 25, Jordan formally announced his return, claiming that he would again play because of "his love of the game," a repackaging of a slogan used to promote a book he had done earlier on basketball. Not everyone was pleased that Jordan had chosen to make another comeback. Some, like his good friend Charles Barkley, feared that he might fail, disappointing his fans and letting himself down. Others felt that the NBA needed to cultivate new stars and heroes, and that Jordan should allow them the spotlight and opportunity to fill his shoes. Promoters and advertisers worried about the consequences of a Michael Jordan failure adversely affecting NBA profits and advertising revenues.[16]

Speculation raged concerning why Jordan had chosen to return to the game. Some believed it was ego and a need to continually challenge himself and succeed. Others thought he needed the adrenaline rush and fix of the game and adulation of the fans. Yet others speculated that it was business that motivated Jordan, who believed that he could help build up a profitable franchise with his participation and position himself as a key force once again in NBA basketball and media spectacle. As is often the case, it was probably all these motivations and more that led the by then 38-year-old Jordan to get his aging body back in shape and become once again a media spectacle.

In the fall 2001 season, Jordan did return and performed reasonably well. Although he was sluggish in his initial highly publicized game with the fabled NY Knicks, missing crucial last-minute shots and the possibility of hitting the "money" in a close 93–91 loss, Jordan's playing picked up and he turned a losing team into a winning one. Jordan indeed provided a big boost to the sagging fortunes of the NBA, as he sold out almost every game he played in, generated increased television interest, and thus generally helped NBA revenues and image.

In 2002, however, Michael Jordan faced the greatest image crisis and most potentially destructive media spectacle of his career, when his wife, Juanita, filed for divorce on January 4, citing "irreconcilable differences." There had long been rumors of Jordan's womanizing, and tabloids had published stories of women claiming to have had sex with Jordan, but on the whole he had maintained a positive family image. Jordan's initial media figure was that of a squeaky-clean good kid from Carolina, who refused to party with the more rowdy Chicago Bulls, and was a devoted son who had appropriated strict family values. In fact, Jordan's closeness to his parents was legendary, and his handlers continued to project images of Jordan as an ideal father and husband after he married and had three children. Jordan had continually projected the image of a wholesome family man, an image necessary to secure his lucrative promotions and to serve as a black role model and man of good American values.

In short, Michael Jordan had become part of the US mythology, combining the values of individualism, hard work, competition, success, and unparalleled athletic achievement with morality, family values, honesty, and rectitude. To be sure, there were recurrent stories of excessive gambling, which were recounted even by his adulatory biographers and journalists, but by and large Michael Jordan was seen as a man of strong moral values. Yet this myth was severely challenged by the stories that were now emerging as the prospects of a divorce entered into play.

The tabloids had a field day exploiting stories of his alleged sexual adventures and his wife, Juanita, suing him for divorce, demanding custody of their three children, their house, and an equitable financial settlement. If one believed the tabloid stories, Jordan was a serial philanderer who had countless affairs with strippers and lap dancers, girls in every town, and a whole collection of cell phones for communicating with his various paramours. These stories circulated through the mainstream media, which was also returning to Michael Jordan gambling stories. Cumulatively, these tales were creating media spectacles of Michael Jordan as a sex and gambling addict, a rather heavy burden for the repository of all-American mythologies to bear.

Jordan had, in fact, long carried contradictory connotations in the dominant representations of his body and physical activity. Representations of male athletes, especially basketball players such as Jordan, present a sexual dimension through images of their physical bodies in a state of undress and as potent and powerful. Jordan also emphasized sensuality in his fragrance ads as an essential part of his being, and his bald head and glistening hard body easily led to his appropriation as a sex symbol. Yet Jordan's potentially potent and potentially transgressive sexuality was always contained in the framework of family values and apparent morality.[17]

It appeared that this crisis was in the process of being resolved on February 4 when in a "joint statement of Juanita and Michael Jordan," a fax was sent out stating that: "We have decided to attempt a reconciliation and our efforts to do so will be greatly enhanced if the privacy of our personal lives is respected." This was a message to the media to lay off, and apparently Jordan was extremely angry about the excessive coverage his marriage problems were receiving and the speculation about the causes. Then, in the midst of this cauldron of bad publicity and image challenges, Jordan suffered a serious injury that might bring his career as an active basketball player to a close.

At the time of the February all-star game, Jordan was appearing a bit worn, had begun to limp, and was facing injuries that were forcing him to have fluid drained from his right knee. On February 27 Jordan underwent arthoscopic surgery to repair torn knee cartilage. Although the surgery was deemed a success, there was a wealth of speculation concerning whether Jordan's career was finished and, although he returned some weeks later, his future was uncertain, adding a spectacle of mortality and bodily wear, tear, and breakdown to the now copious repertoire of Michael Jordan mythologies.

Jordan sat out only twelve games after his surgery, returning to play on March 20. He was obviously in great pain, playing only in reserve, and managing a career-low twelve minutes and a career-low two points in a 113–93 loss to the LA Lakers on April 2. The comeback saga came to a provisional end on April 3, when Jordan announced that he was packing it in for the season, although he hoped to return the next year, for which he had signed on to play, thereby guaranteeing a spectacle of speculation over whether Jordan would or would not be able to play again.[18]

The "third coming" was thus a mixed experience, with Jordan generating his customary excitement, turning a losing team into one that, before his departure at least, had a shot at the play-offs. Jordan himself averaged 22.9 points, the second lowest of his career, but certainly respectable. (He had averaged 22.7 in his second season with the Chicago Bulls in 1985–86, when he played only eighteen games because of a broken foot; otherwise he rarely missed a game and had not previously missed a game because of injuries since 1992.) Although Jordan had some very good moments, it was clear that he could not defeat the unbeatable Father Time and the finitude of an aging body. Hence, Michael Jordan added the spectacle of mortality and aging to his collection of representations.

Contradictions of Michael Jordan

Over the now wide span of a spectacular career, the media figure of Michael Jordan has accumulated highly contradictory representations and effects. Although he was a symbol of making it in the corporate United States, his success record has been patchy since his 1999 retirement and he has become tarnished with the scandals and negative portrayals of excessive greed, competitiveness, predatory sexuality, and hypocrisy. Earlier, Jordan had embodied the contradictions of capitalist globalization as he was tainted with the negative images with which corporations to whom he had sold himself were fouled, such as Nike's exploitative labor practices, as well as embodying positive images of corporate power and success.

Now Jordan is fated to live out not only the contradictions of corporate global capitalism, but his own moral contradictions and conflicts. In a sense, these contradictions, as well as his array of successes and failures, make Jordan more remarkable, more human, and in many ways a more engaging and more compelling media spectacle. Michael Jordan the all-American mythology was always something of a fraud and an ideological gloss over the seamy side of corporate business, the sports/entertainment colossus, and the inevitable imperfections of a mortal human being. As a bearer of complexity and contradiction, however, Jordan presents the drama of a human life that could evolve in any number of directions, ranging from yet further unforeseen success and greatness to moral abjection and failure.

Although Jordan's contradictions and tensions were somewhat suppressed by his ideological halo, to some extent Jordan always was his own contradictions. The representations of his magical athletic body and his presentation of the body in advertising combined the well-behaved corporate black athlete and endorser with a sexy, powerful, and potentially threatening masculine image. Michael Jordan's combination of athletic prowess and his association with fashion, cologne, and the good life always made him a potential transgressor of bourgeois middle-class family values and propriety. Although Jordan's family values images articulated well with the conservative ethos of the Reagan–Bush I era (1980–92), there was always an aura of threatening sexuality and masculinity in Jordan, who was a potentially transgressive figure.

Moreover, in an era of media spectacle, avaricious and competitive media machines are eager to exploit every scandal and weakness of its stars and celebrities, even those such as Michael Jordan who have provided so much to so many. It is an irony of media spectacle, however, that what appears as scandal and transgression can augment the power and wealth of the bearer of such negativity. Dennis Rodman built a career on his bad-boy image, and Bill Clinton's popularity seemed to go up with every new revelation of scandal and transgression, although this dialectic, as I will discuss in Chapter 6, is itself complex, overdetermined, and risky to practice.

Reading Jordan critically

Jordan thus seems fated to live out the cultural contradictions of contemporary US capitalism and his own personal conflicts, embodying a multifarious mixture of images and mythologies. Since Jordan's spectacle is open and ongoing, and could yield future surprises, critical interrogation of the Jordan effect and of how the media constructs and the public appropriates and lives out the Michael Jordan spectacle emerges as an important challenge for critical cultural studies.

To begin, it could be argued that Jordan represents an overvaluation of sports in contemporary US and indeed global culture. Although it is positive for members of the underclass to have role models and aspirations to better themselves, it is not clear that sports can provide a means to success for any but a few. A revealing 1991 documentary, *Michael Jordan's Playground*, features a fantasy about a young African American boy who, like Michael Jordan, had been cut from his school basketball team. Jordan appears to tell the boy not to give up, to apply himself, and to struggle to make it. The rest of the story interweaves the young boy's hard work with images of Jordan's heroic basketball accomplishments, providing at once a morality tale for youth and a self-glorification of Michael Jordan as role model and teacher of youth as well as basketball deity.

The 1994 Nike-financed PLAY program, in which Jordan participated, provided images of antithesis between gangs and sports, urging youth to choose the latter. But this is arguably a false antithesis, and there are surely other choices for inner-city and poor youth, such as education, learning computer skills, or training for a profession. The 1995 documentary *Hoop Dreams* brilliantly documented the failed hopes and illusory dreams of ghetto youth making it in college basketball and the NBA. For most would-be stars, it is a false hope to dream of fame and athletic glory, thus it is not clear that Jordan's "Be like Mike" is going to be of much real use to youth. Moreover, the widespread limitation of figures from the black spectacle to sports and entertainment might also contribute to the stereotype, as Mercer (1994) suggests, that blacks are all brawn and no brain, or merely spectacular bodies and not substantive persons. Yet some criticism of Jordan as a basketball player has also circulated. Amidst the accolades after his announced retirement, some negative evaluations emerged of his style and influence on the game. Stating baldly, "I hate Michael Jordan," Jonathan Chait wrote:

> Whenever I declare this in public, I am met with stammering disbelief, as if
> I had expressed my desire to rape nuns. But I have my reasons. First, he has

helped to change the culture of sports from one emphasizing teamwork to one emphasizing individualism. The NBA has contributed to this by promoting superstars ("Come see Charles Barkley take on Hakeem Olajuwan!"), but Jordan buys into it, too. Once he referred to his teammates as his "supporting cast," and in last year's finals he yelled at a teammate for taking a shot in the clutch moments that he, Jordan, should have taken – after his teammate made the shot. The result is a generation of basketball players who don't know or care how to play as a team.

(*Slate,* January 19, 1999)

Chait also complained that Jordan was "the beneficiary of extremely favorable officiating," and that "Jordan has been so spoiled and pampered by his special treatment that he expects a trip to the foul line every time an opponent gets near him, and he whines if he doesn't get it … The prevailing ethic in American sports used to be teamwork, fair play, and rooting for the underdog. Michael Jordan has inverted this ethic."[19]

Others noted that Jordan was so competitive and obsessed with winning that he was downright "predatory," as team-mate Luc Longley put it, "Opposing player Danny Ainge described Jordan as destroying one opponent like 'an assassin who comes to kill you and then cut your heart out.' Jordan, 'skilled at verbal blood sport,' is hard on teammates and harder still, even merciless, in baiting and belittling his nemesis [Chicago Bulls manager], Jerry Krause" (Novak 1999: X3).

Thus, it is important to read the spectacle of Michael Jordan critically for its multifarious social and political meanings, as well as the wealth of meanings generated by Jordan as sports and race spectacle, and the complexity of his life. Jordan's obsession with wealth, highlighted in Spike Lee's nickname for Jordan ("Money"), circulates capitalist values and ideals, promoting the commercialization of sports and greed, which many claim has despoiled the noble terrain of athletics. Jordan is the prototypical overachiever, pushing to win at all costs with his eyes on all the possible prizes of the rewards of competition and winning. Yet, so far, Jordan has not assumed the political responsibilities taken on by other athletic idols of his race, such as Paul Robeson, Jessie Owens, Joe Louis, Jackie Robinson, or Muhammad Ali.[20] As Touré put it:

Any cause he might have championed – from something as morally simple as supporting the candidacy of fellow North Carolinian Harvey Gantt, who lost two close Senate races against Satan's cousin, Jesse Helms, to any stand against any sort of American injustice – would have been taken seriously because it was endorsed by Jordan. Yet as careful as he has been at vacuuming every possible penny into his pocket … he has been equally diligent about leaving every bit of political potential on the table. Couldn't the world's greatest endorser have sold us something besides shoes?

(*Village Voice,* January 27–February 5, 1999)

Jordan has generally symbolized the decline of politics and replacement of all social values by monetary ones, which has characterized the past couple of decades in which he became a major media spectacle of our era.[21] Such issues are relevant in assessing the Jordan effect because superstar celebrities such as Michael Jordan mobilize desire into specific role models, ideals of behavior and values. They produce an active fantasy life whereby individuals dream that they can "be like Mike," to cite the mantra of the Gatorade commercial, and emulate their idol's behavior and values. Thus, part of the "Jordan effect" is the creation of role models, cultural ideals, values, and modes of behavior. Consequently, critical scrutiny of what sort of values and behavior the Jordan spectacle promotes is relevant to assessing its cultural significance.

In the more somber and serious cultural milieu in the United States after the September 11 terrorist attacks, questions arise as to whether so much celebrity and adulation should be invested in sports figures, who themselves are ever more subject to commercialization and commodification, of which Michael Jordan serves as the model. In any case, as the figures of media culture play such an important role in the culture of the spectacle, it is important to develop insight into how media culture is constructed and functions. In this study, I have attempted to theorize the role of the sports spectacle, and in particular the significance of the Jordan–Nike nexus in the postindustrial United States, and to articulate the importance for media culture of sports and the representations of a sports megaspectacle. I have tried to provide critical insights into the contradictory meanings and effects of the sports spectacle, the ways in which sports provide figures and ideologies to reproduce existing values, and the complex meanings and effects of a superstar such as Michael Jordan.

Understanding how media culture works and generates social meanings and ideologies requires a critical media literacy, which empowers individuals and under-mines the mesmerizing and manipulative aspects of the media spectacle (Kellner 1995, 1998). Critical cultural studies are thus necessary to help demystify media culture and produce insights into contemporary society and culture. Reflection on the Jordan–Nike nexus reminds us that media culture is one of the sites of construc-tion of the sports/entertainment colossus and of the icons of contemporary society. Media culture is also the stage on which social conflicts unfold and social reality is constructed, so that the ways in which the dynamics of gender, race, class, nation, and dominant values are played out is crucial for the construction of individuals and society in contemporary culture. Since Michael Jordan embodies the crucial dynamics of media culture, it is important to understand how the Jordan spectacle functions, its manifold and contradictory effects, and the ways in which the Jordan sports/entertainment spectacle embodies social meanings and circulates multiple Jordan effects. As the Michael Jordan adventure is not yet over, his figure remains a source of fascination that should evoke evaluative enquiry by critical cultural studies and social theory.

Notes

1 On the China and Bosnia references, see Dan McGraw and Mike Tharp, "Going out on top" (*US News and World Report*, January 25, 1999: 55). Summing up Jordan's achievements, Jerry Crowe writes: "His resumé includes five most-valuable-player awards, 12 All-Star appearances, two Olympic gold medals and a worldwide popularity that filled arenas and boosted the stock of the companies with which he was

affiliated" (*Los Angeles Times*, January 13, 1999: D1). In addition, Jordan garnered six NBA championship rings, ten NBA scoring titles (a record), a 31.5 regular-season scoring average (best of all times), a record sixty-three points in a playoff game, 5,987 career playoff points (best all-time), and made the game-winning shot a record twenty-six times during his NBA career. Tributes were numerous: Indiana coach Bob Knight, who mentored the budding superstar in the 1984 Los Angeles Olympics, called Jordan "the greatest basketball player ever ... the best player involved in a team sport of any kind"; coach Pat Riley of the Miami Heat described him as "the greatest influence that sports has ever had"; Jerry West, former NBA superstar and executive vice president of the Los Angeles Lakers, labeled Jordan "the modern day Babe Ruth"; and Chicago Bulls Chairman Jerry Reinsdorf enthused: "Michael is simply the best player who ever put on a basketball uniform. He has defined the Bulls, the city and the NBA for more than a decade. He will always represent the state of excellence."

2 Halberstam, quoted in *People* (January 25, 1999: 56). In its front-page story on Jordan's retirement, *USA Today* employed three "greats," five "greatests," one "greatness," two "marvelouses," three "extraordinarys," one "unbelievable," one "unmatched," two "awe-inspirings," two "staggerings," one "superstar," and a hyperhyperbolic "great superstar" (*Sports Illustrated*, January 25, 1999: 32). Television talking heads commenting on Jordan's retirement speculated over whether he would run for president or "compete with Bill Gates in the business arena" (ibid.), while in a completely earnest front-page story the *Chicago Tribune* suggested that Jordan could be an astronaut (cited in *Time*, January 25, 1999: 68). But the winner in the Michael Jordan Retirement Hyperbole Contest is Bill Plaschke: "Hearing that you'll never see Michael Jordan play competitive basketball again is hearing that sunsets have been canceled. That star-filled skies have been revoked. That babies are no longer allowed to smile" (*Los Angeles Times*, January 12, 1999: D1).

3 ABC bought ESPN in 1985, and its official website states that ESPN now "doesn't stand for anything, but the story is this ... When ESPN started in 1979 we were the Entertainment and Sports Programming Network (thus, ESPN). However, the full name was dropped in February 1985 when the company adopted a new corporate name – ESPN, Inc. – and a new logo. We are a subsidiary of ABC, Inc., which is a wholly owned subsidiary of The Walt Disney Co. The Hearst Corporation has a 20 percent interest in ESPN." The connection with Disney and Hearst signifies how sports have become absorbed into the infotainment society and are a crucial part of a globalized entertainment/sports colossus.

4 On Falk's role in promoting the Jordan spectacle, see Halberstam (1999: 136ff. and *passim*). Following Jordan, basketball players began to be promoted as entertainment stars and were becoming top dog icons of the spectacle and major corporate endorsers.

5 For the complex events that led Jordan to this seemingly bizarre decision, see Smith (1995) and Halberstam (1999). During 1993, Jordan's gambling habits were criticized and increasingly the subject of inquiry, and when his father was mysteriously murdered there were speculations that the murder was related to gambling debts. The NBA and media intensified its scrutiny of Jordan, and he abruptly quit basketball to pursue a quixotic and failed minor-league baseball career, returning to professional basketball 18 months later to achieve his greatest athletic triumphs.

6 Football superstar O. J. Simpson preceded Jordan as an African American icon who crossed the color-line in the world of celebrity endorsements, and his tumultuous media spectacle will be the topic of the next chapter.

7 The claim that Jordan transcended race frequently appeared in interviews upon Jordan's retirement by Mark Vancil, who edited the *Rare Air Jordan* photography books, and it has been repeated regularly by commentators since the mid-1990s. Frank Deford argued in the *Sports Illustrated* collector's issue, published after Jordan's retirement, that Jordan is not "a creature of color" and transcends the racial divisions that have so

sundered US society. Matthew DeBord has written that Jordan is "trans-racial, the first African American cultural hero to massively evade blaxploitation by rising above it, elevating to a zone of rarefied commerce where the only pigment that anyone worries about is green" (DeBord 1999). At times in Jordan's reception, this transcendence of race appears to be taking place, but such claims ignore the negative press of 1993 and the fact that African American celebrities can easily become whipping boys as well as poster boys. For a more nuanced analysis of the stages of Jordan's racial signification, see Andrews (2001). For a critique of the oft-cited claim that Jordan transcends race, see the article by Leon E. Wynter, "The Jordan effect: What's race got to do with it?" (*Salon*, January 29, 1999).

8 For fuller development of this concept of a black aesthetic, see Boyd (1997b).

9 Of course, Malcolm X, Martin Luther King, and the civil rights movement did more to dramatize and ameliorate the plight of African Americans, but I would argue that sports and entertainment helped significantly to promote the interests of people of color. Moreover, I believe that the tremendous achievements of black athletes, music performers, and entertainers were essential in getting the mainstream United States to accept and respect blacks and to allow them into the mainstream – in however limited and problematic a fashion.

10 Although the problem of sexual abuse in the Catholic Church had been festering for years, the issue emerged into the media focus for the first time in 2002; Church abusers were, by and large, white men.

11 See Dyson (1993) and Hutchinson (1996) on the demonization of black figures in contemporary media culture.

12 See the analysis of Nike's ads and culture by Goldman and Papson (1998) and Klein (2002). For a dossier of material assembled on Nike's labor practices and campaigns against them, see Michael Moore's site (www.dogeatdogfilms.com/mikenike.html) and the highly impressive website constructed by David M. Boje (cbae.mnsu.edu/~davidboje/nike/nikemain.html).

13 For analysis of analysis of Nike's PLAY, see Cole (1996), reprinted in Andrews (2001), and Goldman and Papson (1998).

14 For a detailed critique of Young's report, see the study by Glass (1997).

15 On the concept of sign value, see Baudrillard (1981), Goldman (1992), and Goldman and Papson (1996).

16 Doubters included *Los Angeles Times* sportswriter Bill Plaschke, whose rhapsodic eulogy to Jordan in his retirement I cited in note 2 above; see also "From Air Jordan to Err Jordan" (*Los Angeles Times*, September 11, 2001: D1 and 6), Allen Barra, "Air Ball. Michael Jordan's rumored return to the court sounds like a great idea for the NBA. It isn't" (*Salon*, April 18, 2001), and Mark Hyman, "Betting that His Airness will soar again" (*Business Week*, October 8, 2001).

17 Mary G. McDonald's study, "Safe sex symbol? Michael Jordan and the politics of representation" (2001), written before the 2002 Jordan sex scandals, adroitly lays out the contradictions between Jordan's sexual and potentially transgressive black male body and the ideology of family values and morality, with which he has packaged his image.

18 Michael Jordan's website in April 2002 featured an *Associated Press* story headlined "Pollin says Jordan will return" (April 9, 2002), claiming that the owner of the Washington Wizards said that he expects Michael Jordan to return next season "and that his comeback was a 'great success,' even though a knee injury cut short his season." But Washington Wizards coach Doug Collins stated that he would be "surprised" if Jordan returned; see Steve Wyche, "Collins wary of Jordan's return to Wizards next year" (*Washington Post*, March 28, 2002: D1). Jordan announced himself that he would return to play again; see "Jordan will play another season" (*Associated Press*, September 26, 2002).

19 David Halberstam in his study *Playing for Keeps: Michael Jordan and the World He*

Made (1999: 57ff.) notes how the University of North Carolina's basketball team, in which Jordan had his start, embodied the team ethic of playing for the group, while sacrificing individual ambition and showboating, exactly the model that the emergence of superstar icons, such as Jordan, eventually reversed. Chicago sportswriter Sam Smith (1992; 1995) wrote two extremely engaging books about Jordan and the Chicago Bulls which provide demythologizing descriptions of Jordan as highly competitive, often nasty to teammates, and a less than stellar human being. Jordan reportedly called Smith an "asshole" after the first book and never spoke to him again.

20   For a probing comparison of Paul Robeson and Michael Jordan, see Harrison in Andrews (2001).

21   On the decline of politics in the contemporary era, see Boggs (2000).

4 Megaspectacle

The O. J. Simpson murder trial*

Media spectacles are often constructed and played out in the form of megaspectacles whereby events such as the Gulf War, sensational murder cases such as the O. J. Simpson trials, celebrity and political sex scandals, or terrorist bombings come to dominate an ever-mushrooming tabloid and infotainment culture.[1] Megaspectacles fixate attention on events that distract people from the pressing issues of their everyday lives with endless hype on shocking crimes, sports contests and personalities, political scandals, natural disasters, and the self-promoting hype of media culture itself. As cable channels and talk shows dedicated to media celebrities and products multiply, megaspectacles come to define entire periods of culture and politics, as did the O. J. Simpson trials and the Clinton sex scandals in the mid- to late 1990s.

As technocapitalism moves into a new information–entertainment society, mergers between the media giants are proliferating, competition is intensifying, and the media are generating spectacles to attract audiences to the programs and advertisements that fuel the mighty money machines (see Chapter 1). Media culture, in turn, arbitrates social and political issues, deciding what is real, important, and vital. Especially spectacular events, such as the 1995 LA freeway flight of O. J. Simpson, the 1996 explosion of a TWA plane outside New York, the 1997 death and funeral of Princess Diana, the Clinton sex scandals in the late 1990s, the plane crash that took the life of John F. Kennedy Jr. in 1999, or the September 11, 2001 terrorist attacks, bring the TV day to a halt and produce ongoing megaspectacle. The cable television and other news media suspend regular programming to cover the events of the minute, and the megaspectacle is discussed endlessly in talk shows on television and radio, on the Internet, and in conversations of everyday life.

Key megaspectacles come to dominate media culture as a whole for long periods of time, as when television, radio, the Internet, and other media focus on

*This study of the O. J. Simpson megaspectacle has never been published. I began following the Simpson case as it unfolded in 1994, presented several conference papers on the topic, and prepared a text as an article for a book that was never published. I also worked on the text with Steve Best for inclusion in what became *The Postmodern Turn* (1997) and *The Postmodern Adventure* (2001), but the study was not included in those books because of space limitations. Thanks to Steve Best, Carl Boggs, and Rhonda Hammer for discussion of the Simpson spectacle over the past few years and comments on various drafts of the text.

the extravaganza of the moment, excluding other events and issues from media focus. Guy Debord described the "society of the spectacle" in which individuals were transfixed by the packaging, display, and consumption of commodities and the play of media events (Debord 1967).[2] We are now at a stage of the spectacle at which it dominates the mediascape, politics, and more and more domains of everyday life as computers bring a proliferating rush of information and images into the house by means of the Internet, competing with television as the dominant medium of our time. The result is a spectacularization of politics, of culture, and of consciousness as media proliferate and new forms of culture colonize consciousness and everyday life.

The O. J. Simpson murder case was the major media spectacle of the mid-1990s. It became a national obsession and cultural arena, which dramatized society's conflicts around race, gender, class, and celebrity and demonstrated that contemporary US politics was being fragmented into what became known as "identity politics."[3] Issues of personal identity and identity politics were initially a largely academic affair, the concern of intellectuals in the university. Yet one could argue that the origins of identity politics were in the social movements of the 1970s, especially as more separatist strains of feminism surfaced, various nationalisms appeared in ethnic and race-based movements, and gay and lesbian movements highlighted connections between sexuality and identity, while a general fragmentation and splitting of different groups emerged in a politics of difference. An intense focus on issues of identity, identity politics, multiculturalism, and the like was a burning center of attention within academic debates in the 1980s and 1990s. But the academic discussions were never entirely separate from political and social struggles (although the arcane specialized languages that developed might have made it appear to be so), and by the 1990s identity politics was strikingly evident throughout the polity and mediascapes of the current era. Thus, engaging the issue of identity politics is much more than a merely academic affair, in that it touches on the crucial political and social issues of the day and is an essential part of contemporary media politics.

Accordingly, I argue that the response to the O. J. Simpson trials indicates an explosion of identity politics and the proliferation of conflicting political discourses in the new technologies and media (i.e. public access television, talk and community radio, the Internet, etc.). Identity politics is bound up with the increased political role of media culture and the ways in which the media frame, mobilize, and influence political issues. The Simpson megaspectacle discloses the important role of celebrity culture in the contemporary era, the ubiquitous role of media spectacle, and the ways in which highly polarizing and controversial cases in a media society can fragment and divide the population.

Murder and media spectacle in Brentwood

Everything about the O. J. Simpson murder saga was mega. The killing of Simpson's wife, Nicole Brown Simpson, and her friend R on Goldman was one of the most publicized homicides in US history, and the subsequent trial of ex-football star and media celebrity O. J. Simpson for murder was called "the trial of the century." The courtroom spectacle was the longest trial ever held in California and cost over $20 million to fight and defend, producing over 50,000 pages of trial transcripts. The megaspectacle played to one of the largest audiences in TV history and was deemed the major news story of 1995.[4]

From the first reports of the murder of two victims in Ms Simpson's condo in Brentwood on the night of June 12, 1994, the media focused intently on the crime as a major event, as a prime spectacle of media culture. The initial coverage highlighted the fact that Nicole Simpson was the wife of football hall of famer and celebrity O. J. Simpson. Simpson was a star African American college football player at the University of Southern California and also had a distinguished career as a pro with the Buffalo Bills, becoming one of the great running backs in NFL history. After his retirement, Simpson continued his celebrity career as a sports commentator, did popular TV ads for Hertz, which showed him running through an airport to get a rental car, and appeared in TV shows and movies such as *The Naked Gun* series, in which he played a lovable but bumbling cop.

In the light of Simpson's celebrity, the media swarmed to the scene of the murder and to his Brentwood estate on June 13, beginning the circus that would surround the event for the months to come. Of the myriad stories, and countless murders and crimes that occur daily, the media focus on some events and neglect others. Stories attract public attention when the media returns to them day after day, when they enter the circuit of talk and commentary shows, and when the public displays genuine interest. In the case of the Simpson murder case and subsequent trials, the events became a major megaspectacle that dominated the media and emerged as the most discussed and controversial event of its era.

The murders of Simpson's wife, Nicole, and her friend Ron Goldman were of initial interest because of the celebrity status of O. J. Simpson, who was a well-known sports star and media figure. In a media society, the media focus on celebrities, and the public seems fascinated by the trials and tribulations of its luminaries. The first CNN reports indicated that Simpson was not a suspect, though later in the day on June 13, a Los Angeles police commander stated in a news conference that: "We're not going to rule anyone out, and I will pursue whoever I need to pursue until I bring the party to justice." This statement implied that Simpson was indeed under suspicion. By June 14, every major newspaper and TV outlet in the country was on the story. From the beginning the Los Angeles police leaked information to the media, incriminating Simpson and provoking his friends and defenders to proclaim his innocence, attempting in turn to manipulate the media and shape public opinion.

On June 18, a warrant was issued for Simpson's arrest and, instead of surrendering himself to his lawyer as promised, he fled with his friend A. C. Cowlings. TV cameras zeroed in on Simpson in a white Bronco being pursued by police during a live chase along the Los Angeles freeways, thus transfixing media attention on the event. Simpson and his faithful sidekick Al Cowlings thus participated in a real-life buddy and chase film, hooking the TV nation on the live drama: Butch Simpson and the Cowlings Kid, attempting an end run around the long arm of the law (or was it just the bumbling Norberg, whom Simpson played in the *Naked Gun* film series, getting himself deeper into trouble?). That famous Friday night drama gripped the nation and hooked millions of people on the Simpson saga, replicating the car chase epic beloved of Hollywood, with outlaws on the run and the forces of law and order in hot pursuit. The images of the spectators stopping and applauding on the freeway uncannily resembled Steven Spielberg's *Sugarland Express*, as the star-crossed lovers fled the law through small-town Texas. Would the ending be *Bonnie and Clyde,* with the fleeing outlaws a victim of systemic violence, or would they escape the panopticon surveillance in the urban jungle à la *The Getaway*?[5]

After some hours on the freeway, during which more than ten TV helicopters broadcast live pictures, Cowlings and Simpson returned to OJ's Brentwood mansion, and after an hour of negotiations surrendered to the police. The ensuing pre-trial hearing and 1995 murder trial were televised live and attracted phenomenal attention, which continued throughout the civil court case in fall 1996 after Simpson was acquitted of murder in October 1995.[6] The entire set of trials and their aftermath provides a vivid lens to illuminate contemporary society and culture constituted by media spectacles, celebrity fetishism, ubiquitous violence, and increasingly fractious and fragmenting culture wars and identity politics. The intense media scrutiny and passionate interest in the spectacle reveals a country in which media culture functions as an arena where social conflicts are fought out, dominant values are negotiated, role models are produced, debates are generated, and politics takes explosive forms. The divisions of opinion around the Simpson trial disclose a deep split between the various social groups, who saw the case very differently according to their race, gender, and class loyalties, and who experienced it within sharply diverse social constructions of reality. The contending opinions about the spectacle from the beginning and the heated debate over Simpson's acquittal revealed that diverse groups had dramatically dissimilar perceptions of the affair and that identity politics, developing since the 1960s, had polarized the country, shattered civil society, and put in question major institutions.

The impassioned response to the trial disclosed a situation in which individuals live out their real social and political strife in media spectacles that transform the virulent divisions of class, race, and gender into spectacular infotainment. These megaspectacles divert attention from the actual causes of inequality and injustice and the social and political movements that attempt to address them. The Simpson spectacle reveals how the media have taken over politics in the United States, displacing party and social movement politics with media politics, in which the media articulate the resonant issues and play out conflicts within their own frames, creating a pseudo-participation, while decreasing involvement in actual sociopolitical struggles. The tremendous resources that the mainstream media put into the event revealed that the commercial media have sacrificed the imperatives of journalism and news in the public interest for focus on spectacle and entertainment. Thus, the Simpson affair is an important episode in the transformation of news into infotainment and the decline of journalism in a media culture. Far more than just a murder trial, the Simpson incident is a pivotal event in the advent of megaspectacle, as it becomes a defining feature of contemporary mediascapes with important political implications.

The Simpson affair initially appeared to the public as a *murder spectacle*, though it soon brought into play all of the major forms of media culture. Its spectacle ranged from the crime genre to melodrama to tabloid exposé of the lifestyles of the rich and famous, to the courtroom trial, to social drama, which articulated a wide array of current social issues such as spousal violence. This was an upper-class melodrama with an inter-racial romance gone awry, a family torn apart by intense passions, and a violent murder, resulting in intense courtroom drama and fascination with the case as a whole. The Simpson extravaganza contained all the ingredients of pulp fiction with the protagonist rising from ghetto slums to immense wealth and celebrity, marrying the white goddess and fairytale princess. But, as often happens in such pulp sagas, the marriage turned sour, with excessive drugs and extramarital sex, wife battering, separations and reunions, stalking and violent confrontations, and the eventual murder and trial. The story was thus a narrative of the rise and fall of an American hero with every melodramatic complication necessary to hook a nation addicted to pulp entertainment.

Although it would be an exaggeration to present the drama as a Greek tragedy, as Simpson was a mere celebrity and, at best, a highly flawed individual and hardly a king or noble figure, it was a thoroughly US tragedy, as Simpson had risen to a high pinnacle of success as a very popular all-round celebrity. Moreover, the parallels with Shakespeare's *Othello* were obvious, with Simpson possessed by jealousy and periodically violent in his obsession with Nicole. The story was saturated with soap opera complications, as the many books detailing the complex love lives of both Simpson and his former wife and their circles of friends make clear (see Resnick 1994; Weller 1995). In short, the Simpson drama employed the dominant genres of media culture and engaged a nation hooked on its formulas and pleasures. It is precisely this mobilizing of dominant codes and themes of media culture that caught the nation's attention and created "OJ addicts" and a national obsession with the case.

The Simpson case played out as a *TV spectacle*, and when the pre-trial hearing and the trial were televised live daily on CNN, Court TV, E! Television, and other networks, it involved its audience in *live* drama, with the possibility of surprise and the ups and downs of daily excitement and suspense. The main networks televised key segments and had daily summaries and frequent news specials, and the case dominated the evening news programming and talk programs. Ratings soared on the cable channels, and tabloid shows, such as *Hard Copy* and *A Current Affair*, had regular features on the case and the players, with even minor characters getting the fifteen minutes of fame promised by Andy Warhol.

Thus, the TV day was dominated by the Simpson megaspectacle for almost two years from the murder, through the criminal and then the civil trial.[7] The Simpson case was also an *Internet spectacle*, featuring 24/7 chat-lines and discussion, news bulletins and summaries, and websites, which compiled court transcripts, articles, trivia, and other pro- and anti-Simpson information and arguments. In chat-rooms and Usenet discussion groups, there was endless debate about every detail of the case, with daily battles between ProJs, who believed that Simpson was innocent, and NoJs, who were sure that he was guilty. Every imaginable conspiracy theory was vented, and today one can still find copious Internet evidence of OJ mania.[8]

As a megaspectacle, the Simpson murder trial pushed all the hot buttons. It provided an explosive *race spectacle* in which the wide chasm between the races in the United States – especially blacks and whites – became all too visible. Although Simpson's legal team initially said that they were not going to bring race into the trial, it unavoidably entered through the fact that Simpson was a famous African American sports hero and celebrity, that the murder victims were white, and that one of the key police officers, Mark Fuhrman, was alleged to be a rabid racist.[9] Moreover, as I document below, members of different races were experiencing the affair in dramatically opposed ways. Indeed, the image of a black man handcuffed by the police even before any charges had been made against him, the dramatic spectacle of Simpson's LA freeway run with a black friend, his arrest and incarceration – with *Time* magazine even darkening the mug shot of Simpson's face on its cover after he was accused of the murders – inevitably made the event a race problem, which ultimately led to intense divisions on the Simpson spectacle along color lines.

The Simpson saga was also a *multicultural spectacle* and a specifically *Los Angeles spectacle*. Among the motley crew of trial players, there were a wide range of witnesses, people who testified in the trial, the police, and the Simpson ensemble that included Hollywood wanabees such as Kato Kaelin and the would-be screenwriter Laura McKinney, immigrants such as his maid Rosa Lopez, and a large number of Asian police or experts, including Dr Henry Lee, LAPD criminologists Colin Yamauchi and Dennis Fung, and Judge Lance Ito. The Simpson and Brown families and friends contained a panorama of southern California character types, and part of the attraction of the spectacle was the unending array of fascinating characters from diverse races and ethnicities and walks of life.

From the beginning, the Simpson murder trial was also a *gender spectacle*, which unfolded detailed exposés of wife battering, generating intense discussions on the abuse of women. The June 23, 1994 release of the 911 (emergency) tape of a menacing OJ threatening Nicole in 1989 brought the "domestic violence" element of the story to the fore. The tape, repeatedly played in the media, suggested that Simpson had a previously unperceived violent and dangerous side to his personality, with the entire nation listening intently to every detail of his savagery against Nicole. This was the first release of an emergency telephone 911 call to national audiences, and the episode spawned a discourse around so-called "spousal abuse" (a euphemism for wife beating), dramatizing the problem, much as Anita Hill's accusations against Supreme Court Justice nominee Clarence Thomas had thematized the issue of sexual harassment.[10]

The Simpson affair was also a *class spectacle*, which revealed that money could buy the best lawyers and technical experts and ultimately an acquittal. If commodity logic saturates everything, truth can be bartered and justice bought. The trial put on display the privileges of wealth, as it portrayed the affluent lifestyles of Simpson, Nicole, and their social circles. Indeed, part of the seduction of the trial was the fascination with class and wealth in a hypercapitalist society. The entire megaspectacle spawned a proliferation of books, articles, TV tabloid exposés, and other artifacts that displayed the opulence of upper-class life and intimate details of the affluence and decadence of the Simpson circles.

In addition, Simpson himself, like Richard Nixon and Ronald Reagan, testified to the possibilities of class mobility in US society, rising from a life in the ghetto slums of San Francisco to the lifestyle of the rich and famous. Simpson was thus an icon of class mobility, demonstrating that even African Americans could climb the class ladder, hob-nobbing with the elite, partying with the world's most beautiful people, and enjoying the benefits of an affluent society. But the trial also put on display the underclass and class differences, with the appearance of maids, servants, waiters, and other witnesses demonstrating the existence of immense class distinctions and the existence of a large service class to literally serve the wealthy.

The Simpson affair was thus also inevitably a *commodity spectacle*, with the live televised chase in Simpson's white Bronco focusing attention on the commodities associated with Simpson the night of the murders. Attention was called in the case to his Bentley parked in front of his house, a mysterious knife, expensive gloves and shoes that were part of the evidence, Simpson's golf equipment and luggage, and his expensive house and upscale lifestyle. Curiously, the McDonald's spectacle was also part of the Simpson case as Simpson and his house guest Kato Kaelin went to McDonald's the night of the murder and OJ wolfed down a couple of Big Macs.[11]

The affair was a *celebrity spectacle* as well, with the tabloids and mainstream media alike focused on every detail of Simpson's life and the coverage creating new celebrities with every twist and turn of the investigation and trial. Celebrity, in turn, mobilizes cash and class privilege, and it was obvious that the wealthy Simpson was not sparing expense to hire the best lawyers, legal experts, and publicity agents that his money could buy, thus pointing to the commodification of law and the privileges of celebrities. Indeed, a media culture is a culture of celebrity in which sports stars, film and TV actors, and media personalities themselves are the idols and gods of the society, who crystallize people's aspirations and structure their fantasy lives.

O. J. Simpson himself was a superstar athlete, a popular sports commentator, a minor player in film and television, and an all-round celebrity who performed cheerfully in TV ads and promoted corporate interests. The initial disbelief that Simpson could have committed the murders was due to his celebrity status and the "nice guy" image that he had projected for decades, showing the extent to which media frames and images determine perceptions of reality.[12] The intense focus on the case month after month derived in part from Simpson's superstar celebrity status, while his ability to buy a costly legal team was also one of the prerogatives of celebrity and class. Yet, the high visibility and notoriety of media celebrity can also focus unwanted attention on individual personalities and contribute to their downfall. Those who live by the media can also be undone by it – as Simpson came to find out, reflecting on the trial from his prison cell and circumnavigating a hostile social world after his acquittal.

In addition, the event was a *commercial media spectacle* on all sides, with broadcast and print media fighting for ratings and with major participants selling stories to the tabloid press or getting lucrative book contracts (including the jury, members of the prosecution and defense, and friends and foes of Simpson and his murdered wife). Those involved in the case also established 1-900 pay-telephone numbers on which one could hear messages from Al Cowlings and other Simpson associates, giving their version of events, and one jury member even posed for pictures in *Playboy* magazine. Other individuals, often only remotely connected to the case, sold stories to tabloid media, while hucksters hawking trial memorabilia of all sorts were part of the daily spectacle.

Thus, the Simpson case was a *media-mediated spectacle,* with the media itself part and parcel of the story as print and broadcast journalists swarmed to Los Angeles, the scene of the murder and trial, creating one of the greatest media circuses of all time. Indeed, new celebrities emerged from the media themselves, ranging from the CNN and Court TV commentators, to journalists and legal experts who made regular appearances to discourse on the trial, while established news anchors also attempted to get into the act, mobilizing their star power to create a Big Event. The spectacle also brought tabloid journalism to national attention, with the weekly print magazines, such as *The National Enquirer,* and nightly TV tabloids seemingly the only ones doing investigative reporting. The tabloids provided week after week of headline scoops, delving deeply into the protagonists lives, rooting out every little piece of gossip and trivia to feed the insatiable audience desire for clues and infotainment, while creating new targets for its dubious pleasures.

Interestingly, the tabloids, especially *The National Enquirer*, had their first moments of respectability, as even the *New York Times* and ABC's Ted Koppel noted their aggressive investigative reporting.[13] On the other hand, during the trial, the distinction between mainstream and tabloid journalism – and more generally between news and entertainment – collapsed, with important world events almost completely eclipsed by the trial. The *Tyndall Report*, which provides a weekly analysis of evening network news programming, claimed that between January 1 and September 29, 1995 the nightly news programs on ABC, CBS, and NBC devoted 1,392 minutes to covering the Simpson trial. Coverage exceeded the combined attention to the war in Bosnia and the Oklahoma bombings, which, with a total of 1,292 minutes, were the second and third most covered stories of the period (*In These Times*, October 16, 1995: 10).

It is, in fact, a national tragedy that the Simpson spectacle became the major focus of TV news in 1995 during a period of unprecedented change and turmoil. The middle 1990s period was marked by the global restructuring of capitalism with its dramatic transformation of work, everyday life, and experience through new technologies. It was a period in which the Republican Party was attempting to dismantle the public sector, which had been developing since the 1930s New Deal, while the Clinton administration helped to undo the welfare state. The Simpson era was a time of over thirty civil wars throughout the world, indicating a dangerous "new world disorder," which would eventually surface to the center of attention after the September 11 terrorist attacks and subsequent Terror War. The Simpson era was also marked by an increase in environmental destruction, deadly diseases, and general social deterioration. But the O. J. Simpson megaspectacle came to dominate the national mediascape for years, displacing other issues from the forefront of attention.

During the Simpson murder trial, CNN often broadcast live coverage throughout the day, had daily thirty-minute trial summaries, repeated several times a day, and filled regular news with reports as well. For TV news, 1995 was the year of the Simpson spectacle, thus making clear that the priorities of corporate journalism are infotainment and profits, merging news into entertainment and journalism into business. Yet the investigative reporting that is supposed to be the virtue of mainstream journalism was apparently taken over by the tabloids, whose reports were then transmitted by the national media, which became more and more tabloid themselves. In fact, the mainstream media garnered few scoops and did little in-depth reporting during the trial. The tremendous number of print and broadcast media personnel who hung out in "Camp OJ," as the area for the media around the Los Angeles courthouse was called, appeared merely to be standing around watching. The reporters and talking heads of the mainstream media for the most part described what was obvious to the TV audience, rather than probing into what was behind the media circus, or doing any sustained enquiry into the case. Given the saturation coverage by the corporate media, it is curious that more probing reporting was not actually done by the mainstream media. The media circus and lack of investigative reporting by the mainstream perhaps signifies the end of an era of investigative journalism and its replacement by journalism that is dependent more on pictures and leaks than in-depth "behind the scenes" inquiry. During this period, the broadcast networks in particular become conduits for media spectacle and endless talking heads engaging in verbal culture wars rather than investigative reporting or more analytical writing valorized by traditional journalism.

The Simpson megaspectacle thus revealed the mainstream media to be bankrupt in relation to traditional journalistic priorities. It was almost as if the mainstream had given up real investigative reporting, or providing context and insight, in favor of merely transmitting images of media events and "breaking news." The latter often consisted of cameras cutting to the Simpson trial courthouse and an interview with participants, or news summaries concerning what had happened during the trial that day. Moreover, according to more informed experts, the talking-head media commentators, mostly law professors or members of the legal profession, were often mediocre, unilluminating, and, whether purposely or not, tended to help Simpson get off by exaggerating events of the day and failing to put the case in a broader legal context (Bugliosi 1996: 50ff. and *passim*).

Thus, the Simpson saga is a key event in the decline of journalism in a nation, and perhaps a globe, hooked on infotainment and tabloid culture. The Simpson megaspectacle marks a shift in TV news from journalism to infotainment, culminating a process that had been going on for years (Kellner 1990; 1992). Yet although the Simpson saga was clearly a sensationalistic media spectacle, it was also concerned with substance, and for some audiences it provided highly educational instruction concerning how the legal system works (or fails to) and how society is split around the axes of gender, race, and class. Watching the trial unfold, one could learn about the intricate machinations of lawyers, judges, and others involved in the criminal justice system, and how the media is playing an ever greater role in all facets of present-day life. An attentive audience could learn about male abuse of women and wife beating, racist prejudice and violence against blacks, police corruption, the privileges of class and celebrity, and the ways in which society is polarized into conflicting groups. Although much of the commentary focused on arcane legal issues, there was also useful debate about law, gender and race issues, the role of the media in contemporary society, and the legal system and social justice. Furthermore, for our purposes, the Simpson spectacle is a useful lens for analyzing the centrality of media spectacle in contemporary culture and its growing power in every realm of life.

Spectacle culture and the social construction of reality

The TV nation was utterly fascinated by the O. J. Simpson spectacle, which took over everyday life, with the audience living in a media world of tabloid infotainment for month after month, totally engrossed in every detail of the trial. The spectacle represented the merging together of law, money, celebrity, politics, and media culture, with massive audiences becoming totally immersed in the megaspectacle, living their lives through passionate immersion in the murder case and trial. The audience fascination with the Simpson case discloses a culture colonized by the media, which is prepared to put aside the concrete problems of everyday life to escape into the media world, whose celebrities and characters seem to be more compelling and seductive than the figures of everyday life. As Baudrillard (1983b; 1993) argues, media "reality" is a "hyperreality," a world of artificially constructed experience that is "realer than real," that purifies the banality of everyday life to create an exciting world of mass mediated, technologically processed experience that is often far more involving and intense than ordinary life.[14]

TV addicts of whatever genre (soap opera, sports, talk shows, news, etc.) regularly live in the world of the media hyperreality, and media spectacles periodically appear to focus audience attention and take over everyday life. Just as the Gulf War dominated and militarized US and global culture in 1991 (Kellner 1992; 1995), so too did the Simpson case dominate media culture and everyday life for large sectors of the public during 1994–96. Thus, the obsession with the Simpson case signifies the triumph of media spectacle over reality and the immense power of media culture to define what is real, important, and worthy of attention. Indeed, the very ability to hook a nation on a single murder trial, despite so many important political and social issues on the agenda, shows the immense significance of media culture and its megaspectacles. The ability to attract vast audiences day after day to follow a murder case is itself a sign of power, as is its ability to create a nation of OJ addicts whose time, energy, and lives were fixated on the spectacle.[15]

The obsessive fascination with minute detail and unending daily portrayal and debate over every conceivable aspect of the life of the protagonists in the case also exemplifies Baudrillard's concept of the ecstasy of communication (Baudrillard 1983a). In a media culture, the private sphere disappears and the most intimate details of everyday life are revealed in the white-hot glare of media focus. In a society under the surveillance of ubiquitous media, there seems to be nothing sacred or immune from media scrutiny, leading to an implosion of private and public life.

In this environment, tabloids are merely the vanguard of media culture that feasts daily on public and private misery and problems that are packaged and sold to mass audiences. Moreover, during the Simpson spectacle, some previous taboos disintegrated, and it seemed that everything pertaining to the trial was permitted media exposure (i.e. never before had one heard so many and such vile racial epithets, such obscenity, and so many intimate details of domestic life as the daily fare of the mainstream media).

The Simpson trial was thus the country's first major *legal media spectacle* in which, day after day, massive audiences followed courtroom drama live on cable channels such as CNN, Court TV, and E! Television, all of which provided full trial coverage, daily news summaries, and ongoing commentary on the case. There have been murder trials and scandals many times before in US history, but never a live, televised media spectacle on this scale. The OJ junkies also had computer discussion groups and sites to debate the trial and copious websites on the Internet to read trial transcripts, articles, commentaries, jokes, and arguments over the case. TV shows, talk radio, and daily press and tabloid exposés of the antics of various characters in the trial made it possible to immerse oneself totally in the trial. There was even a cruise ship for those who wanted to enclose themselves in the total OJ spectacle and to get away from the more trivial distractions of everyday life.

The Simpson spectacle thus revealed a postmodernization of culture in which daily life is colonized by a total media environment, perhaps providing glimpses of the information–entertainment culture of the future, when people will be given even more extravagant technologies and spectacles to escape into media and virtual reality. Disparate audiences, however, lived the event very differently, and the sharply divergent reactions revealed the extent to which social reality is constructed and lived according to one's race, class, and gender constituents, mediated by one's life experiences and media interaction. The social construction of reality is generated in part through symbolic interaction between life experience and appropriation of media culture. This is, of course, a dialectical process by which personal experience is mediated, articulated, and focused by media culture, but in which interpretations and uses of the media are constructed by individuals in real-life situations. As I will indicate below, the disparate responses to the event by diverse audiences were in part constructed through the media representations and frames. Yet, which portrayals audiences appropriated and how they used media material depended on their own gender, race, class, and ideological perspectives.

Perhaps never before has the perspectival construction of social reality been put so dramatically on display. The wildly divergent responses to the Simpson spectacle made it clear that people of different races, for instance, have fundamentally different perspectives, life experiences, and views of the world. It was widely recognized during the Simpson affair that black and white audiences simply saw and experienced the world differently and had opposing social constructions of reality. Consistently, from early in the trial to the aftermath, the majority of blacks polled believed that Simpson was innocent, while the majority of whites considered him guilty, disclosing a fundamentally different construction of social reality, and demonstrating that US society is divided along "multiple realities" into parallel but divergent social worlds.[16]

At first, during the summer pre-trial hearings, the issue of race was suppressed in both media analyses and the legal proceedings. But discussion began to emerge during the trial itself in fall 1994 indicating that the case was fundamentally about race. It was also recognized that black and white audiences were perceiving the events, issues, and personalities in markedly dissimilar ways. Blacks, on the whole, saw the case as an issue of racial justice and supported Simpson, whereas many whites reacted strongly against this response and were angry that issues of domestic violence, murder, and the legal issues were overwhelmed by the race issue. Yet the white response to the spectacle might also be conditioned by the fact that Simpson was alleged to have killed two whites, including his former wife and mother of his children. Had it been a black-on-black crime, it is doubtful that whites would have reacted so passionately and that the media would have been able to dramatize the case so intensely.

Yet it is probable that never before have so many African Americans been able to articulate their views and circulate their version of social reality through the mainstream media. Never before had so many black commentators appeared on television, ranging from legal experts to men and women in the street. Many African American reporters were put on the case and the panels on the ubiquitous talk shows were often racially balanced between whites and blacks. Rarely, if ever, had so many black discourses critical of the police and legal system circulated through the media, and these discourses in turn spread through the black community, focusing attitudes and manufacturing a consensus that O. J. Simpson was innocent and a victim of racial injustice – a construction that sharply contrasted with the version of social reality dominant in the white community.

In a sense, the case put on display the growing power of African Americans in US society, who had become major lawyers and public prosecutors, legal and media commentators, and a cohesive social group able to forge consensus among its members and assert its interests as a community. Yet it was ultimately the white-male-controlled media establishment that constructed Simpson as "guilty," which helped to swing the majority of the country against him, assisting in producing a "guilty" verdict in the 1996 civil trial. Moreover, the successful assertion of black identity politics and power and subsequent white backlash has helped to render civil society and coalitions between black and white groups ever more precarious, as my analysis of the jury verdicts of the criminal and subsequent civil case will indicate. Indeed, the Simpson megaspectacle revealed that racial divisions in US society were deeply rooted, with racial hostility and tensions at a boiling point. The affair raised serious questions concerning the possibility of racial harmony and understanding in the United States, and, as I argue, put into question the entire set of legal and judiciary institutions, ranging from the police to the jury system.

The verdict and the aftermath

As the criminal trial proceeded, race became more and more a central factor, partly as a result of media frames, which often pitted black and white commentators and pundits against each other, with most of the blacks represented as defending

Simpson and the "not guilty" criminal jury verdict, while whites were presented as outraged by what they saw as a miscarriage of justice. Person-in-the-street interviews tended to further reinforce this racial polarization, as did talk radio programs and the ubiquitous polls, which invariably suggested a major racial divide in response to the trial. The case thus revealed an extremely polarized society along the vector of race. Certainly, the entire cast of characters in the Simpson drama represented a cross-section of ethnicities, presenting the United States as an intensely multicultural society. Audiences in turn often reacted positively to their own identity markers and responded angrily throughout the trial to what they perceived as mistreatment of members of their own ethnic or peer groups (i.e. as when Asians got angry at racist slurs of Judge Ito or the defense badgering of Asian witnesses, or when Hispanics got angry at what they perceived as mistreatment of Hispanic witnesses, and so on).

Judge Lance Ito became literally and symbolically the middleman in the trial, himself a man of color – an ethnic Japanese American – but not too colored. Ito mediated daily between the bickering lawyers and attempted to stay above the fray, arbitrating the disputes and attempting to portray an image of even-handedness and a fair-minded justice system. Yet Ito regularly allowed Hollywood celebrities to sit in the court and delayed proceedings to chat with them. As Asian American scholar Darrell Hamamoto wrote (1995), Ito evidently also craved the media attention usually denied to Asian Americans, and a *Los Angeles Times* article described how the judge would play "Dancing Ito" skits from Jay Leno's *Tonight* show for the attorneys while in chambers. Moreover, since Judge Ito was certain to offend proponents of both sides as the months went on, both he and the criminal justice system as a whole came under increasing attack.[17]

Judge Ito defended the presence of the camera in the courtroom on the grounds that it provided the public with a more objective and unbiased access to the trial:

> The problem with not having a camera is that one must trust the evaluation and analysis of a reporter who is telling you what occurred in the courtroom, and anytime you allow somebody to report an event, you have to take into consideration the filtering effect of that person's own biases. Whereas if you have a camera in the courtroom, there is no filtering. What you see is what's there.[18]

But against this view, one could argue that the very presence of the camera elevates the significance of the event, producing a TV spectacle that more directly involves viewers in the drama than other print and broadcast media, and thus provides television with the power to frame the event. The camera creates a mediatization of the courtroom that does not merely mirror an event objectively, but alters what is happening. Televising an event live is always subject to media commentary that frames the issues and defines what is important and what "really" happened. Thus, the media frames and interpretations help constitute the "reality" of the situation. In addition, the presence of the televisual apparatus seduces both sides into playing to the camera, and thus inevitably transforms the dynamics of the trial. Its presence also enables the public to participate in a daily media ritual and to get deeply involved in the events.

During the closing arguments, the skills of Simpson's formidable legal team were obvious. Although media culture privileges visual and photographic evidence, the power of the spoken word to frame interpretations and construct meanings was also conspicuous in the trial. While there was a wealth of evidence from photographs, videos, audiotapes, graphics, and visual exhibits mounted by both sides, their meanings were constructed through the discourse of the protagonists.[19] Indeed, the power of the spoken word was evident in the closing statements. Both sides deployed narrative arguments, trying to tell stories that would indict Simpson or raise reasonable doubts concerning the accusations. Thus, the trial can also be seen as a clash of narratives. The prosecution constructed a scientifically based account, grounded in the forensic evidence, while the defense constructed a narrative of police corruption and incompetence, using its forensic experts to question the validity of prosecution evidence that was claimed to be corrupted and tainted.

Prosecutor Marcia Clark and her team were constantly appealing to reason, logic, and scientific evidence in their arguments. By contrast, the defense was able to turn the trial into an indictment of police racism and corruption and to make it a forum on racial injustice rather than a murder case. In their closing arguments, prosecutors Christopher Darden and Marcia Clark attempted to combine narratives concerning Simpson's propensities for jealousy and wife abuse with a marshalling of the scientific evidence. In his closing arguments, Simpson's African American lawyer, Johnnie Cochran, evoked civil rights rhetoric and figures, biblical phrases, and clever slogans, repeated over and over for hypnotic effect, to cast doubt on the prosecution case and to mobilize the jurors emotionally to acquit Simpson. More controversially, Cochran deployed holocaust rhetoric, implying an equation of policeman Mark Fuhrman with Hitler and attacking Fuhrman's "big lies" and "genocidal racism." This phrase led the father of murder victim Ron Goldman to lash out at Cochran at a dramatic press conference after the closing argument, and led Simpson's lawyer Robert Shapiro to distance himself from the play of "the race card" and Cochran's rhetoric immediately after the trial.

But the defense also skillfully presented forensic testimony by Barry Scheck in its closing argument that raised questions about the validity of the prosecution's evidence.[20] The defense strategy appeared to work when a "not guilty" verdict was handed down in record time after the closing arguments. On Monday, October 2, 1995, the jury reported that it had reached a decision after only 4 hours of deliberation. Lead prosecutors and lawyers, expecting that the decision would not be attained for days, were not available, and Judge Ito postponed the reading of the verdict for the next day at 10 am, creating a tremendously theatrical situation and intense interest and speculation concerning the outcome.

The reading of the verdict was one of the more dramatic events in TV history, and much of the nation watched it live, as did people throughout the world.[21] Many television networks canceled all of their regular morning programming, hyping the verdict as a major event. Nine TV networks chose to cover the Simpson verdict live, and many local stations replaced their normal programming with the coverage. People gathered in their homes, in public places, in classrooms, and even the stock market stopped doing business and airline flights were delayed so that the TV nation and indeed the Global Village could watch the verdict. The reading of the acquittal of "not guilty" drew victorious smirks and smiles from Simpson and his lawyers, though members of the victims' families sobbed and cried out in grief and disbelief.

There was immediately a sharply polarized national response, with black audiences shown cheering the verdict, while many whites were presented reacting with shock and dismay. Pundits began dissecting the event and all major participants – as well as the jury members – were sought out for statements and talk show appearances. Reactions to the trial and the verdict were distributed according to the factors of gender, race, and class, which were crucial for determining audience attitudes toward the trial. Individuals often identify with those to whom their own personal identity is most closely linked – with African Americans largely identifying with Simpson and believing in his innocence, while whites tended to sympathize with the victims and to consider Simpson guilty. Of course, there were conflicts and overdetermined loyalties, with black women, for instance, feeling the pressure to identify with the plight of a black man, but also perhaps sympathizing with an abused and murdered woman.[22] The case certainly dramatized the racial and gender divides in US society, and the ways in which they are articulated in media culture, but the final jury verdict seemed to indicate that race clearly overshadowed gender and other determinants, with the predominantly African American jury declaring Simpson not guilty.

, Polls registering agreement or disagreement with the jury's verdict indicated that the overwhelming majority of African Americans clearly responded to defense lawyer Johnnie Cochran's closing arguments appealing to racial solidarity and justice, painting O. J. Simpson as a victim of racial targeting. Policeman Mark Fuhrman's vitriolic racism became the core of the defense argument and successfully mobilized revulsion against the LA police, while also raising questions about the status of the evidence. Reaction to the Rodney King beating and disgust with the acquittal of the white police officers videotaped viciously beating him had galvanized African American hostility toward the police and legal system, and these events helped mobilize African American support for Simpson.[23] Many African Americans openly cheered the jury decision while many whites were outraged. Polls taken after the verdict indicated that blacks overwhelmingly thought the decision was just, while the majority of whites polled opposed the acquittal. The aftermath of the case indeed revealed sharp racial divisions, with blacks and whites having two symbolically constructed worldviews and life experiences, obviously at odds.[24]

There was much discussion of the Simpson murder case verdict being parallel to the Simi Valley jury verdict, which acquitted the policemen accused of exercising excessive force against Rodney King in 1992. The King verdict helped elicit the so-called "LA uprisings," the worst urban violence since the 1960s, and by some accounts one of the most explosive urban uprisings of the twentieth century. In both cases, it was argued that juries ignored visual and "scientific" evidence to acquit the accused, and in both cases the juries operated along racial lines, with white suburban jurors acquitting the white police officers despite the video of the officers viciously beating King and black jurors acquitting Simpson despite the mountains of evidence against him. In the Simi Valley case, the defense lawyers appealed to white fears of black urban violence and the need for stronger policing and law and order. In the Simpson affair, the defense appealed to black anger over police brutality and corruption and made the case into a vote for racial justice.

The problem with this interpretation, however, is that it symmetrizes social groups into equals and opposites rather than seeing society as a matrix of hierarchical groups existing in relations of opposition, inequality, and subordination. The Simi Valley jury decision reveals the fears of dominant white groups, while the O. J. Simpson decision testifies to the growing power of black groups, who are able to mobilize their constituencies into cohesive opposition to racial injustice and domination. That is, the Simi Valley verdict was a validation of the existing form of hegemonic power, while the O. J. Simpson verdict represented a challenge to it.[25] In both cases, however, identity politics came to the fore and arguably put into question legal rationality and logic, making the law subordinate to politics and justice and morality subordinate to group interests and identity politics.

The Simpson spectacle, identity politics, and postmodernization

The O. J. Simpson murder case demonstrates the extent to which the legal system and politics are deeply influenced by media spectacle and how dramatic trials and legal decisions and the political responses of the public are fundamentally mediated through the media. The intense fascination with the O. J. Simpson megaspectacle displays how people have come to live out society's major conflicts in a mass-mediated space that becomes the arbiter of what is real and important, with highly unpredictable and complex effects. The courtroom drama and melodrama surrounding the trial created a national media megaspectacle perhaps unparalleled in its intensity and explosive in its effects.

The Simpson case demonstrates, as well, how key political and legal issues are played out through the media and the postmodernization of law, involving fundamental changes concerning how legal issues are processed and resolved. Computer databases have changed the nature of legal research and argumentation by providing instantaneous information, which can be deployed on the spot, often without sufficient reflection or thought. Such computerized data played a major role in the trial, with judges and lawyers constantly consulting computer databases for facts on the case or previous rulings pertinent to the issues. This results in a more fragmented and disjointed presentation of facts and evidence rather than carefully crafted argumentation. It also makes possible the instant filing of briefs, motions, and other papers that deluge judges and often prolong judicial decisions.

Deployment of hi-tech information and the use of multimedia in trials and press conferences help produce a postmodernization of law. New information technology transforms law firms into information-processing corporations, privileging technical knowledge over legal experience and courtroom skills. In addition, postmodern law is more dependent on video depositions and exhibits and even virtual reality simulations of evidence, tipping the scales of justice even further to the advantage of those who can afford to pay for expensive hi-tech legal expertise and gadgetry. Finally, postmodern law is subject to "mediatization," with participants in high-profile trials becoming media celebrities and both sides playing to the media and using the media to advance their positions.

All of these features of postmodern law were evident in the Simpson murder trial. The court had installed a $200,000 computer system, and both prosecutors and defense attorneys used it to present evidence to the jurors on an overhead screen. Judge Ito, the attorneys, and witnesses had fifteen-inch monitors on which to observe the evidence, and laptop computers were visible and in use by defense, prosecution, and the judge. Both sides had fax machines for receiving information from the outside or sending requests to colleagues. Never before in such a public forum had so many hi-tech exhibits and displays presented the evidence and revealed to the public the ways in which new technologies were transforming the legal profession.

In addition, major participants in the trial became celebrities, with both sides playing to the media and attempting to cultivate positive media images from the beginning. In fact, the trial made clear that the identities of participants in trials, politics, or any event of the public sphere were constructed through the manufacture of images in a media culture, and that trials dealing with celebrities had to take into account the already constructed media images of the protagonists. O. J. Simpson was known and loved by millions as a congenial personality, as "a great guy," depicted as an outstanding athlete, familiar figure in ads, amiable sports commentator, and entertaining movie and TV star. Simpson's image was that of an affable personality, and his smile came to define him as likeable and popular – much as Ronald Reagan's smile presented him as pleasant and genial, as did Michael Jordan's personality and demeanor.[26]

From the beginning, the prosecution therefore had to create a negative image of Simpson and used a recording of the 911 call in which Nicole described his threatening behavior to police with Simpson raging in the background. The prosecution also engaged in systematic leaks to tabloids and news media, circulated images of the suspect with a knife and committing violence in a TV show and film, and leaked testimonies of witnesses to create a negative impression. The defense attempted to circulate positive images of Simpson and used, in turn, the tabloids and mainstream media to question prosecution evidence, witnesses, and prosecutors, going after Detective Mark Fuhrman with crucial leaks to the media from the beginning of the case.

Hence, media images mediate how individuals perceive people, as looks, image, and style become more and more fundamental constituents of social identities, shaping how people are publicly viewed and defined (see Kellner 1995). Just as Michael Jackson undertook a media campaign to refurbish his image after he was accused of child molestation, so too did Simpson attempt to recreate a positive image – with decidedly mixed results. After making a deal to go live on NBC TV in October 1995, immediately after the verdict, to explain his case to the nation,

Simpson backed out at the last minute. He promised he would do everything pos-
sible to find the killer of his wife and Ron Goldman – and then went off to Florida
to play golf and pursue model Paula Barbieri. He publicly proclaimed his love for
Paula and his intention to marry her – and then locked himself up in his estate with
Gretchen Stockdale, a blonde model and former pro football cheerleader, angering
Paula, who publicly broke off the relationship.[27]

During the first half of 1996, Simpson made a major effort to rehabilitate his
image. His demeanor on his January 24, 1996 Black Entertainment Television
interview, his talks at black churches and other sites in which he criticized racism
and the media, his May 1996 trip to England to lecture at Oxford and appear on
television, and other 1996 public appearances, seemed to suggest that tabloid stories
of Simpson's disintegration were exaggerated. Trying desperately to recreate a
positive image, Simpson began presenting himself as a critic of racism, as a media
critic, as a victim of a racist society, and as a supporter of battered women in a
fundraiser at his Brentwood estate. So the "new" O. J. Simpson became a man of
family values and religion, a black man who has returned to his people and roots,
and a social critic and activist assailing the distortions of the media, who has
discovered identity politics and how to play the race card.

But then during his civil court case in late 1996 and the simultaneous court
battle for custody of his children, negative stories predominated in the mainstream
news and tabloid media, as more and more evidence surfaced against Simpson.
Photographs turned up of Simpson in the Bruno Magli shoes, footprints from which
had appeared at the murder site and which Simpson denied he had owned, claiming
he would never buy such "ugly ass" shoes. In the civil case, mountains of evidence
were amassed and presented to the jury, Simpson responded unconvincingly to the
case against him, and he was found guilty (see Petrocelli 1998). The unprecedent-
edly high $33.5 million judgment against Simpson disclosed the intensity of the
passions around the case, and this time, with the judgment reversed, whites for
the most part applauded the verdict whereas many blacks attacked it, once again
inflaming racial passions and aggravating racial relations.

Identity and identity politics

The O. J. Simpson case also revealed that, in the current media culture, politics is
defined through the media-mobilizing issues with which individuals and groups
identify. In this section, I discuss how the Simpson megaspectacle was bound up
with the promotion of a postmodern identity politics, which became another defining
feature of the case. The term "identity" is extremely complex and overdetermined,
with meanings flowing and overlapping from a variety of discursive sites.[28] In philosophy, the term was used to characterize the concrete singularity and particularity
of an individual, such as the "essence" of the self that abides through time and
change. Yet a dialectic of identity and difference runs through Western thought,
with some theories privileging a substantive or metaphysical identity and others
privileging difference, as when the French philosopher Jacques Derrida argues that

language functions through establishing systems of differences. Personal identity became a major philosophical issue with Hume and Kant, as the former dissolved the self into a bundle of sensations, whereas the latter anchored it in a transcendental ground and unity, a presupposition of experience that itself transcended experience. During the twentieth century, philosophical and psychological themes combined in the existential drama of theorists attempting to define what constituted identity and individuals striving to discover or create their own personal identities and selves.

The quest for identity mutated into an identity politics in the 1960s, with many individuals searching the history of their affiliated social groups to discover their cultural identities (i.e. as African Americans, Chicanos, gays and lesbians, women, and so forth). Identity politics emerged when individuals within oppressed groups linked their identities with movements that attempted to promote their interests. Previously, people constructed identities through their interaction with family, religious affiliation, community groups, profession, or political ideologies and attachment. In a media age, people began identifying with celebrities, acquiring their role and gender models, ideals, style, and aspirations from media culture (see Kellner 1995).[29] Since the 1960s, politics has been increasingly played out through the media, and individuals have been able to identify with groups, issues, icons, and struggles presented through the media. New modes of identity have thus circulated through media culture, such as feminist, gay and lesbian, conservative white male, militia, environmentalist, anti-globalization activist, and other figures generated by social movements and conflicts. In turn, audiences connected with these political models, or associated with gender, race, or sexual issues and positions, as key features of their personal identities.

During the 1960s, identity politics constituted an expansion of the political into new realms, beginning with the efforts in the civil rights movement to construct positive identities for African Americans and to reverse the negative signification of blackness. In feminism, the motto "the personal is the political" emerged, in which the "private" domain of relationships, sexuality, child rearing, domestic labor, and other issues relegated to the sphere of the non-political were reinterpreted as political, as constituted by relationships of power and domination. This necessarily led to a redefinition of the political, to an expansion of the concept beyond the politics of the state to encompass issues of culture, everyday life, and identity. In this discursive register, personal identity became bound up with ethnicity, gender, sexuality, history, culture, and the whole register of society and history.

Identity politics begins with a negative experience of oppression in which one's identity markers (skin color, gender, race, sexuality, and so on) are deemed to be inferior, subordinate, and subject to oppression. Often, the experience of denigration and domination leads to positive affirmation of what has been defamed and attacked, reversing the valorization (i.e. "black is beautiful," women are deemed superior to men because they are more nurturing and relational, and so on). Identity politics really takes off, however, when anger and affirmation take the form of institutional organization and social action. Yet identity politics often becomes defuse and apolitical, as the media create spectacles that divide individuals around gender, race, and class issues, and as proliferating new media (i.e. the Internet) fragment audiences according to their (identity politics) preferences. The result is often that groups bicker among themselves and fragment into smaller social atoms, as, for example, when feminists split into ever smaller divisions according to race, class, political affiliations, sexual preferences, and the like, or when vegetarians and vegans squabble over such things as the legitimacy of consuming dairy products.

There are a variety of reasons why identity politics emerged as a major component of US politics from the 1990s into the present. With the decline of the nation-state and class as sources of social identity, people turned to gender, race, ethnicity, sexual preference, religion, and other sources of social belonging. The decline of community in an era of suburbs, media culture, and consumerism led people to need greater units or groupings than their immediate social relations, to be part of something bigger. In the 1960s, new social movements mobilized individuals into such formations, generating black, feminist, and gay consciousness and pride, and in some cases spawning separatism and nationalism. There has been, as well, to be sure, a politics of solidarity and alliance, manifested in the anti-war movement and what indeed was referred to as The Movement in the 1960s, that has continued to some extent into the anti-globalization movement of the present. Yet during the past decades, after the fragmentation of the 1960s movement, which had held the different alliances together, there has been an intensification of the pitting of group against group of the sort evident in the responses to the Simpson trial.

In the contemporary era, the issue of identity is thus becoming bound up with which particular identity marker individuals especially identify, the intensity of the identification, and the struggle for recognition, rights, and benefits among different social groups. When the media articulate a race, gender, or other political issue, people who identify with one or another form of identity politics are mobilized to take a position on the issue at question. The Simpson case is interesting because it mobilized varying, sometimes conflicting, political issues and identities, causing intense discord and controversy around the case. The passionate debate in the aftermath of the Simpson murder trial reveals the dramatic differences in the constructions of people's social identities and realities, showing too how antagonisms between people's diverse social identities are an important part of social contestation. The affair reveals the divisions that threaten the stability of contemporary US society, and that civil society in the United States is more and more uncivil and fragile; its institutions are vulnerable to contestation and challenge; and fundamental conflicts in the society are played out on the stage of media culture and may be, as I suggest below, exacerbated by the harsh focus of the media on dichotomized competing positions.

The playing out of identity politics on the terrain of media spectacle is a highly ambiguous process. On the one hand, the dichotomized conflicts suggest that people have the power to contest and change dominant institutions and configurations of power when basic institutions, such as the police, the legal system, or the political system, are being challenged. On the other hand, the intense divergences on controversial issues such as the Simpson case threaten alliances between oppressed groups that might carry out positive social change, and harsh media polarization may contribute to producing a backlash against groups perceived as single-interest or grievance groups. Identity politics promotes highly passionate identification with one's own group and undermines solidarity with other oppressed groups and alliances, which might generate movements that could address the shared and common problems and grievances as well as particular issues of specific oppressed groups and individuals.

In fact, the responses to the verdict in the Simpson spectacle raise questions concerning how identity politics polarizes and fragments civil society into warring special interest groups. In principle, every individual possesses shifting and fluid identities mobilized in specific configurations, in which sometimes one issue is fundamental in the construction of identities, and sometimes other factors. However, there is also the possibility that individuals will identify with one dimension to the exclusion of others and engage in identity politics that solely pushes the interests of one's chosen group and identity marker to the exclusion of all other groups and concerns.

In general, an individual's identity is subject to contradictory overdeterminations and contextual constraints, in which sometimes gender comes to the fore, sometimes race or ethnicity, sometimes class, sometimes sexuality, sometimes ideology, or sometimes even species (i.e. in animal rights disputes), depending on the context and issues. But identity politics can freeze individual identities into one determinant, such as race or gender. It can also sunder society into fixed and warring group identities in which the politics of one group sharply clashes with other groups that produce obstacles to mediation or consensus. There is thus a danger that identity politics can essentialize and fetishize a single defining feature of one's identity, covering over commonalities and shared interests with other oppressed groups against which one's identity politics pits one (i.e. as when black nationalists cover over shared interests with poor whites or Latinos, or when underclass white racist groups fail to see their common interests with subjugated people of color, or when liberal feminists fail to address issues of women of color or of the developing world). Against the fetishism of one identity marker to the exclusion of others, we should be aware that identity is multiple, flexible, and overdetermined, that oppression takes place on many dimensions, and that an oppositional political identity requires solidarity and alliance with other subjugated groups against common oppressors and institutions and practices that produce inequality and injustice.[30]

The O. J. Simpson trial reveals the effects of a mass-mediated identity politics in US society and the ways in which the mainstream media exploit and escalate differences in a manner that propagates a divide-and-conquer cultural climate, which benefits ruling elites. Especially in the aftermath of the event, responses seemed to be constituted primarily by an individual's identity politics. Most African Americans interviewed about the trial interpreted it in relation to race and used the media to attack racism or to make some point about race. Many of the white women who commented on the trial stressed the gender issue and the messages sent out by the verdict concerning domestic violence. Many Jews stressed the inappropriateness of Johnnie Cochran's comparisons of Mark Fuhrman to Hitler and his misuse of the holocaust experience, as well as his deployment of Nation of Islam bodyguards. And numerous white males made negative remarks about African Americans, or expressed resentment of various sorts – as was especially virulent on the Internet and talk radio.

Identity politics has become in general heavily media oriented, with contending groups articulating and circulating their views through the media. It generates a politics of confrontation and promotes an adversary culture, with each group asserting its own interests and grievances as loudly and dramatically as possible in order to get media attention. The very structure of the media encourages such an adversarial culture and politics of confrontation. The media frame controversies, such as the Simpson case, in terms of competing positions and thus mobilize spokespeople for both sides, who tend to take extreme and one-sided positions. In fact, there was little real dialogue about the Simpson trial in the media, with the talking heads for the most part talking past each other, revealing a society fragmented into warring groups and provoking further fragmentation. The media, in turn, intensify such adversarial politics through their use of sound bites and the playing off of differing groups and positions.

Defenders of Simpson, or the verdict, who appeared on the broadcast media were almost always African American, whereas its critics were mostly white; thus the racial polarization was in part a function of the media spectacle of the affair. The Internet also was fragmented into its ProJ's, who were pro-Simpson, and the NoJ's, who were anti-, and controversy here too was polarized and vicious. Media polarization in general intensifies tensions between oppressed groups, which undermines potential alliances and vitiates the just claims in the Simpson megaspectacle by both African Americans' and women's political demands for justice and equality. Instead, women and people of color appeared as being merely special interest advocacy in the polarized contestation. Dichotomous media coverage thus arguably sharpens differences between groups with common interests, and in turn circulates and reproduces the discourses and tropes of identity politics. Indeed, the dominant media frames that pitted black against white in the Simpson case excessively polarized reactions, especially after the verdict, when African Americans were represented as jubilant and whites appeared dismayed or angry. CNN and all the major TV networks played image after image of the diametrically opposed responses and had one panel discussion after another, with African Americans proclaiming Simpson's innocence or at least the correctness of the jury decision, contrasted with whites claiming that he was guilty and attacking the jury. Local television and press coverage also replicated these frames, suggesting that all African Americans were ecstatic about the decision, whereas whites were all angry. One of the few exceptions to this polarizing and essentializing coverage was a *Newsweek* account of the verdict aftermath (October 16, 1995: 35):

> While the media focused on the celebrations, a *Newsweek* Poll found that a quarter of blacks surveyed thought that Simpson was guilty. And an even greater number regretted the in-your-face rejoicing. "I cringed at those scenes of jubilation," said the Rev. Emanuel Cleaver, mayor of Kansas City, Mo., "not because I didn't know how black people felt, but because of the fear and misunderstanding it would generate." Meanwhile, *Newsweek*'s Poll found that

a third of the whites agreed with the verdict, and half thought the jury had been fair and impartial.

Obviously, reaction to the Simpson verdict was polarized, and the generally divided responses to the verdict *do* reveal deep racial divides in the country. On the other hand, it should be noted how the media frames exaggerate the black/white divisions and give the impression that *all* African Americans believed Simpson was innocent and/or rejoiced in his acquittal, whereas *all* whites thought that he was innocent and were angry. Such a dichotomy heightens harmful relations between the races, giving the impression that African Americans in general are contemptuous of the justice system and support a possible murderer, and that whites believe that Simpson was guilty and that the jury acted emotionally and from racial solidarity, rather than following the facts of the case and the legal evidence, which might indeed provide "reasonable doubt" in the light of racist attitudes in the police and possible tampering with evidence.

In fact, *Newsweek* also cited a white liberal backlash against black "grievance politics" and "groupthink" (October 16, 1995: 35) and the feeling of betrayal of liberal ideals of justice on behalf of a group whom they had supported. Liberal women, ranging from prosecutor Marcia Clark to leaders of NOW (the National Organization for Women), were especially critical of the decision and appeared to join the white backlash against blacks.[31] Of course, conservatives were more aggressive and outspoken in their denunciation of African American racial politics in the case, and the Internet and talk radio was full of rancorous racism and attacks on African Americans, who were accused of being more racist than whites for putting race before everything else. The conservative threat to gain revenge by attacking political programs that benefited blacks was graphically expressed in an e-mail message by conservative Ben Stein to liberal *New York Times* columnist Frank Rich: "When OJ gets off, the whites will riot the way we whites do: leave the cities, go to Idaho or Oregon or Arizona, vote for Gingrich. .. and punish the blacks by closing their day-care programs and cutting off their Medicaid" (cited in *Newsweek*, October 16, 1995: 66).

Indeed, in the days following the trial, California Governor Pete Wilson proposed dramatic changes in the jury system, banning TV cameras from the courtroom, and prohibiting lawyers from sending political messages to jurors. Various other "reform" groups began drafting proposals to make it easier to convict criminals (of color). Of course, the more extremist whites openly threatened the lives of O. J. Simpson, Johnnie Cochran, and other African Americans involved in the case, forcing them to hire bodyguards, or use volunteers from the Nation of Islam for protection.

As noted, during the 1996 civil trial Simpson was found guilty and was required to pay $33.5 million in damages (see Petrocelli 1998). Simpson reportedly never paid much in damages to the Goldman family, continued to live his affluent life-style, recurrently had scrapes with the law, and had a high-profile and tempestuous relationship with a blonde who looked like Nicole, all of which has kept Simpson in the tabloids until the present. Forced out of the private golf clubs that he had long inhabited and unable to eat in his favorite local LA restaurants, or hang out in his preferred clubs, because of the uproar that his presence continued to provoke, Simpson went to Miami in 2000 and became imbricated in a series of police and tabloid scandals. He was involved in a tumultuous relationship with his Nicole-lookalike girlfriend, Christie Prody, and after one breakup she told the *National Enquirer* that OJ had confessed murdering Nicole to her and had threatened to kill her. In another scandal, Simpson, Prody, and a third woman were stung by tabloid reporters, who claimed that they had documented an attempt by the three to make a porn movie for which they could be paid millions.[32]

In October 2001, Simpson was involved in a road-rage trial, when he reportedly assaulted a man who had honked and flashed his headlights at him after OJ ran a red light, but he was acquitted of the charges. In December 2001, Simpson's home was raided in an investigation of an international drug ring and theft of satellite TV programming. Soon after, the home of Simpson's girlfriend, Christie Prody, was broken into and a cat was killed, an event that the tabloids interpreted as a message to her and Simpson not to reveal what they knew about the drug ring under investigation.[33]

Hence, the Simpson spectacle continues as a sordid celebrity scandal, signaling the unending fascination with the trials, tribulations, and lifestyles of the rich and famous and the notorious and infamous. The Simpson saga therefore, like the Michael Jordan spectacle, remains open and has been narrated and theorized in countless ways. I conclude, therefore, with a discussion of the contradictory effects of the O. J. Simpson megaspectacle.

The Simpson effect: contradictions of a megaspectacle

The Simpson murder trial was thus a megaspectacle that put on display competing versions of social reality, intense identity politics, and resultant social fragmentation. It will continue to resonate for years, with unpredictable effects. At its most obvious, it has intensified racial divisions and conflicts, and helped promote a white backlash that has endangered programs helping blacks and other minority groups. It sent out a message that men might be able to get away with violence against their spouses, even murder, though it also promoted passionate debates about domestic violence and might eventually help construct a consensus that it is unacceptable. Likewise, it focused scrutiny on police racism and corruption and might have helped efforts to reform the police. Yet the Simpson megaspectacle also intensified racial divisions and passions to such an extent that it worsened relations between blacks and whites that may set back reform efforts and intensify racial conflict.

Indeed, media images, such as those of O. J. Simpson brutalizing his wife, or Mark Fuhrman's vile racist discourse and behavior, can be mobilized positively to organize women against wife abuse and citizens against police racism and corruption. Yet the transformation of politics into media spectacle also results in a displacement of political movements and struggles, substituting the trials and tribulations of OJ and Nicole Simpson for the real problems of African Americans, women, and the oppressed. As identity politics moves toward an anti-politics of identity, with real-life grievances acted out in variegated forms, politics become more divorced from actual social movements, replacing organized struggle with assorted diffuse and inchoate configurations and contradictory effects. Thus, some acted out racial grievances through identifying with O. J. Simpson whereas others identified with his murdered wife, Nicole, and concern with issues such as police corruption and racial or domestic violence found release in arguments over the Simpson case, rather than organized political struggle and action.

On the other hand, the Simpson case could motivate individuals to involve themselves with issues that the case dramatized and arguably had a pedagogical function in educating the public at large about complex issues involving the legal system, police, domestic violence, and police corruption. Consequently, the effects of the Simpson megaspectacle are highly contradictory and demonstrate that media spectacles are involved in a complex process of disseminating images, discourses, and narratives that are received and constructed in opposing ways by different groups. Clearly, the media do not affect audiences in a simplistic casual nexus, but instead proliferate effects by generating a profusion of role models, morality tales, spectacles, discourses, and figures with which individuals identify and appropriate in diverse ways (Kellner 1995). While celebrities construct and market their images within media culture, individuals take the resources of their culture as material with which to construct their own social identities. The Simpson affair discloses that the identities created by people are fundamentally shaped by such things as race, gender, and class, and the ways in which people appropriate and live out these constituents of social identity.[34]

The Simpson megaspectacle thus calls attention to the complex ways in which the media construct social reality and in which audiences interact with and appropriate media spectacle. In terms of how the Simpson megaspectacle presented the social system and its major institutions, the trial and its aftermath has arguably delegitimated major institutions and exacerbated tensions between the races. In general, media culture provides rituals and spectacles that celebrate the society's basic institutions and values and plays an important part, along with education and the family, in social reproduction. Yet, because the media construct and mediate fundamental social controversies, they may have contradictory effects, partly legitimating the social system and partly delegitimating it. Although many of the official legal commentators employed by the mainstream media repeatedly said that the Simpson legal proceedings demonstrated how well the US justice system worked, the trial ultimately failed as a legitimating media spectacle because the country was so divided over the case. So many people were disappointed with the outcome, which was clearly determined by money, celebrity, identity politics, and the media spectacle of the events themselves, that it tended to intensify social criticism rather than make people feel good about the social system.

In the Simpson trial, major institutions of the legal and political system appeared to be dysfunctional. The trial and its aftermath revealed that the police were incompetent in their gathering of evidence, and their questionable procedures in collecting and handling evidence allowed the defense to raise questions and doubts in the jurors' minds. The racism of Detective Mark Fuhrman, captured on audiotapes, raised the specter of a police force permeated with racism, while the defense was able to suggest the possibility of police corruption, thus posing questions about the legitimacy of the police in the United States.

The trial itself also raised questions about the competency and legitimacy of the legal system. Analyses of the trial by knowledgeable legal authorities were highly critical of prosecution decisions to assent to a downtown Los Angeles trial site rather than Santa Monica, which was the appropriate site for a Brentwood murder trial; the selection of jury candidates; the sloppy presentation of evidence; the choice and handling of witnesses; and actual jury room performance (Bugliosi 1996; Toobin 1996; Petrocelli 1998). Judge Lance Ito was severely criticized for letting the trial go on for so long and for not controlling procedures appropriately, for letting the defense get away with too much, for grandstanding to the media, and for making many questionable decisions on a daily basis (Bugliosi 1996: Chapter III). And the defense was chastised for playing the race card and for making many mistakes, despite ultimately winning the case.

Indeed, the intense media scrutiny of the trial and its participants put in question the entire criminal justice system, from the police, and their methods of evidence gathering, to the jury system, including the legal profession and trial procedures. The decision left many members of the public feeling violated and denied a proper cathartic experience. Thus, whereas modernity required the legitimation of modern institutions of the state, congress, the judiciary and legal system, the military, the media, and other institutions (Blumenberg 1983), postmodernization has involved the delegitimation of these institutions. One could argue that the Vietnam War and subsequent military crimes and misdeeds delegitimated the US military; that Watergate and subsequent presidential misdeeds delegitimated the presidency; that failures to gather crucial information and its copious misdeeds delegitimated the CIA; that Congress was delegitimated after abundant revelations of corruption, the 1995–96 gridlock, involving the first government shutdown in history, and the 1997 campaign finance scandals; that the Clarence Thomas nomination delegitimated the Supreme Court, seen as a political football in which a cynical president could nominate an obviously unqualified Justice; and that the O. J. Simpson case delegitimated the US justice system in its entirety from the police to the trial and jury system.[35]

On the other hand, in each of these events, the media attempted to gain legitimation as the defender and repository of fundamental American values and strove to increase its own power after each of these spectacles. Indeed, the Simpson spectacle could be seen as a minor victory or at least boon for the media, which was able to attract tremendous numbers of people to its programming and augmented its social power once again at the cost of other institutions. Yet the media also arguably delegitimated itself through constructing a media spectacle that made television especially appear as a circus of paparazzi more concerned with dramatizing than with informing or illuminating. The lack of investigative reporting by the mainstream media and their constant circulation of stories and rumors uncovered by the tabloids revealed both a sacrifice of the norms and values of traditional journalism and a tabloidization of journalism. Thus, during the Simpson megaspectacle, the values of entertainment and scandal permeated the mainstream media in a period in which competition for audiences intensified and the media machines fed the audiences what they believed they craved.

And so the Simpson spectacle turned out to be a US tragedy without proper resolution, rather than a ritual that legitimated the legal system. In a sense, "the trial of the century" was, in the words of Melanie Lomax, "the disgrace of the century."[36] In the trial's aftermath, the participants signed multimillion-dollar book deals and churned out instant books, vindicating their own roles in the trial and heaping blame on others. But surely there was enough blame to go around, and Lomax argued that all of the participants disgraced themselves, ranging from the prosecution, which made many incredible mistakes; to the judge, who played to the cameras, lost control of the courtroom, and made many questionable calls; to the defense, which overplayed the race card; and to the media, which inflated a sordid murder trial to the spectacle of the era, collapsed mainstream journalism into tabloid infotainment, and ignored more important public responsibilities. Every participant, from jury members to prosecutors and defense lawyers, who sought to capitalize on the affair with instant books and publicity tours disgraced themselves, and almost everyone in the Simpson circles came out looking bad, revealing the culture of celebrity itself to be a scandal.

Thus, in an era of celebrity and media spectacle, the media have come to define social reality and the key issues and dramas of an epoch. Megaspectacles signal to the public what is important and generate a media bandwagon effect. They can elevate squalid scandal into the defining issues of the day, as they did in the 1990s with the Simpson murder trials and the Clinton sex scandals. The O. J. Simpson megaspectacle signaled a new era of tabloid journalism, in which the media would pursue celebrity and media scandals that would dominate the news cycles and become obsessive phenomena of everyday life.

For a diagnostic critique, the Simpson megaspectacle indicated various problems in US society and the need to address a multiplicity of issues of gender, race, class, and politics in addressing a complex case such as the Simpson one. Moreover, while the OJ trials unfolded amidst elaborate conspiracy scenarios, including an alleged LA police plot, which his defense manipulated to help acquit Simpson of murder charges, conspiracies and paranoia concerning dominant US institutions were becoming a pop culture phenomenon in the popular TV series *The X-Files* (1993–2002). Media spectacles such as *The X-Files* articulate and help to define the political ethos and atmosphere of an era, as I will discuss in the next chapter. And they have also, as I argue in Chapter 6, helped to define the presidencies and success or failure of various US political administrations and personalities in the contemporary era.

Notes

1   The term "megaspectacle" was developed in work with Steve Best for our book *The Postmodern Adventure*. We distinguish between regularly scheduled megaspectacle, such as the Oscars, sports events such as the World Series, the Super Bowl, and the Olympics, presidential elections, and other mega-events that I discussed in Chapter 1,

and media extravaganzas, such as the Gulf War, the O. J. Simpson trial, the Clinton sex scandals, or the September 11 terrorist attacks, that come to dominate the media and define an entire era of politics and culture.

2   On Debord and the "society of the spectacle," see the discussion in Chapter 1 of this work and in Best and Kellner (1997: Chapter 2).

3   "Identity politics" has a quite complex genealogy, different constructions, and is highly contested in the present age. It generally refers, in my use of the term, to a politics in which individuals construct their cultural and political identities through engaging in struggles and actions that advance the interests of the groups with which they identify. In this chapter, I suggest that in an age of media spectacle "identity politics" is not just an academic category or one that refers to oppositional groups, but also one that plays out in mainstream society and culture. For a useful overview of different conceptions of identity politics, see Castells (1997).

4   "CNN viewership increased fivefold, topping their Gulf war ratings; while E!'s daytime rating quadrupled; Court TV viewership swelled significantly and it became a national institution" (*Entertainment Weekly*, October 13, 1995: 8–9). In addition, the major national networks devoted the overwhelming majority of their news coverage to the case, as I document below, as did many local TV news outlets, talk radio and television discussion shows, and Internet discussion groups and websites.

5   Prime-time programs and even major sports events were interrupted as a fascinated nation watched OJ's flight down the LA freeways in the white Ford Bronco, wondering how this live drama was going to play itself out. Andrea Ford, one of the *Los Angeles Times* reporters who covered the case, said that the Bronco chase was "the defining moment. It locked people into this common emotional experience" (*Los Angeles Times*, October 9, 1995: S3). Interestingly, according to some accounts, Simpson identified himself during his run with the figure in the popular TV series and 1993 film *The Fugitive*, who was unjustly accused of murdering his wife (*The Daily Mail*, June 20, 1994).

6   According to US laws, one cannot be tried twice for murder, so Simpson's second trial involved wrongful death complaints against him by the Goldman and Brown families, and Goldman's mother Sharon Rufo; see Petrocelli (1998). Civil trials require that the plaintiff must prove that the accused committed the murders only by a preponderance of the evidence and not beyond reasonable doubt; civil jury verdicts need not be unanimous and in California a 9–3 verdict is sufficient to resolve the case; and, thirdly, Simpson could and was required to testify at the trial.

7   To some extent, the Simpson affair was a global spectacle, as I discovered while teaching in Finland and Sweden during the trial in 1995 and visiting the United Kingdom, where I observed guests in a hotel in Wales watching the Sky Television broadcasting of the trial. It is, however, predominantly a highly Americanized spectacle and it is from this angle that I will focus in my account.

8   For an overview of sites on "OJ and the Internet," which was developed for a University of Florida law course, see www.fsu.edu/~crimdo/lecture11.html. Proponents of conspiracy theories of the Simpson spectacle include A. G. Coleman ("The O. J. Simpson affair: more and better conspiracy theories"), who worked out the drug cartel assassination theory that allegedly targeted Nicole and which had been floated by the Simpson defense, throwing in speculations about other conspiracies as well (see www.policenet/com/ojcons1.hmtl). The long-time conspiracy theorist Sherman Skolnick circulated conspiracy theories about drug cartel murder plots involving Nicole Simpson and Ron Goldman in the home page of his website (www.skolnicksreport.com/) and they were widely distributed by *Conspiracy Nation* (whose web archives are collected at www.conspiracynet.com/archives/consphtml/conspnation.shtm). "The framing of OJ Simpson" sets out the theory that Ron Goldman was the main target of the murders (www.geocities.com/CapitolHill/5244/). And Dave Wagner developed the thesis that

Simpson was framed by a mob involved with a sports betting ring, which Simpson had worked with and then broken with at Nicole's insistence, and that the mob subsequently killed her and framed OJ in retaliation (www.wagnerandson.com/oj/OJ.htm). Some of the web conspiracy material was developed in books such as J. Neil Schulman's *The Frame of the Century* (1999), which claims that Simpson's former cop friend Ron Shipp, who testified against him in the trial, was the murderer! William C. Dear's *OJ Is Guilty But Not of Murder* (2000) alleged that Simpson's son Jason was the murderer! Peter Roberts provided an overview of the Simpson conspiracy theories in *OJ: 101 Theories, Conspiracies and Alibis* (1995). I discuss the nature and role of conspiracy theory in contemporary media spectacle in the next chapter. On the whole, the wealth of conspiracy theories helped to promote legitimation of those who claimed that there was doubt concerning Simpson's guilt in the murders and puts on display the weirdness that is the United States in the contemporary era.

9 Fuhrman was the police officer who was called to the scene at Simpson's Brentwood home and who found the bloody glove and other evidence on the site that was to help indict Simpson. There were rumors that Fuhrman had a troubled and a racist past and he was trapped on the witness stand, where he denied having used the "N-word," and then tapes were discovered in which Fuhrman repeatedly used that highly charged racist epithet and engaged in highly offensive racist discourse. The defense was able to imply successfully that Fuhrman might have planted evidence and conspired to make Simpson the culprit.

10 On the media and the social construction of "domestic violence," see Hammer (2002). The media are able to focus national attention on issues, calling attention to problems often neglected or covered over. But the coverage cuts two ways. There were reports in domestic abuse centers that just as some women were becoming more able to articulate the problem of domestic violence, others were becoming afraid to call for help because their spouses snarled that they would "OJ" them, threatening to murder wives who would not submit to their will. African American commentators called attention to the fact that it was a black male celebrity, O. J. Simpson, who became the magnet for discussions of domestic violence, just as black male celebrities Mike Tyson and Michael Jackson spawned discourses on date rape and the issue of the sexual exploitation of children respectively (see Dyson 1993; Hutchinson 1996) for discussion on the targeting of black celebrities for domestic problems that cut across class and race lines). Obviously, countless members of all races had engaged in these unsavory activities, but the media seem to make them focal topics of intense debate when black male celebrities were caught in public exposure, leading many blacks to claim that white media culture is intent on bringing down successful and powerful black males.

11 Would-be actor and house guest Kato Kaelin became part of the Simpson spectacle with his crucial testimony as to Simpson's comings and goings the night of the murder. In the civil trial, Kaelin testified that Simpson wolfed down his burger earlier in the evening of the fateful killings: "I think he ate it before we left McDonald's. It was, like, immediate ... It was right out of the parking lot and it was gone" (in Petrocelli 1998: 203). Some speculate that Simpson used Kaelin the night of the murder to provide an alibi and that McDonald's was a site that would normalize Simpson's behavior; no doubt, Simpson's choice pointed to McDonald's popularity in the era and how people from all walks of life participated in the fast-food spectacle. On the role of commodities and marketing in the Simpson case, see Lipsitz (1997).

12 Carl Boggs argued that "celebrity (far more than race) was the decisive factor in the Simpson case – in the superstar's privileged treatment, in the refusal of people (among all ethnic groups) to believe he could have been the murderer, in the verdict itself ... The Simpson fiasco shows how difficult it is for people to relinquish celebrity worship in a society of vast divisions and inequality, where little else remains fixed or

stable, where attacks on celebrity may seem like attacks on the self ... Thanks in great measure to the narcotizing impact of TV on our lives, we project so much of our hopes and dreams onto these personae, seeking to live vicariously through the medium of celebrity" (*Los Angeles View*, November 10–16, 1995: 10). I agree with Boggs on the importance of celebrity, but believe that gender, race, and postmodern identity politics were equally salient.

13 After the trial, the *Los Angeles Times Magazine* published a long article on the *National Enquirer* and how it pursued investigative journalism and feminist issues during the trial; see Katy Butler, "The accidental feminist" (*Los Angeles Times Magazine*, December 10, 1995). In fact, of the mainstream media, it was perhaps only the *Los Angeles Times* that did in-depth investigative reporting into the various dimensions of the crime, evident in a series of comprehensive overviews of the affair after the verdict in October 1995.

14 On Baudrillard and the culture of simulation and hyperreality, see Kellner (1989b).

15 Parenthetically, one could argue that the O. J. Simpson trial indicates that a large majority of the public still lives in a television-centered media culture and that the computer-generated cyberculture is still of secondary cultural and political importance. For the Simpson trial, as for the 2000 election and the battle for the White House (Kellner 2001) and the September 11 terrorist attacks and subsequent Terror War (Kellner, forthcoming), the broadcast media appear to be still the most powerful arbiters of social reality. This suggests that TV culture remains the center of contemporary politics and everyday life, putting into question claims that the computer and the Internet are now the dominant media forms. On the other hand, computer culture also played a significant role in disseminating and constructing OJ mania and addiction, and the many bulletin boards, websites, and computer communications dedicated to the trial and its aftermath anticipates an ever-growing role for computer culture in the new millennium. One poignant story tells of how OJ addicts were spending hundreds of dollars a month on chat-lines on the trial and on accessing Internet material at a time when one still paid in the United States according to the length of time logged on to the Internet.

16 On the social construction of reality, see Berger and Luckman (1967). A July 20–22, 1994 *Newsweek* poll found that 60 percent of African American respondents believed that Simpson was "set up" for the double murder, compared with 23 percent of whites polled. A *Los Angeles Times* poll, taken the following week, indicated that 70 percent of black audiences were "very" or "somewhat" sympathetic toward Simpson compared with 38 percent of whites polled. By the end of the trial, over 70 percent of blacks thought that he was innocent, while over 70 percent of whites believed that he was guilty, thus showing a significant polarization of opinion between the races. Yet, there were also studies indicating that from the beginning the response in the African American community was more complex than the polls might indicate; see the stories in the *LA Weekly* (June 24–30, 1994: 33) and the *Los Angeles Times* (July 10, 1994: A1 and A22–23). On the primacy of race in the Simpson spectacle, see the dialogue between white and black reporters Tom Elias and Dennis Schatzman (1996), who have diametrically opposed opinions on almost every aspect of the Simpson case. One could do a diagnostic critique of that book uncovering the extremely one-sided positions held by both sides in the Simpson case. On the race issue in the Simpson case, see also the collection of articles in Morrison and Lacour (1997) and Cose (1997). Indeed, every book on the Simpson trial has extended reflections on the role of race in the trial and there is general agreement over its significance. Williams (2001) puts the representations of race that played out in the Simpson megaspectacle into a historical perspective.

17 Senator Alphonse D'Amato (Republican, NY) was forced to make a public apology for mocking Judge Ito's non-existent "Asian" accent, revealing that Ito had become the butt of many racist jokes, as well as an object of sympathy. Participants in the trial,

and others, were harshly critical of Ito, including Darden (1996), Dershowitz (1996), Bugliosi (1996), and Petrocelli (1998).

18 Judge Lance Ito, in a videotaped interview with Gayle Former, a journalism student at California State University, Northridge. Transcript distributed on the Internet in the CNN O. J. Simpson home page, October 24, 1995.

19 This was also the case in the Simi Valley verdict, which acquitted the police officers accused of violence against Rodney King, despite the videotaped evidence to the contrary. Images of King raising his hands to fend off police blows were interpreted as his resisting arrest, and claims that the police brutality shown on the video was commensurate with the situation was accepted by the all-white jury that acquitted the police officers. Obviously, the Simi Valley jury was predisposed to acquit the police, just as the predominantly black jury was predisposed to acquit Simpson in the criminal case, but powerful words were needed in both cases to legitimate the countermining of visual evidence.

20 Jurors interviewed after the trial said that they were especially impressed by Barry Scheck's performance. In their post-trial analyses, Vincent Bugliosi (1996) and Alan Dershowitz (1996) marshaled arguments against the prosecution case and blamed prosecutors Marcia Clark and Christopher Darden for extremely poor performances, claiming that they had made a series of blunders. Bugliosi, however, believed that Simpson was clearly guilty, whereas Dershowitz argued the case for "reasonable doubts" and acquittal; Christopher Darden (1996), in turn, blamed the jury, the judge, and the defense playing of the "race card," and Marcia Clark (1997) attempted to vindicate the prosecution and place the blame for Simpson's acquittal elsewhere. In his book on the civil trial, lawyer Daniel Petrocelli (1998) clearly put the blame for the murders on Simpson and told the inside story of how he came to persecute Simpson and win the civil lawsuit case.

21 The overnight Nielsen ratings reported that 42.9 percent of the nation's TV homes – a total of about 41 million – were tuned in to see the verdict. But many, many more viewers were watching at work, in restaurants and public places, and wherever there was a television, so it was estimated the next day that about 107.7 million people or 57 percent of the nation's adult population watched the verdict live, according to a CNN poll (*New York Times*, October 3, 1995: A10). The weekly Nielsen ratings concurred with this figure and indicated that an additional 62.4 million had watched the verdict later in the day. CBS ratings researcher David Poltrack estimated the audience at 150 million, roughly 90 percent of the adult population of the United States. He noted that 96 percent watched the 1969 moon landing, 93 percent the funeral of JFK, and 84.5 percent the first day of the Gulf War; thus, with a greatly increased population, the ratings for the Simpson murder verdict qualify it as the most watched event in TV history, according to the number of viewers. Despite the huge figures, networks reportedly had difficulty selling advertising during their coverage of the verdict and its aftermath. The *New York Daily News* observed that advertisers viewed the Simpson coverage as "the wrong environment" (October 4, 1995).

22 See the studies in Morrison and Lacour (1997), which attempt to mediate the concerns between gender, race, class, and other issues in the Simpson case.

23 Rodney King was an African American male who had been arrested by the LA police and was brutally beaten by them. Despite a dramatic videotaping of this evident, an all-white jury acquitted the police, leading to major rioting in Los Angeles; for an excellent cultural studies analysis of the King affair, see Fiske (1994). Fiske opens his book with an account of the Simpson case, which argues that the mainstream media first used racist framing to construct Simpson's guilt and then decentered the race issue in favor of domestic violence and other issues; this may have been true of one stage of the trial, but later, after Fiske's book was in press, the race issue came to the fore and dominated public perception and media coverage of the trial and its aftermath.

24 See the letters to the editor in the *Los Angeles Times* in the days following the verdict

for indicators of the race and gender divisions and intense passions over the trial. A large number of letters, however, also cited the class dimension, indicating that it was Simpson's wealth and celebrity that contributed greatly to his acquittal. Talk radio buzzed with controversy for months after the verdict, as did the Internet, TV talk shows, and print media. The controversy continued through the civil trial in fall 1996 and over the next few years as articles, books, and other media continued to debate the case and to follow the trials and tribulations of the participants.

25 Many argued that there were "reasonable doubts" in the Simpson case concerning police contamination of and tampering with evidence, and an extremely poor presentation of the evidence by the prosecution (see Dershowitz 1996), whereas there was no doubt that the LA police had brutally beaten Rodney King.

26 In the civil trial, Daniel Petrocelli quoted to Simpson extracts from a co-authored autobiography that highlighted the importance of image for Simpson and his image-consciousness. Chapter 1 of Simpson's autobiography was titled "A question of image," and the text indicates the importance for sports celebrities and others of producing the proper image in order to succeed in a world of media spectacle (Petrocelli 1998: 486f.).

27 Initially, the tabloids were merciless in negative presentations of Simpson. According to the *Globe* (November 21, 1995: 6–7), the suicidal Simpson was "a muttering, unshaven wreck wandering around in his underpants" who "locks himself in [his daughter] Sydney's room and sobs like a baby for hours on end." Rejected by his hoped-for fiancée Paula Barbieri, shunned by his Brentwood neighbors, unable to play golf at his favorite links or visit his favorite restaurants and stores, Simpson was even rebuffed on Halloween: after he decorated his Brentwood home with "cobwebs, ghosts and goblins" and bought "bags of candy in eager anticipation of a fun night," no one visited Simpson's house for trick or treat, leaving him "so depressed the next day he didn't get out of bed" (ibid.). The *Star* tabloid, by contrast, published exclusive and highly paid photos of an ecstatic Simpson after his release (October 24, 1995). But by November 14 *The Star* reported that Simpson had exploded with rage at Paula Barbieri, accusing her of sleeping with other men and berating her for her clothes and make-up. Simpson then turned to former Buffalo Bills cheerleader Gretchen Stockdale for solace, but was reportedly chagrined to discover that she was a former Las Vegas stripper and thus bad for his image. There were also stories of Simpson's impotency, his money problems, and new allegations against him, especially as witnesses began to give depositions in the civil case against him in spring and summer 1996, and more incriminating evidence turned up against him in the civil trial itself. Negative tabloid stories continue to this day about Simpson and partisan debates persist on the Internet, as I will discuss later in this chapter.

28 There has been a proliferation of discourses on identity that take up the shifting fortunes of the self in the contemporary era. It is indeed interesting how identity talk has replaced the discourse of the self and subject as a major focus of philosophical discussion. Self/subject discourse became weighted with too much metaphysical (and anti-metaphysical) baggage, reifying in idealist forms, and then dissolving, the concept of the subject and self (poststructuralism), thus decentering and disabling agency. The discourse of identity has, by and large, replaced the debates over the subject and self in the contemporary era, taking up some of the same metaphysical, ethical, and political themes in a different context with a seemingly more concrete language.

29 Sociological discourses of identity articulate the social bases of identity, how it is socially constructed, how individuals change identity, and its key social constituents (i.e. gender, race, class, sexuality, and so on). Cultural representations help construct identity in the current age and media culture provides resources for creating identities. Further, media spectacle is producing a postmodernization of identity by promoting an identity politics through which individuals identify with certain groups, subject positions, and discourses that together help produce personal and political identities.

30 For an elaboration of a politics of alliance and solidarity, see Best and Kellner (1997; 2001).

31 Shortly after the trial Marcia Clark was quoted by CNN as saying that: "Liberals won't admit that a black jury won't find a black defendant guilty in a case like this. They [i.e. black jurists] won't seek justice." Clark soon resigned as public prosecutor, after receiving an allegedly $4 million contract to write a book on the trial, which she published in 1997. She then pursued a career in public speaking and the media.

32 See "Ex-lover tells all. OJ's murder confession" (*National Enquirer*, October 17, 2000) and "Gotcha! OJ's sleazy porn flick" (*Globe*, March 6, 2001). Of course, in the world of sleaze spectacle, it is difficult to discern which sleazoid to believe, a problem throughout the Simpson saga.

33 See "Simpson road rage trial opens" (*Los Angeles Times*, October 19, 2001); "OJ's home searched in drug probe" (*Associated Press*, December 4, 2001); "O. J. Simpson's home raided in drug theft ring inquiry" (*Los Angeles Times*, December 5, 2001); and "OJ's terror. Disgraced grid great fears he's marked for death" (*Star*, February 12, 2002).

34 Before the murder case, O. J. Simpson chose to construct himself in a way that downplayed race. *Time* (October 16, 1995: 43) makes the interesting point that O. J. Simpson "entered the trial as a fellow white man and grew darker as the proceedings went on." Simpson was fond of saying, "I'm not black, I'm OJ!" Thus, Simpson previously appeared to be the perfectly assimilated black male for whom race seemed not to matter and was apparently transcended. He had indeed shown little interest in civil rights politics or the African American community; after marrying his African American high-school sweetheart, Simpson seemed primarily interested in white women and in socializing in upscale white society. Yet after *Time* colored him darker on a cover of the magazine after his arrest in June 1994, OJ indeed became blacker to the African American community. For an excellent account of Simpson's previous politics and role in breaking through as an African American marketing spokesperson, see Johnson and Roediger (1997).

35 Of course, legitimation is an intensely complex process that is constantly renegotiated and is transformed as social events evolve. After dramatic examples of delegitimation, certain institutions and individuals attempt relegitimation, sometimes successfully. As I suggest, O. J. Simpson has failed to relegitimate himself, and is seen by many as a brutal murderer who has got away with his crimes. The Los Angeles police went through other cycles of scandal after the Simpson case, including the Ramparts case, and are thus still in a legitimation crisis. The theft of election 2000, I have argued, puts into question the basic institutions of the US political system of democracy (Kellner 2001), and in a forthcoming book I will argue that the events of the September 11 terrorist attacks on the United States have put in question the institutions of the National Security State. Hence, in my view, the institutions of US society have been in constant crisis since the 1960s and the system is constantly attempting to relegitimate itself after the legitimacy of major institutions has been put into question.

36 Lomax made this argument on several *Rivera Live* shows in March 1996 and thereafter.

5   TV spectacle

Aliens, conspiracies, and biotechnology in *The X-Files*

The X-Files TV spectacle is an exemplar of a popular TV series that became a global cult hit, with fans and followers all over the world. When it first appeared on Fox Television in 1993, the series initially appealed to fans fascinated by extraterrestrials and aliens and/or the paranormal. By the mid-1990s, however, it had become a megahit pop culture phenomenon attracting legions of viewers, who often had *X-Files* gatherings or parties to see the program on its Friday and then Sunday night spots. This was the era of the rapid growth of the Internet and X-Philes developed chat-rooms, websites, list-serves, and other domains to discuss their passion and to connect with like-minded enthusiasts in fan communities.

The X-Files also received respectful critical acclaim, receiving over fifty Emmy nominations, and winning seventeen, as well as several Golden Globe awards and a coveted Peabody Award for TV excellence. By the mid-1990s, its ratings had soared, it usually won its time-slot, and at its height in 1998 it had over twenty million regular viewers and an additional ten million per week on its syndicated reruns, making it one of the most popular TV series of its era. The TV series spun off a movie deal, *X-Files* conventions and product-line sales, and made its creators and stars rich and famous. It continues to be a global popular and as it winds down to its US finale in May 2002, it is seen regularly in the United Kingdom and many other European countries, as well as in Latin America, Australia, Asia, and a variety of other places throughout the world.

In retrospect, *The X-Files* tapped into a pre-millennial upsurge in spirituality and belief in the occult, deepening fear and distrust of government, inchoate fears of science and technology getting out of control, and worries about disaster and apocalypse. On the whole, *The X-Files* presented a vision of a world heading for catastrophe, driven by unseen government, corporate, technological, and alien forces, which have overwhelmed contemporary individuals in a world that threatens individual autonomy and well-being, and even the viability of life on earth.

The X-Files spectacle cumulatively presents a polysemic and multi-layered complex text that can be read on multiple levels.[1] On the most overt level, *The X-Files* can be seen as an occult text, which deals with various modalities of the paranormal and supernatural. The occult subtext points to widespread faith in the supernatural in contemporary society and belief in the existence of extraterrestrial aliens. Yet one can also provide a theological reading of the series, and various plotlines and episodes are full of theology and religious imagery, motifs, and overtones, articulating hopes for transcendence and even an afterlife.

On the existential level, *The X-Files* deals with primal fears, horrors, and hopes of human beings in the contemporary era. Episodes of the series often take place on various levels of consciousness, fantasy, hallucination, or madness, providing unusual psychological depth. The main male and female characters are used to probe gender roles and psychology, relationships, and such issues as sexuality, pregnancy, birth, and death. Indeed, frequent medical tragedies, comas, and the demise of significant characters provide an unusually powerful existential pathos to a series that deals with the significant issues of life and death.

The existential dimension brings up the connection of the series with genre fiction, such as horror and gothic romance. The series combines these with science fiction and political conspiracy motifs to provide an especially rich and engaging example of high-quality series television. Specific episodes deal with a panorama of primal fears, while others project fantasies of religious transcendence, and the series as a whole arguably puts on display deep desires for love, community, truth, knowledge, and religious revelation and salvation.

The series' extensive fandom relates to either some specific aspects or all of these dimensions, with groups of fans focused on the relationship between the main male and female characters, while others follow the intricate details of the show's mythology, or its depiction of aliens and monsters. Many fans obsessively dwell on the personalities of the show's creators or the actors in the series, often collapsing the person into their TV role. Some fans write convoluted scripts that they publish in 'zines or on the 'net, frequently fleshing out their fantasies about the characters or directions that they would like the series to take.

The X-Files thus presents a spectacle of highly involved fans, who relate to and use the series in a diversity and multiplicity of ways. Its popularity makes the text and audience response a productive vehicle for a diagnostic critique of what *The X-Files* spectacle tells us about contemporary US and global society over the past decade. From the perspective of diagnostic critique, the theme of political and governmental conspiracies in *The X-Files* resonates with growing concern with corporate and political machinations within US society and the global economy over the past decade. The series thus articulates the populist suspicions of Americans and others throughout the world concerning US politics, corporations, and culture.

Many theorists have raised questions concerning whether we are living in an age of conspiracy and paranoia, and what the prevalence of conspiracy theories and popular TV series such as *The X-Files* tell us about our contemporary condition.[2] In the United States and elsewhere, books about aliens and extraterrestrial abductions have become bestsellers, and TV documentaries on these topics proliferate. Rightwing paramilitary groups in the United States allege a myriad of political conspiracies and strike out at government targets. Internet conspiracy sites and chat-rooms abound and talk radio prospers on political rumors and controversy. Popular TV series and films feature government, corporate, and extraterrestrial conspiracies galore. At the same time, US politics, media culture, and everyday life seem to be saturated with fears and fascination with conspiracy, generating a paranoid sense that individuals have lost control of their institutions and even the ability to map and understand the machinations of a complex global society and culture.

Although conspiracy thinking has long been characteristic of the American experience, as has been what Richard Hofstadter (1996) has called "the paranoid style of American politics," there seems to be an explosion of popular paranoia and conspiracy thinking in the contemporary moment, of which *The X-Files* is a significant and symptomatic part. In this study, I carry out a diagnostic critique using *The X-Files* to provide a critical analysis of contemporary US society and culture. I distinguish between a *clinical paranoia,* which demonizes irrationally dominant institutions and which often projects evil on to occult, supernatural, or all-powerful authority figures, and a *critical paranoia,* which is rationally suspicious of hegemonic institutions such as the state, the military, or corporations. On my reading, *The X-Files* combines rational social critique and mistrust with occultist projection on to the supernatural, which deflects attention from the real sources of social oppression, and thus is itself highly ideologically contradictory and ambiguous.[3]

The X-Files also articulates fears about technology creating monstrosities and eluding human control. In its last two seasons (2000–2), the series put on display frightening products of biotechnology and genetic engineering, as I discuss below. Thus, critical interrogation of technologies, medical practices, and the ways in which new technologies are producing novel and frightening new species and forms of life are other concerns of the series, which put into question the ideology of unfettered technological development and raise disquieting questions concerning the role of science and technology in the present world.

My analysis will suggest a growing crisis of confidence in the institutions of US society and an openness to criticize its structures and ideology on the part of network television, previously a rather conservative ideology machine. However, the critical discourse of *The X-Files* is itself ideological in many ways, and is frequently undercut by its occultism, its conservative, traditional American work ethic, its covert religiosity, and the long-established tropes of romantic individualism. Nonetheless, *The X-Files* spectacle raises questions about the workings of contemporary society, puts into question the opposition between science and reason and their "other," and subverts the conventions of traditional commercial television to an unparalleled extent. Consequently, the series provides challenging texts through which we can engage, via diagnostic critique, some fundamental sociopolitical and cultural issues of our time.

Conspiracy, paranoia, and postmodern aesthetics in *The X-Files*

In the 1960s and 1970s, a popular discourse concerning widespread and virulent conspiracies within US society and politics flourished. After the assassinations of John and Robert Kennedy and black political leaders, such as Malcolm X, Martin Luther King, and figures in the Black Panther party, reports of political conspiracies circulated, often implicating agencies such as the FBI, CIA, and other arms of the

National Security State. There was the seemingly endless continuation of the Vietnam War, the US covert and overt interventions throughout the world, and the flourishing of a steady stream of revelations of US government-sanctioned crimes. With the disclosure of systematic wrongdoing in the Nixon administration during the Watergate scandals and the revelations of nefarious US interventions throughout the globe in the post-World War II period, the mainstream media began taking up conspiracy themes. Subsequently, its discourses provided tools of critique of institutions that had previously been sacrosanct during the Cold War, when denigration of the National Security State was equivalent to treason.

During the same period, revelations of US corporations producing unsafe cars and other products, willfully and knowingly engaging in environmental destruction, and promoting potentially catastrophic nuclear energy plants and weapons helped to create a distrust of major economic organizations and practices. The widespread suspicion of dominant government and corporate forces was translated within media culture into new genres of conspiracy films. Political conspiracy films, such as *Executive Action* (1973), *The Parallax View* (1974), *Three Days of the Condor* (1974), *The Domino Principle* (1975), *All the President's Men* (1976), and *Twilight's Last Gleaming* (1979), are significant because they reverse the polarities of earlier Hollywood political thrillers. Most pre-1960s Hollywood political films generally affirmed US institutions, while 1970s Hollywood corporate and political conspiracy films, and later *The X-Files,* suggested that evil was within those very agencies. The political conspiracy films transcoded fear and distrust of government, a theme that would return with a vengeance in the 1990s, and nurtured a paranoid sense that political power was out of the reach of ordinary citizens and democratic political processes.[4]

The X-Files takes up the conspiracy and paranoia motifs of its Hollywood predecessors and goes even further in its critique of dominant institutions and depictions of depravity and intrigue. The series is generally acclaimed to be *the* TV cult hit of the 1990s, and rarely has a popular artifact of media culture exuded so many layers of conspiracy and paranoia. Its world of shadowy government and corporate conspiracies, its excursions into the occult, paranormal, and supernatural, its anxious injunction to "trust no one," and its paranoid presentation of the US system have touched a responsive chord during an era when belief in the fantastic, aliens, and government conspiracies has accelerated.

Featuring the exploits of two Federal Bureau of Investigation (FBI) agents, Fox Mulder (David Duchovny) and Dana Scully (Gillian Armstrong), *The X-Files* articulates a panorama of contemporary fears and fantasies. Drawing on classical figures of the occult, present-day horrors, developments and misfirings of science and technology, and political machinations as material for its stories, it deployed the forms and iconic figures of media culture and references to contemporary historical individuals and events to present and comment upon present-day issues. Through dealing with salient disturbing aspects of the current era, the series has raised questions concerning powerful US institutions and practices.

The X-Files takes up classical genres of science fiction, horror, occult, fantasy, crime drama, and political and corporate conspiracy, which are reconfigured from conservative TV legitimations of the established system to instruments of critique. In terms of *The X-Files'* thematics, its questioning of the epistemology of truth and erosion of binary oppositions between science and faith, the irrational and rational, and the natural and the supernatural enacts a deconstructive postmodern epistemology. Accordingly, its themes of aliens and the supernatural can be read as allegorical figures for a postmodern implosion of technology and the human, a theme I will highlight in a later section. Moreover, its paranoid politics constitute a version of pop postmodernism that deploys suspicion and mistrust to help to map a difficult-to-represent political complexity and heterogeneity, which seems to defy conceptual mapping and representation. Yet *The X-Files'* aesthetics and thematics exhibit some classical modernist features as well as novel postmodern ones, thus the series navigates the tricky and hazardous shoals between the modern and the postmodern.[5]

A founding gesture of high modernist aesthetics created a great divide between high and low culture. On this view, the artifacts of high culture were alleged to reside in an elevated sphere of beauty, truth, originality, and value, while the debased artifacts of mass culture were perceived to be infected with commercialism, banality, ideology, and the lack of aesthetic form or value. The postmodern turn in aesthetics, however, rejected this distinction, arguing that what is now acclaimed as high culture was once popular (i.e. Greek drama, Shakespeare, Bach, Wagner, etc.), while the popular has its own aesthetic pleasures and values. A postmodern take on media culture thus opens aesthetics to the artifacts of the popular and legitimates and sanctions aesthetic and thematic analysis of such forms as series television, pop music, and the other artifacts of media culture. In the following analysis, I will accordingly subject *The X-Files* to aesthetic and political scrutiny, taking it seriously as a media spectacle that offers a symptomatic and interesting artifact of the contemporary, which reveals significant cultural shifts in both the forms of culture and societal values.

The X-Files pilot and the succeeding episode, "Deep Throat" (1-1 and 1-2; 1993),[6] combine the forms of the political conspiracy and science fiction genres to present the characters, plotlines, and themes of the show. The early episodes utilized rather conventional TV-narrative (pseudo-)realist aesthetics with standard plot structures and character presentation. To play on quasi-documentary narrative realism, thought to be essential to TV credibility, the series opened – for the first and last time – with a text saying that the story was "inspired by actual documented accounts." The series opener shows Dana Scully, a new FBI agent, trained as a medical scientist, entering a dark government chamber in which she learns that she will be assigned to the X-Files. Her partner in this enterprise is Fox Mulder, an Oxford-educated psychologist who is reputed to be an expert in crime profiling, but who was known in the FBI academy as "Spooky" Mulder because of his interest in the occult and supernatural. The actor Charles Cioffi, who plays the FBI bureaucrat informing Scully of her assignment, was the murderous psychopath in Alan Pakula's *Klute* and villains in other political conspiracy films, thus contributing to the disturbing aura of sinister government bureaucrats surrounding the young agents.

Scully goes down to Mulder's basement office to meet her new partner, who is initially framed against a poster with a small flying saucer, which reads "I want to believe." This trope will identify Mulder's quest for truth and passion for knowledge. He ironically introduces himself as "the FBI's least wanted" and correctly assesses that Scully was "sent to spy on me," highlighting his (justified) paranoia. Yet Mulder also indicates that he is impressed with her scientific credentials, which include senior thesis *Einstein's Twin Paradox: A New Interpretation*, which Mulder assures her he has read. But, he explains, "It's just that in most of my work, the laws of physics rarely seem to apply."

Their initial assignment in the 1993 pilot episode (1-1) involves exploring the murder of young teenagers, whom Mulder suspects were victims of alien abduction and experimentation. Scully, of course, is skeptical, setting up an opposition contrasting the scientific rationalist with the paranormal supernaturalist, Mulder, who wants to believe. This common delineation between reason and faith, science and the paranormal, functions critically in *The X-Files* since the usual gender associations are reversed. Moreover, as the series proceeds, it deconstructs the oppositions, with Mulder often becoming more critical and skeptical, and Scully becoming more open to extra-scientific explanations, faith, and what are referred to as "extreme possibilities."

The X-Files also calls into constant question its own mythology of aliens and government conspiracies. In a classic two-part episode, "Duane Barry" (2-5; 1994) and "Ascension" (2-6; 1994), Mulder is sent to negotiate with an individual who has claimed alien abduction and who has escaped a psychiatric institution and is holding hostages. Scully calls Mulder to tell him that Barry is a former FBI agent who was shot and had key parts of his brain destroyed, producing a rare form of psychosis and bizarre hallucinations. Yet the episodes show Barry being abducted and introduce FBI and government agents who seem to be involved in the alien conspiracy. Thus, the series raises questions over whether those portrayed as alien abductees are insane or victims, and whether the government itself is involved in alien conspiracies, issues that repeatedly reappear in future episodes throughout the series.

Although most mainstream US television classically follows a simplistic representational strategy that involves clear-cut characters, plotlines, and series codes, *The X-Files* questions and reconfigures traditional television forms, providing its own set of aesthetic pleasures. While US television usually follows norms of simplicity, familiarity, and predictability, *The X-Files*, by contrast, revels in complexity and ambiguity. Whereas most network television uses a banal realism and neither strives for nor is interested in aesthetic values, *The X-Files* employs production teams that pursue high creative values and produce some of the most aesthetically pleasing, stylized, and intellectually challenging television yet to appear. The series thus has affiliations with classical modernism and its ideal of the complex and open text, which invites multiple readings and requires an active audience.

There are other distinctly modernist aspects of the series as well. Scully and Mulder are first and foremost truth seekers. The series has adopted as its motto, which concludes the opening title sequence, "The truth is out there," thus projecting a strong concept of truth. In addition, the series exhibits something like a modernist authorial vision, defined by series creator Chris Carter, who wrote and directed many of the episodes and played an extremely involved supervisory role over production details. The show thus projects a personal vision, style, and aesthetic characteristic of the auteurs of modernism.

Indeed, *The X-Files* excels in the production of aesthetic pleasures, including the visual delight of seeing the unknown, of gaining ocular access to the supernatural and paranormal. The opening sequence unfolds with Mark Snow's mysterious music and the show title positioned against a black background. The image jumps to what appears to be a computer-generated montage of an unidentified flying object and then to what appear to be alien hieroglyphics and a strange technology that mutates into a fearful face, itself morphing into an abstract image of terror with background graphics stating "Paranormal activity" appearing. The montage then cuts to an FBI office and Agent Mulder's badge and face, punctuated by a dimly flickering title, "Government denies knowledge," pointing to the conspiracy motif of the series. Next, Agent Scully's face and badge appear, followed by images of Mulder and Scully entering through the door into a dangerous site, succeeded by what looks like an X-ray of a hand with a glimmering red finger and then a strange body.

Near the end of the opening title sequence, there is a morph to an image of a giant eye, which then cuts to a dramatically cloudy sky, usually emblazoned with the motto "The truth is out there." The opening sequence thus signals to the viewer that she or he is about to enter unknown and mysterious spaces and to see something different, perhaps frightening and shocking. The show deals with the pleasures of seeing and knowing as the FBI agents, Scully and Mulder, discover and perceive novelties, bizarre and paranormal phenomena, and the secret and villainous machinations of government.

Most interpretations of *The X-Files* perceive it as one-sidedly modern or postmodern, failing to see how it negotiates the boundaries between them, participating in both sides of the great divide. In an otherwise illuminating and interesting article, Reeves *et al.* (1996: 34) write: "Although the generic sampling and episodic/serial straddle of *The X-Files* could be interpreted as boundary blurring, other aspects of the program are explicitly anti-postmodern." According to these authors, *X-Files* is "post-postmodern" because of the committed and sustained quest for truth on behalf of its protagonists, its seriousness, and its lack of the sort of postmodern cynicism, irony, and play with generic codes characteristic of such TV programs as *Beavis and Butt-Head* (1993–97) or *Mystery Science Theater 3000* (1988–99). I claim, by contrast, that *The X-Files* does embody postmodern aesthetic strategies, themes, and vision, despite the fact that its characters often exhibit arguably modern characteristics, which inform some of the plots and vision of the series (i.e. questing for truth, a traditional American work ethic and professionalism, belief in scientific rationality, and so on).

My argument is that the series on the whole subverts the modern paradigm of truth, representation, and subjectivity, while presenting new postmodern paradigms. Moreover, from the perspective of aesthetic strategy, *The X-Files* systematically uses postmodern pastiche, combining classical cinematic and literary genres, traditional folklore, and references to contemporary urban legend and political events.[7] It brings this material together in an original and intriguing mixing of classical generic codes, material from a diverse realm of media culture, and journalistic engagement with current events, resulting in a postmodern blend of the traditional and the contemporary. The specific postmodern aesthetic at play in the series is that proposed by Linda Hutcheon

(1988; 1989), who advances a model of postmodern appropriation and hybridity as a way of commenting on traditional generic forms and material. For Hutcheon, the best postmodern texts make critical comments in regard to history and contemporary social forces and events. This notion is opposed to Jameson's (1984; 1991) more ludic notion of postmodernism, which sees it as a play with codes more interested in surface form than social commentary or critique.

For Hutcheon, a critical postmodernism inscribes *and* contests previous forms of culture, which it sets out to undermine (1988: xiii and 3), and thus has a "contradictory dependence on and independence from that which temporally preceded it and which literally made it possible" (1988: 18). Hutcheon agrees with Jameson, Huyssen, and others on the point that postmodern culture is inherently quotational, reiterative, and parasitic on previous cultural forms, but she claims that the postmodern mode of quotation is intertextual parody rather than mere pastiche, as Jameson holds (1984; 1991). For example, Jameson (1991: 21f.) presents novelist E. L. Doctorow and *Ragtime* as illustrating a postmodern reduction of history to stereotypes and quotations. Hutcheon (1988: 61–2), by contrast, reads Doctorow as being exemplary of a postmodern interrogation of the boundaries between fiction and history, which opens up history to critical examination. Moreover, she argues that Doctorow breaks with the perspective of the historical novel as the voice of ruling elites, decenters unifying historical narratives, and brings out a plurality of oppositional voices and perspectives.

In his 1991 revision of his earlier 1984 essay on postmodernism, Jameson retorts that in a postmodern context audiences for the most part cannot interpret the narrative historically and that the mixing of historical figures with fictional ones reduces the text to dehistoricized "fantasy signifiers from a variety of ideologemes in a kind of hologram" (Jameson 1991: 22–3). In general, Hutcheon's model of postmodernism is preferable for interpreting some types of postmodern texts that interrogate and engage history and politics, while other types of texts (many nostalgia films and forms of media culture, much contemporary painting, and some forms of writing) are better described by Jameson's paradigm. My argument here is that Hutcheon's notion of a critical postmodernism provides a more useful take on key aspects of *The X-Files* than Jameson's ludic conception, though his model also illuminates some of its features.

The X-Files' postmodern aesthetic can be characterized by its aggressive use of pastiche and quotation. The series borrows from a large number of classical TV and Hollywood film genres – science fiction, horror, fantasy, the occult, political conspiracy, melodrama, the crime drama, the medical and forensic series, and others. It also mines the hoary figures of the werewolf, vampire, and alien for contemporary relevance and significance, reappropriating these figures to comment on contemporary problems and issues. It features police and medical authorities, typical social types, and more specific figures drawn from the domains of political culture, urban legend, and contemporary news and tabloid sensation. But whereas the classical forms of these genres often reproduced conservative ideological themes, *The X-Files* points to problems in dominant ideologies and classical generic codes.

The X-Files most obviously draws on 1950s science fiction (hereafter SF) movies and 1970s political conspiracy films, and the representational and semiotic codes of these genres. The alien and flying saucer motifs were popularized in a series of 1950s Hollywood science fiction films that portrayed alien invasions, which were either friendly and benevolent (i.e. *The Day the Earth Stood Still*), or hostile and malevolent (i.e. *The War of the Worlds*). It also borrows from popular TV series such as *The Twilight Zone*, *The Outer Limits*, *Star Trek*, and *Kolchak, The Night Stalker*. As the characters, conspiracies, and complexities of the plotlines and mythologies evolved, however, it was indeterminate what sorts of aliens *The X-Files* was presenting. As I note below, it was often unclear in the unfolding of the series whether the mythology of the aliens was a government conspiracy to cover over military misdeeds, or whether there were actual aliens that posed a threat to the survival of the human species. Indeed, the growing complexity of the series exemplifies a postmodern indeterminacy that characterizes *The X-Files* as a whole.

Moreover, no previous TV series had presented such critical visions of the US government as *The X-Files*. The series creator and chief creative force, Chris Carter, has said that the Watergate trials were his formative political experience. Indeed, in some ways Scully and Mulder resemble *Washington Post* reporters Bob Woodward and Carl Bernstein in their tireless efforts to get to the truth, to unravel the conspiracies, to find out who did what, to lay their hands on the "smoking gun," and to provide irrefutable evidence of the conspiracies that they seek to expose. There are countless references to other 1970s conspiracy motifs of media culture: the motto "Trust no one" echoes Don Corleone's advice to his son ("Keep your friends close, but keep your enemies closer"). And as Graham (1996: 59) summarizes:

> Mulder quotes Dirty Harry and, like Harry Caul in *The Conversation*, tears up his apartment looking for surveillance devices, bodies are suspended in *Coma*like tanks; the government attempts to assassinate Mulder the way it did the CIA worker played by Robert Redford in *Three Days of the Condor*; people are possessed in *Exorcist*-like fashion (a film which producer Carter certainly remembers was set in post-Watergate Washington). The "lone gunman" theory of political assassinations so mocked in *The Parallax View* is given short shrift here as well through Mulder's friendship with "conspiracy nuts" who publish a bulletin called *The Lone Gunman*. In case anyone thinks this all merely random pastiche, the boss who sets the whole scenario in motion in the first episode – and who brings Scully and Mulder together – is played by Charles Cioffi, the Nixon-clone murderer in *Klute* (Nixon's visage even appears in cartoon form on one of the Lone Gunman's screensavers, complete with the bulled caption, "I am not a crook.").

Specific episodes of the series draw on popular generic texts in the mode of postmodern appropriation and pastiche, deploying familiar horror and SF stories in various episodes. For example, an early thriller, "Ice" (1-8; 1993), is a pastiche of the situation of the popular 1950s SF movie *The Thing*, with a group of scientists isolated in the Arctic, terrorized by a strange alien creature, which is inhabiting various characters and setting them off against each other in paranoid fear; the episode "Eve" (1-11; 1993) exploits the evil demon child horror genre and cloning of child monsters à la *The Boys From Brazil*; "Wetwired" (3-23; 1996) appropriates the themes of David Cronenberg's film *Videodrome*; "Talitha Cumi" (3-24; 1996) replays the section featuring the Grand Inquisitor of Dostoyevsky's *The Brothers Karamazov*; "Herrenvolk" (4-1; 1996) deploys the iconography of *Children of the Damned*; "Anasazi" (2-25; 1995) quotes passages from the political conspiracy film *Three Days of the Condor;* "War of the Coprophages" (3-12; 1996) plays on a *Twilight Zone, the Movie* episode about fear of roaches and roach invasion; a 1997 episode, "The Post-Modern Prometheus" (5-6; 1997), broadcast in black and white, drew on figures and the iconography of *Frankenstein*; the hoary werewolf appears in "Shapes" (1-18; 1994) while a modern vampire emerges in "3" (2-7; 1994); "Roadrunners" (8-5; 2000) presents a homage to the Spencer Tracy movie *Bad Day at Black Rock*; "Dreamland I and II" (6-4 and 6-5; 1998) provide pastiches of the TV series *Quantum Leap*; and the episode "X-Cops" (7-12; 2000) offers a homage in form and content to the video vérité TV series *Cops* (1989 onwards).

Other episodes model their villains on well-known mass murderers such as Jeffrey Dahmer and Henry Lee Lucas, and there are copious intertextual references to political events and figures and artifacts of media culture, including a plethora of in-group references to the series itself, its producers, and a variety of contemporary issues. Thus, *The X-Files* appropriates many genres, artifacts, and specific texts of media culture, utilizing postmodern strategies of pastiche and quotation. The Scully character is modeled to some extent on the ascetic and dedicated female FBI detective Clarice Starling in *The Silence of the Lambs*. In one episode, "2Shy" (3-6; 1995), Scully and Mulder pursue a vampire-like killer who consumes the fat of lonely, overweight women, whom he contacts through an Internet chat-room, "Big and Beautiful." A conservative police officer questions whether a woman like Scully should be doing autopsies of the murdered women and whether a woman detective can retain her critical distance in such cases in which the victims are women. Scully, of course, maintains her objectivity, and in a final scene, drawing on the confrontation of the woman FBI agent in *The Silence of the Lambs* with the murderous but intellectual killer Hannibal Lecter, she effectively confronts the murderer. This iconography of the woman officer alone in a cell with a vicious criminal was replicated in *The X-Files* episode "The List" (3-5; 1995).[8]

In addition to the problematics and forms of the horror and SF genres already cited, the series draws on the formats of the crime drama, the coming-of-age drama, and the medical drama. Scully and Mulder are FBI agents, and each program presents a crime or mystery that needs to be investigated. As the agents gain experience and knowledge, they mature, overcoming their previous one-sidedness and naiveté, thus presenting models of growth and development. The fact that Scully is a medical doctor ensures numerous medical scenes and problems, and her police work involves forensic and autopsy work. The series itself is thus a postmodern TV hybrid, mixing the codes of a variety of genres, while providing metacommentary on standard television forms and their ideological thematics.

Moreover, *The X-Files* exhibits a level of narrative ambiguity rarely encountered in mainstream media culture. In many episodes it is not clear whether the rationalist or supernaturalist explanation is more salient, scores of mysteries are not unraveled, the resolving of some problems often creates numerous new ones, and it is often not clear what actually happened in a lot of episodes. As noted, the series as a whole exhibits significant postmodern ambiguity concerning its villains, the source of its evils, and its own beliefs and values.

Another interesting aspect to *The X-Files* spectacle's contradictions and ambiguity is that the series was broadcast throughout its tenure by the conservative Fox TV network, owned by rightwing media mogul Rupert Murdoch. *The X-Files* was one of Fox's first break-out dramatic series hits and the fledging network probably allowed its creators more leeway to explore "extreme possibilities" and engage in edgy material than the more stodgy US television networks. To win viewers from the big three US networks, Fox targeted youth, African Americans, and audiences with more off-center interests. Conspiracy theorists might see the Fox sponsorship of the show as a covert political form of promoting the FBI or hidden conservative ideologies beneath the seemingly critical and liberal ethos of the show. But, in fact, because the series was such a megahit for Fox, the network was probably happy with whatever weirdness the series creators produced to keep eyeballs glued to its wares, as long as it continued to get good ratings.[9]

Series television as social critique: "Trust no one"

The X-Files spectacle shares some of the thematic and stylistic frames of film noir. Its plots are saturated with ambiguity and mystery, while a quest to unravel the machinations of unscrupulous individuals and institutions drives the narrative. Like noir, *The X-Files* has voice-overs, flashbacks, convoluted plots, expressionist visual styles, dark shadows and night shots, and often-ambiguous resolutions and even failure to attain closure. For the noir detective confronting threatening femme fatales, who literally trusts no one but himself, *The X-Files* substitutes the partnership of Scully and Mulder, who do come to trust each other. Yet, like noir, *The X-Files* protagonists face an incomprehensible and overpowering universe that they find difficult, if not impossible, to understand and master.

While film noir emerged at the end of World War II during an era marked by fear of nuclear annihilation, political repression, and economic change, *The X-Files* appeared in a period of proliferating new technologies with dramatic and perhaps unanticipated effects, accompanied by political fragmentation and conflict on both local and global levels. The era of *The X-Files* was one marked by a dramatic restructuring of global capitalism and the rise and fall of the dot.com economy, resulting in corporate downsizing, loss of jobs and economic security, and a general unease during an era of highly turbulent and volatile economic development. Beneath the surface placidity of prosperity during the Clinton years, there lurked as well fierce cultural wars between the left and right, economic insecurities, fears of new technology, such as the Internet and biotechnology, and feelings of the loss of power and autonomy that *The X-Files* expressed in allegorical form.

Hence, a diagnostic critique reveals that *The X-Files* taps into salient fears and uncertainties of the present, which it articulates in its often disturbing narratives, and, like film noir, uses stylized forms of media culture to provide allegorical critiques of aspects of contemporary society and culture. Structurally, *The X-Files* oscillated between episodes featuring aliens and government conspiracies and episodes highlighting more classic figures of the horror and fantasy genres such as the werewolf, vampire, psychotic killer, and mutant monsters (referred to by commentators as "The Monster Movie of the Week" or MMTW). Demonic figures of the occult often project society's most prevalent fears and anxieties and soothe them by having the evil destroyed. Such conservative horror/occult texts usually legitimate dominant societal forces, such as the military or police, as protection against evil and threats to normality. *The X-Files*, however, is more ambivalent in its use of classical horror figures.

While the reactionary occult genre shows its monsters as inexplicable, as forces of nature, as if nature itself was full of evil, threatening, and in need of control and domination, *The X-Files* often shows monstrosity to be a creation of social forces, of societal ills rather than the incomprehensible forces of nature. For instance, illegal strip-mining of old trees unleashed dormant insect larvae in "Darkness Falls" (1-20; 1994); the "Flukeman" mutant in the popular episode "The Host" (2-2; 1994) is a product of nuclear wastes from the accident in Chernobyl, born "in a primordial soup of radioactive sewage," which produced mutants and monstrosities. And "Hungry" (7-3; 1999) can be read as a parable about the dehumanizing effects of working in a fast-food restaurant and how it creates pathological eating habits.

"Sleepless" (2-4; 1994) depicts Vietnam veterans who are victims of a sleep elimination program, which would make them superkillers, and are subsequently driven mad by the US government military program. One, the Preacher, becomes an avenging angel who kills the soldiers who had been involved in war crimes against the Vietnamese. In "The Walk" (3-7; 1995), a Vietnam veteran who had his limbs amputated develops murderous telekinetic powers to compensate for the loss of his limbs, fabricating yet another monster created by the US military. And "Unrequited" (4-16; 1997) tells the story of a Vietnam POW who is left behind in Vietnam, is rescued by a US rightwing paramilitary group, and returns to the United States to assassinate the generals responsible for the decision to cover up the existence of American POWs still captive in Vietnam. The Vietnam War is obviously an unhealed wound for Chris Carter's generation, which keeps festering and generating tales to capture its hideousness and horrors.

Thus, many of *The X-Files* monsters are shown to be the products of human meddling with nature, or malicious government and/or corporate policies, rather than the inexplicable forces of nature. Yet some demonic figures are associated with Native Americans, or developing world countries, utilizing reactionary stereotypes that equate native peoples with the primitive and the monstrous. "Shapes" (1-18; 1994) associates werewolf-like creatures with Native Americans; "Fresh Bones" (2-15; 1995) links diabolic events with Haitian voodoo rituals; "Teso Dos Bichos" (3-18; 1996) portrays evil unleashed by moving artifacts from a sacred South American burial ground; and "Teliko" (4-4; 1996) depicts an African skin-eating immigrant, while "Biogenesis" (6-22; 1999) and "The Third Extinction" (7-1; 1999) use Africa as a site of primitivist superstition and malevolence.

The theme of the origins and nature of the monsters in *The X-Files* calls attention to the significant folkloric element in the series. Rarely has a TV series drawn so heavily on urban legend and traditional mythic beliefs, cures for disease, and modes of warding off evil. The folkloric motifs often provide the format for a cautionary morality tale that warns of the dangers of tampering with nature for excessive profit or power, or producing genetic mutations and entities that may have unforeseeable consequences. A wide variety of episodes deal with monstrosities emerging in far-off regions – the Arctic, the rainforests in Central America, or the woods of the Pacific Northwest. In many cases, the monster is the result of a quest for a wonderdrug, weapon, or exploitable product that awakens a dormant parasite or creates a new life form through genetic engineering. These episodes show a highly toxic parasite, fungus, or other entity, safely contained in a natural habitat, which is awakened or released through tampering and meddling in the pursuit of power or profit. The many episodes that deal with genetic engineering run amok are obviously contemporary cautionary warnings against tampering with the natural order, thus articulating fears of technology eluding human management, replaying the Frankenstein myth, which is probably *the* archetypal myth of *The X-Files* and, more broadly, contemporary culture.

Yet, as noted, some of the folkloric episodes reproduce negative stereotypes of "primitive" cultures. However, *The X-Files* spectacle also calls attention to how the representation of "otherness," of groups and individuals who are not part of the usual repertoire of mainstream media culture, is politically charged and volatile. The series continually engages "otherness" and challenges societal normality and rationality, opening itself to what it calls "extreme possibilities." This process involves an exploration of cultures and beliefs that are marginal to mainstream vision. Yet "otherness" and difference are deployed in a variety of modes, some of which serve as a critique of normality and dominant institutions and discourses, while some of its representations defame marginal and "othered" cultures as dangerous and grotesque.

The X-Files' use of images of folklore and the occult and its monster figures are thus politically ambiguous, used sometimes to criticize dominant US government or business policies and practices and sometimes to demonize or valorize native peoples and cultures. Yet often the evils portrayed are products of contemporary US society. The character who intones in an iconic gesture "Trust no one" is code-named "Deep Throat," inevitably evoking thoughts of the Watergate scandal. *The X-Files* plays on fears of government malfeasance and dangerous state and corporate conspiracies, as well as anxieties over the occult and aliens. Combining these motifs intensifies the atmosphere of paranoia, generating images of a universe haunted by mysterious and evil forces, which are extremely difficult to comprehend, let alone to conquer. This is hardly the typical TV universe with its clear-cut distinctions between good and evil, customary morality tales, sharply drawn generic codes, and usual resolution of the mysteries or problems portrayed. Instead, *The X-Files* explores new ground, drawing on the audience's propensity to believe the worst of its government, to fear what it cannot understand, and to be open to ambiguity and extreme possibilities.

In particular, the alien conspiracy mythology of *The X-Files*, as series creator

Chris Carter christened the continuing plotline, functions as an ongoing vehicle of social critique. Each season, between five and seven episodes directly highlight the ongoing narrative, with many other episodes contributing small pieces. As the series evolved, the plot thickened, the conspiracies became more convoluted, and the viewer was forced to work with a vast amount of complex narrative material concerning whether aliens do or do not exist, their nature and threat, and what sort of government conspiracy is involved in the phenomenon. This complexity calls into question modern conceptions of truth, evidence, and even the nature of human beings and of human and individual identity.

The mythology episodes in *The X-Files* deploy a mode of critical paranoia to subvert received attitudes, beliefs, and ways of seeing that are common to popular television. On the whole, television has taught its viewers to look at established institutions, authorities, and practices positively and threats to established law and order negatively. Thus, television has instilled an attitude of trust toward the existing social system, and fear of those threatening forces outside it. *The X-Files* reverses this way of seeing by instilling distrust toward established authority through representing government and the existing order as exorbitantly flawed, even complicit in the worst crimes and evil imaginable. *The X-Files* feeds on and intensifies the populist paranoia that government is bad, and that the CIA, FBI, military, and other agencies of government are filled with individuals who carry out villainous actions and constitute a threat to traditional humanistic moral values and even human life itself.

In a provocative way, however, the series debunks a certain kind of conspiracy theory that posits a shadowy collective of evil men, with an "invisible Master" pulling the strings and controlling events. Conspiracy paranoia has traditionally taken the form of fear of mysterious groups such as the Masons, Jews, or the Trilateral Commission, influencing events from behind the scenes. Interestingly, the villainous Cigarette-Smoking Man (aka Cancer Man) was put in this position in *The X-Files*. He was connected with a cluster of initially faceless and then increasingly sinister looking men called the "Syndicate." By the time of the movie *X-Files: Fight the Future* (1998), it appeared that this cabal had sold out to the aliens and was helping with their colonization program of taking over the human race. But the Syndicate itself was revealed to be a conflicted and vulnerable group, which had segments trying to develop a vaccine against the virus possessed by the aliens that might conquer and destroy the human race.

The Syndicate appears to be an elite group of global capitalists led by conservative white men who were allied in nefarious ways with the aliens. Its members include the sinister Cigarette-Smoking Man, who, in one key episode, "Musings of a Cigarette-Smoking Man" (4-7; 1996), is shown involved in events from the Kennedy assassination to the fixing of football games to X-Files conspiracies. But he is portrayed as rather ordinary, often ineffectual, and generally alone and isolated. The Cigarette-Smoking Man is eventually killed, and it appears that major members of the Syndicate are also wiped out, thus eliminating a conspiratorial grouping that the audience was positioned to view as running the show. This plot-arc thus deflates fantasies of a conspiratorial consortium of faceless white men behind historical events, forcing viewers to question critically a certain kind of conspiracy theory.

To highlight the paranoia and conspiracy motifs, the series uses expressionistic lighting and camera angles, Mark Snow's moody and often disturbing music and sound effects, and oblique narratives to accentuate the air of mystery. Such devices disorient and perturb the audience, creating an atmosphere of fear and paranoia. Moreover, the continual use of medical technology and procedures, with Scully frequently performing autopsies or medical examinations and with both main characters shown in hospitals in life-threatening situations themselves, plays on fears of disease, doctors, medical incarceration, and technological intrusion into the body.

The X-Files also exploits anxieties over US government conspiracies by depicting experiments to manipulate its citizens or to develop supersoldier weapons [i.e. "Sleepless" (2-4; 1994)] – a theme that became central during the eighth and ninth seasons. In "Wetwired" (3-23; 1996), it appears that a government experiment to manipulate individuals through TV signals produces psychotic behavior (a pastiche of Cronenberg's *Videodrome*). Furthermore, the constant shifts in the plotline concerning whether the government is or is not involved in alien conspiracies raise disturbing questions about the nature and effects of government institutions and the possibility of seeing into their machinations. On a deeper epistemological level, as I will explore in the next section, the series questions whether we can ever discover or know the difference between truth and falsity, or illusion and reality.

The postmodern sublime, or "Is the truth out there"?

By presenting shadowy government figures, covert operatives, and even the agents' FBI bosses and Mulder's father as complicit in heinous crimes, *The X-Files* makes its audiences suspicious of established state institutions and ways of seeing. Critical paranoia thus provides a mode of representing the unrepresentable, of putting on display the horrors of the present, by evoking anxieties over evil forces that are manipulating the existing social system and carrying out abominable actions. This is not to affirm the sort of clinical paranoia in which the paranoid person can easily become dysfunctional if paranoia eclipses rational and critical knowledge. Critical paranoia, by contrast, can help, within proper boundaries, to map the forces that structure the world and turn the subject against oppressive forces. Although clinical paranoia projects itself beyond the world of actual social relationships into a fantasy world of imaginary entities and thereby loses all contact with reality, critical paranoia focuses one on oppressive forces within the world. Although critical paranoia assumes conspiracies and plots, presuming that there are hidden and malevolent forces behind political, social, and personal events, it maintains a judicious and rational outlook on these in order to confirm or refute the paranoid hypothesis. Critical paranoia thus does not disassociate itself from a reality principle, nor does it retreat into a solipsistic world of persecutorial or occult fantasies. As we will see in our reading, *The X-Files* combines critical paranoia, which focuses attention on oppressive institutions, with supernaturalism, which deflects attention from these forces to focus on the occult.

The aesthetic and ethos of *The X-Files* embody Lyotard's notion of a postmodern sublime that utilizes allegory, hyperbolic exaggeration, and otherness to represent the unrepresentable and to convey a sense of the complexity and horrors of the present (1984; 1988). Traditionally, in Burke, Kant, and others, the category of the sublime denominated that which defied naturalistic representation, transcending all representation, such as the divine or the grandeur of nature. Lyotard provides the concept of the sublime with a postmodern inflection, claiming that it is the crucial notion for a contemporary aesthetic. He suggests that in an increasingly complex contemporary world, with a blurring or destruction of previous boundaries and categories, the sublime attempts to represent the unconventional and unrepresentable, to embody the new and complex, and to capture the novelties and heterogeneities of the present. Building on this conception, Jameson (1991) talks of a "technological sublime," replacing the previous aesthetic conception of the sublime, which referred to attempts to stand for the splendor, grandeur, and awe of nature. Today, however, natural environments are being replaced by technological environments that take on the awesome and difficult-to-represent features of nature.

Such a use of postmodern sublime, allegory, and paranoia can help audiences both to question dominant values and practices and to seek new modes of representing the complexities of contemporary life. Distrust in the face of science, technology, government, and orthodox attitudes forces an individual to penetrate beneath the lies and illusions, to attempt to grasp the complex and inexplicable, and to pursue the truth. Thus, while seeking and stating the truth is a modern ideal, *The X-Files* suggests that modern methods (science, rationality, and documentary evidence) may not be adequate for the job, that one must dig deeper, and that new modes of representation and inquiry are necessary.

A highly complex political allegory is employed as the mode of representation in the mythology episodes of the series depicting government and alien conspiracies. The pilot introduces the elements that will come to characterize *The X-Files* mythology. The agents interview several characters who exhibit traits of alien abduction, speaking of lost time, nosebleeds, and mysterious illnesses. They discover a corpse that appears to be a strange mutant, but it disappears. They recover what may be alien tissue samples and a metal nasal implant, which in turn are destroyed in a mysterious fire. Scully and Mulder even experience a blinding flash while driving in the countryside and experience "lost time," as they investigate their case. The conclusion of the episode shows the sinister "Cigarette-Smoking Man" storing the only piece of evidence remaining, a small implant removed from one of the murdered teenagers, in a massive Defense Department storage room, thus evoking the possibility of a US government conspiracy and cover-up.

The succeeding episodes of the government–alien conspiracies unravel an incredibly dense and complex plot, which suggests a government cover-up of alien presence, experiments on humans with alien DNA, attempts to create new breeds of human/alien mutant clones with superhuman powers, and shows the struggles between various groups and government agencies to guide the conspiracies. Yet in a startling development, episodes in the fifth season (1997–98) imply that the whole alien mythology is a government ploy to cover over the really malevolent things that the government and the military have been doing over the past decades since the end of World War II. These episodes suggest that all the evidence of aliens has been a fraudulent creation of political and military agencies, and that "aliens" are a diversion from greater government wickedness during the Cold War.[10]

"Redux" and "Redux II" (5-2 and 5-3; 1997), for instance, show Mulder coming to question his belief in aliens, and beginning to think that he himself was manipulated to promote the existence of aliens as part of a government conspiracy, thus becoming increasingly skeptical. The episodes also imply that the Cigarette-Smoking Man is not in charge and that greater forces are behind the conspiracy. Later in the season, however, and in the summer 1998 *The X-Files* movie, Mulder is again provided with evidence of the existence of extraterrestrials. During the sixth and subsequent seasons, he reverts to playing the role of investigator of the supernatural, although he undergoes many trials and tribulations in his adventures. For the most part, then, the series promotes belief in alien extraterrestrials, alien abductions, and conspiracies to cover up the fantastic occurrences portrayed by depicting the phenomena in question.

However, in one distinctively postmodern episode, "José Chung's 'From Outer Space'" (3-20; 1996), written by Darin Morgan,[11] the alien mythology itself is destabilized and a highly postmodern take on truth and representation is presented. The episode "José Chung" opens with a postmodern verbal pun and trick as portentous music dramatizes an extreme long shot of the night sky, the camera zooms on to what appears to be a massive space ship, while the soundtrack is saturated with a mechanical whirring. Suddenly, however, a jump cut jolts the viewer to see men working in a metal basket on power lines and we hear workmen discussing a power failure. The images draw on *Close Encounters of a Third Kind*, which features a power-line repairman eventually undergoing an alien encounter. But the opening sequence warns you not to trust your eyes, that you can be easily fooled, and that the show itself is engaging in possible trickery. This motif is extended and the camera pans on to a "Klass County, Washington" sign, evoking the figure of Philip Klass, a noted UFO debunker and critic.[12]

After setting up the narrative in the mode of postmodern irony, appropriation, and pastiche, the scene cuts to two teenagers in a car, on their first date, engaging in clichéd conversation. Their car clunks to a stop as a white light fills the screen and awe-inspiring choral music suffuses the scene with drama, a direct representation of the spaceship scene in *Close Encounters*. What seem to be gray aliens appear, and the couple are frightened by the lights and what appears to be a red-eyed alien. But as they express their fear and uncertainty, the camera pans on to young boys dressed up as aliens, who are terrorizing the teenage couple.

In a sense, this episode replays and parodies, in the mode of postmodern irony, the pilot episode that presents teen alien abductions. But whereas the pilot utilized a deadly serious melodramatic science fiction mode and traditional editing and narrative framing, "José Chung" undermines standard television narrative forms, is highly ironic, satirical, and even makes fun of the program's frames and themes. The episode centers on a writer, José Chung, who appears to be neither Hispanic nor Asian, researching a "nonfiction science fiction" novel based on the teen abduction episode. The rest of the program flashes back to the abduction, told from a variety of points of view, all of which are dramatically disparate. In a pastiche of Kurosawa's *Rashomon*, it suggests a postmodern perspectivism, in which there is no unitary truth, but rather each individual has his or her own interpretation of the truth. Thus, in this vision, although the truth "may be out there," it is multiple, complex, difficult to access, and subject to a diversity of interpretations.

A diagnostic critique thus stresses how *The X-Files* questions the modern concept of truth as accessible to proper methods that guarantee secure and indubitable results. Truth in the postmodern register, by contrast, is complex, constructed, and perspectival, and is not subject to an indubitable perception, absolute grounding, or certainty (Best and Kellner 1997: Chapter 5). "José Chung" thus undercuts the series' modernist quest for truth by suggesting that perhaps "the truth is out there," but it is hidden under dramatically conflicting interpretations and perspectives. The "José Chung" episode suggests that sight and experience themselves cannot be trusted, that all evidence is a construct subject to multiple readings, and that even documentation does not constitute absolute knowledge or foundation for truth.

In the "José Chung" episode, Mulder produces a photograph with great excitement that seems to show an extraterrestrial object, but later analysis reveals it to be a fraud, thus showing again that visual evidence is not to be trusted. Hence, key tensions run through the series between truth and lies, and between the realism and rationalism of the crime drama in conflict with the occultist fantasy of the supernatural genre. Indeed, it is uncommon for a US network TV series to exploit the generic tension between realism and suprarealism, naturalism and supernaturalism, and the explicable and inexplicable as in *The X-Files*. Further, it is often undecidable whether the bizarre phenomena depicted are subject to a rationalist and naturalist or a supernatural explanation.[13] While some episodes favor one mode and others the opposite, many are undecidable, and rarely has a TV series so consistently exploited such ambiguity and complexity.[14]

It is precisely this epistemological boundary blurring, this narrative indeterminacy of plot and epistemology, this questioning of standard modes of explanation, that renders *The X-Files* a postmodern undoing and questioning of the boundaries and distinctions characteristic of modern culture and rationality. The series' opening image in the title sequence of a misty, hazy object that looks like a flying saucer illustrates this indeterminacy. On one level, the image signifies "flying saucer" and the alien theme of the show. But it is so hazy and blurry that it could be an illusion, a military experimental object, or who knows what? It is coded as a photograph, which everyone knows can be doctored, and thus might not be a trustworthy index of truth. Other images in the opening sequence show strange hieroglyphics and objects that might be alien writing and technology – or human concoctions. Strange figures shown mutating might be aliens – or hallucinations and fantasies. An eyeball looks out at a bright blue sky with clouds dramatically appearing – and may or may not be able to see what is out there.

Moreover, as the series unfolds, there are more and more religious motifs. Scully is constantly renewing her Catholicism, and in the later series there is a proliferation of crosses and other religious imagery. Moreover, when it is disclosed that Mulder's sister Samantha has died, in one episode she is taken to a more blessed domain of the afterlife. Scully and Mulder's entire trajectory on the seasons, in fact, can be read as a quest narrative. The agents start off from a position of innocence in which they trust their elders and the dominant institutions of US society. Mulder then learns of his supposed father's questionable past and involvement with McCarthy-ism and other government conspiracies, discovering as well that his enemy, the Cigarette-Smoking Man, might be his true father. Suffering deep self-doubt, anger, rejection, and failure, Mulder must overcome these problems and reach a more mature and enlightened state.

Likewise, Scully matures as the series proceeds, overcomes the limitations of her scientific rationalism, and takes on the burdens and challenges of childbirth, a task immensely complicated by the series' mythology (I take on the issue of Scully's child, aliens, and biotechnology in a later section). Moreover, the constant death and resurrection of major figures on the show transcode Christian rebirth motifs and there is a salvational dimension to Mulder and Scully's search for the truth throughout the series.

It is therefore undecidable whether *The X-Files* promotes the supernatural or a critical scientific naturalism, and whether it ultimately upholds the deepest values and ideologies of the existing society or puts them into question. In some episodes, the occult or supernatural explanation is explicitly privileged, as viewers are often shown aliens, supernatural beings and events, and traditional and novel forms of the occult. In other episodes, however, what appears to be supernatural and occult is presented as either the machinations of human agencies and individuals, or a natural phenomenon that just appears to be supernatural. In many episodes, and perhaps in the series as a whole, the line is blurred and it is not clear whether the phenomena displayed are natural or supernatural, the product of government conspiracy or an alien presence that explodes the existing categories of life and being.

Indeed, one can see these opposed readings on display in Internet discussion groups of the series, with some individuals always defending a naturalist reading, or criticizing the show when it does not conform to realist narrative frames, while others delight in the occult and supernatural elements of the show. A website entitled "The Netpicker's Guide to *The X-Files*" lists all departures from realist narrative and scientific rationality, and many fans try to provide rational explanations for the mysterious events, while a book collects "bloopers, inconsistencies, screwed-up plots, technical glitches, and baffling references" (Farrand 1997). Several UFO and occultist sites celebrate the series for its daring subversion of scientific rationality, and many fans are obviously drawn to its supernaturalism. Internet discussion lists and 'zines argue endlessly about the meaning of specific episodes and the series as a whole. That it is able to play to different audiences and generate such passionate debate helps to account for the popularity of the series.

Another major conflict negotiated in the series, which also splits its fans into two opposed camps, concerns the clash between those who want to see Scully and Mulder form a romantic relationship and those who find the idea objection-able and prefer their professional relationship and a focus on the show's themes and mythologies rather than personal relationships and private lives. The former, called "Shippers" (i.e. those who seek a love relationship depicted), are opposed by "NoRomos," who do not want romance to take over the series. So far, *The X-Files* has fitfully negotiated this chasm, providing hints at romance and even a chaste New Year's Eve kiss in one episode and a more passionate kiss to end the eighth season, suggesting that indeed their relationship was significant. For the most part, the series focused on the thematics of individual episodes and the mythology of the series, rather than descending into the details of the main characters' private lives. But in the last two seasons it was clear that Mulder and Scully were deeply involved, and one plotline suggested that they had mysteriously conceived a child together. Next, however, I want to explore how the series also took on major dichotomies of Western thought, which, I argue, it subjects to deconstructive critique.

Postmodern deconstruction: "I want to believe" but …

The X-Files' method is to contrast two opposing epistemological binaries and then to put into question these radical dualistic oppositions, somewhat in the mode and spirit of Derrida's deconstruction. The first and chief dichotomy of Western reason that the series explores is the conflict between science and religion, reason and faith, and the rational and irrational. Consider the poster shown in Mulder's office in the first episode, which becomes an icon of the series, showing a small flying saucer against a deep blue sky with the motto: "I want to believe." Indeed, Mulder is driven by an obsession to experience the existence of aliens and supernatural forms of life, to have experiential confirmation of their existence, and to interact concretely with aliens and occult forces.

Moreover, Mulder desperately wants to *prove* that aliens exist, that the supernatural and aliens are part of the natural order, that occult forces are as real as genes and microbes. Scully is assigned to the X-Files precisely because she is a skeptic, because she believes not in the occult or supernatural but in scientific rationality. The series thus initially equates the female agent, Scully, with science, reason, and skepticism and the male agent, Mulder, with belief, the irrational, and supernaturalism, thus inverting the standard gender equations (i.e. women as irrational, intuitive, and believing, contrasted to men as scientific, rational, and critical).

However, it is the epistemological task of the series to subvert this dichotomy, to deconstruct the fixed oppositions, and to create a more complex and nuanced epistemological vision that encompasses both poles of the opposition. As the series proceeds, Scully comes to believe in government conspiracy, evil, and the inexplicable, and opens herself to "extreme possibilities." Mulder, by contrast, comes to question whether natural or supernatural explanations can account for the bizarre occurrences encountered in every episode, and even if the aliens that he is so diligently pursuing actually do exist. Indeed, although Mulder is initially presented as the representative of belief and openness to the occult, he also constantly deploys scientific rationality and often presents naturalistic explanations of supernaturalist phenomena. Moreover, although he wants to believe literally in the existence of alien forms of life, Mulder begins to query this belief, and several episodes in the fifth season show him coming to believe that the alien conspiracy is a government hoax and cover-up (although the sixth to the ninth seasons return to the alien conspiracy motif, which is itself made even more convoluted and complex, as I discuss below).

In the terms of the modern paradigm, then, the truth is out there, it is the goal of scientific research and police work, but in *The X-Files* it is often inaccessible, always challenged, and is thus a highly elusive Holy Grail. Scully and Mulder are presented as modern truth seekers, but their inability to discover the essential truths for which they are searching suggests, in a postmodern register, that truth is highly elusive, exists on multiple levels, and is perhaps even impossible to ascertain in a confusing and convoluted contemporary world.

While the motto "the truth is out there" signifies a modern drive toward truth, the difficulty in accessing it signifies a postmodern indeterminacy and undecidability, the mark of postmodern epistemology, which on the whole is characteristic of the epistemic vision of *The X-Files*. From this perspective, "belief", and not "truth," is all one can reasonably assert. In almost every episode, it is uncertain whether the phenomena observed are natural or supernatural, can be explained rationally or not, and the plot resolution is often saturated with ambiguity. Frequently, the crime is not solved or the villain is not apprehended, and often there is no clear explanation for what transpired. This marks a distinctive break with the forms of most TV crime dramas, as well as putting into question the efficacy of the FBI and other law enforcement agencies.

The world of *The X-Files* is thus qualitatively different from the previous world of the crime drama. It expresses a postmodern distrust of existing US institutions in the wake of Watergate and the revelation of copious crimes of the system – the October Surprise, Iran-Contra and the other misdeeds of the Reagan, Bush, and Clinton administrations, as well as FBI wrongdoings in Waco, Ruby Ridge, and elsewhere. While, on one level, *The X-Files* is a rehabilitation of an image of the good FBI agent (see Malach 1996 for this argument), on another level, serious doubts are raised about the organization, with the series questioning the motives and actions of the US government itself.[15] Thus, *The X-Files* might be seen as an example of what Hal Foster (1983) calls "critical," or "resistance," postmodernism, which contests existing cultural forms and social organization. The series transcodes critical discourses questioning dominant US institutions that began circulating through the public during the 1960s and 1970s and began to be articulated in media culture (Kellner and Ryan 1988).

As in Hutcheon's concept of postmodernism (1988; 1989), *The X-Files* uses the strategies of postmodernism to contest dominant ideologies, ways of seeing, and modes of explanation, and to provide critical social commentary and insight. Yet, as noted, it is ultimately undecidable who the villains are, what sort of conspiracies are afoot, and whether the phenomena displayed can or cannot be explained by "normal" science. The politics of the series is also ambiguous. While the show often criticizes the FBI and the government, it stretches credibility to believe that government agencies would allow the extent of dissent and insubordination exhibited in the young agents. During the sixth season, when once again the X-Files are closed, Mulder and Scully continue to pursue occult events, despite orders not to, and intensify their conflict with their FBI superiors. Likewise, two new agents, John Doggett (Robert Patrick) and Monica

Reyes (Annabeth Gish), introduced during the eighth and ninth seasons, also become increasingly suspicious of FBI motives and actions, and become highly resistant and rebellious toward agency authority.

Seldom before has patriarchy been under such sustained assault in popular television as in *The X-Files*. Almost all of the villain figures are patriarchal, upper-class men, ranging from American corporate types to Japanese scientists, to US government officials. Mulder's relation to Deep Throat is highly paternal, yet it is not clear whether or not Deep Throat is manipulating Mulder for his own purposes and Mulder comes to distrust him. Moreover, his supposed father, Bill Mulder, appeared to have allowed the government to take his own daughter for secret experiments and was clearly implicated in evil government conspiracies. In one episode, "Travelers" (5-15), Mulder learns that Bill Mulder was involved in McCarthyist witch-hunting and had severely compromised his integrity. In a flashback to the 1950s, a TV set plays the McCarthy–US Army hearings, showing Senator Joseph McCarthy engaged in a search for supposed communists and subversives, and the plotline of the episode reveals that Bill Mulder was involved in McCarthy's dirty dealings.

More shocking, later episodes suggest that the Cigarette-Smoking Man is really Mulder's father! Hence, patriarchy reveals itself to Mulder as a set of faithless and corrupt fathers, who cannot be trusted and whose authority and rule he must overthrow. Indeed, the Cigarette-Smoking Man, who appeared to be behind the most nefarious crimes and conspiracies, is portrayed as an emotional cripple, without a life, without friendship or love, showing the inhumanity of an oppressive patriarchy in the way it destroys even the bearers of patriarchal power.

Thus, in the course of *The X-Files*, Mulder is confronted with a variety of older male figures who could serve as role models, or as models of identification. But he is subsequently disappointed and betrayed by each, as the various figures of authority reveal themselves as unfit: Deep Throat initially relates to Mulder in the mode of benevolent patriarchy as supportive, helpful, honorable, and professional – but then lies, betrays him, and is in turn killed. The mysterious "X" next takes over as Mulder's guide and mentor, but he is excessively violent, destructive, and playing too dangerous a game – and is also brutally murdered. Mulder's supposed father, Bill, who in "Colony" (2-16; 1995) shows himself to be emotionally distant, repressed, and tormented, is revealed to be part of the conspiracy that took Mulder's sister, Samantha, and which was engaged in the unholy experimentation with alien DNA on humans, and thus also demonstrates himself to be unworthy of identification and emulation. And, of course, the male authority figure that is most sinister, the Cigarette-Smoking Man, who had an affair with Mulder's mother and appears to be Mulder's father, is totally unworthy as a role model.

The only older male authority who has not been shown to be thoroughly compromised, contemptible, and villainous is Mulder's boss, Assistant Director Skinner (Mitch Pileggi), who in the first couple of seasons is often depicted negatively as an oppressive and perhaps corrupt authority figure. As the series proceeds, however, he is humanized, becomes openly supportive of Scully and Mulder, and thus becomes the one positive older male authority figure. However, one episode,

"Avatar" (3-21; 1996), showed that Skinner too is of dubious personal morality, depicting him getting divorced from his wife and picking up a woman in a bar, who turns out to be a prostitute. She is found dead in bed with Skinner the next morning, and it appears from the narrative that Skinner's enemies murdered her to pin the killing on Skinner in order to eliminate him. Scully and Mulder manage to uncover the scheme and save Skinner (a GenX fantasy: the sons and daughters save the father), but he is now somewhat morally compromised. Indeed, in this and other episodes, Skinner reveals his involvement in atrocities in Vietnam and is haunted by memories, and thus serves as a flawed, if ultimately decent and positive, member of the older generation.

Scully too has conflicting relations with patriarchal figures and the figure of patriarchy. She is constantly clashing with male authority figures, and, as I discuss in a section below, is abused by the male medical and political establishment. Although she is presented as having warm family relations, in "Beyond the Sea," Scully dreams of her dead military father, who appears to be speaking through the persona of a pathological killer.

On the whole, the US military is presented as villainous and allied with the mysterious Syndicate, aliens, or conspiratorial government forces. From this perspective, *The X-Files* can be read as a GenX projection of a corrupt older generation that has been disloyal to good American and human values. The previous generation is portrayed as thoroughly compromised and unfit to serve as role models for the GenX professionals who are the moral center of *The X-Files*. Many episodes also portray the generation following GenX as mindless teens who engage in stupidity and destructive behavior, and, as with classical crime dramas, often depict members of inferior socioeconomic classes, in particular the lumpen underclass, as potentially immoral and violent. In this sense, the series often reproduces elitist class prejudices, which negatively stereotype individuals in social groups different from one's own.

Thus, *The X-Files* embodies a GenX fantasy condemning – more harshly than any popular artifact in TV history – the previous generation, and raising doubts about the coming generation and even members of its own generation who have sold out or are themselves comprised by complicity in crime and overall societal or governmental wrongdoing. Scully and Mulder are thus the idealized role models for professional GenXers; they are the representatives of virtue, professionalism, and positive values, whereas the previous generation, the generation of the fathers and their system of patriarchal authority, is shown to be highly flawed, and even evil.

Yet, as noted, it is ultimately undecidable who the villains are, what sort of conspiracies are afoot, and whether the phenomena displayed can or cannot be explained by "normal" science. The politics of the series is also highly ambiguous. For while *The X-Files* assaults patriarchal authority and conservative institutions, it celebrates the all-American virtues of the work ethic, professionalism, and individualism, as well as honor, loyalty, commitment, family, religion, and other core values betrayed by the older generation during the Cold War. It is as if the fathers betrayed the authentic American traditional values and the sons and daughters have to redeem them.

From this perspective, *The X-Files* can be read as a document of generational war, of a younger, more liberal generation that is more professional, humane, and dedicated to higher moral values than the previous generation. Like the films *A Few Good Men*, *The Firm*, *Courage Under Fire*, *The Chamber*, and many other post-1980s, corporate and political conspiracy films, *The X-Files* shows the older generation tremendously compromised, especially those in military, political, and corporate bureaucracies. These texts are the revenge of aspiring professionals and the younger generation against the older conservative establishment.

Although on one level *The X-Files* subverts and undermines patriarchy, on another it reinscribes it. Mulder is clearly the senior partner, with Scully assigned in the first episode to work with him on the X-Files. The opening iconic images of the series present Mulder's image first, followed by Scully, and then shows Mulder leading Scully through a closed door into a threatening space – an archetypal image for the series. Mulder typically takes charge, provides the explanations, and is more often than not proven correct, though sometimes Scully's hypotheses seem to be vindicated. Especially during the first two seasons, more often than not Mulder is portrayed as the prime knower and doer, and Scully takes on an ancillary role.

In succeeding seasons the gender imbalance becomes modified, however, and on the whole the series shows both characters coming to respect each other, by depicting Mulder becoming more critical and skeptical and Scully more open to alternative explanations. Moreover, and crucially, as the series proceeds, the two work together more and more as a team and as equals. Indeed, the series is a coming-of-age drama for both, as both agents grow and develop, learn from each other, and become able to see the world from the other's perspective. They thus absorb each other's complementary personality traits and both come to be more rounded individuals. As Wilcox and Williams (1996: 99f.) point out, the phrase "What do you think?" becomes a sign of their mutual respect, their co-operative relationship, and their development of a successful partnership and friendship.

The gender equality on the series is frequently praised, though most of the articles on gender politics in *The X-Files* fail to point out that Mulder's perspective is generally favored over Scully's. Indeed, Mulder is the senior partner, who usually gives the orders and who often – but not always – has the more correct analysis. More episodes also privilege his supernatural explanations. For the most part, the visual elements of the program support Mulder's view as we *see* the supernatural/paranormal occurrences that his explanations attempt to illuminate, and it is by and large Mulder who provides examples of visual or other forms of evidence to support his views. Moreover, it is commonly Scully who, at least through most of the series, represents the conventional wisdom and explanations that the series as a whole challenges.

However, the figure of Dana Scully is a rare example of a competent, active, and intelligent woman, and both male and female viewers have appreciated this representation. Scully has written an MA thesis on Einstein, is a highly competent scientist, is able to perform extremely difficult autopsies and forensic investigations, and is shown as physically active and capable as well. Breaking with gender stereotypes and representational practices, *The X-Files* camera rarely objectifies her body parts and instead shows her as a fit and adept subject.

Still, it is undecidable if *The X-Files* ultimately undermines, subverts, and contests dominant societal forces, ideologies, and authorities, or upholds them. To some extent, it works with the Manichean dichotomies of traditional culture between good and evil, though it arguably complicates these categories. Moreover, the use of the occult and paranormal may promote irrationalism and deflect critical attention from the actual events, structures, and personalities of history, substituting populist paranoia and conspiracy for the real crimes carried out by ruling elites and reducing history to the production of conspiratorial cartoon-like figures. This is particularly egregious in "Musings of a Cigarette-Smoking Man" (4-7; 1996), which places one individual at the center of a variety of conspiracies from the Kennedy assassination to the rigging of Super Bowl games. Such tongue-in-cheek satire deflects attention from actual crimes and conspiracies, as does the figure of the occult, perhaps promoting societal irrationalism and paranoia, or extreme cynicism.

Nonetheless, more than any program in TV history, *The X-Files* at least alludes to government crimes and conspiracies and raises serious doubts concerning the institutions and morality of the National Security State with its covert apparatuses and shadowy operations. But, ultimately, the politics of the series is ambiguous and indeterminate, failing to promote any positive solutions. Its pop postmodernism reproduces the failings of populism, promoting suspicion against the existing social system without specifying how one can actually solve the problems presented. The evil depicted is so vast, the conspiracies are so complex, and the politics are so ambiguous as to promote cynicism and a sense of hopelessness. Yet, the series has obviously touched a responsive chord and displays fear and distrust of dominant authorities, which points to cracks and fissures in a system that obviously needs to be radically changed. Moreover, Mulder and Scully continue to struggle, against all odds, to uncover the conspiracies and provide models of dynamic and intelligent subjects struggling against oppressive forces and institutions.

Postmodern theory, then, is an attempt to depict the novel and complex dynamics of the present era, and postmodern culture provides new representational strategies to characterize the contemporary moment. *The X-Files* shows a society in transition, with its institutions, values, and identities in crisis. Using the generic forms and figures of media culture to comment on some of the most frightening aspects of contemporary society, *The X-Files* spectacle presents government conspiracies and wrongdoing, frightening developments in science and technology, and a multitude of contemporary threats to the body and individual integrity. It provides powerful critical visions and warnings concerning dominant social, political, and technological forces during an era in which novel developments in science and technology are altering human life as we know it, creating new species, and possibly contributing to the end of the human adventure.

Nothing important happened today ... except that everything changed

Although *The X-Files* declined in popularity in its last two seasons, culminating in an announcement in January 2002 that the series would be canceled at the end of its ninth season, its spectacle continued to address key contemporary fears and issues.[16] The narrative trajectories of the eighth and ninth seasons make it clear that the alien and conspiracy motifs intersect in a major way, displaying fears about cloning, the genetic engineering of human beings, and the creation of new species that could surpass and eliminate human beings. The opening of the new millennium was marked by increased public awareness of the dangers of biotechnology and genetic engineering, fierce debates over cloning and stem cell research, and growing fears concerning chemical and biological weapons. It was also a period of breakthroughs in research in biotechnology, with the project to map the human genome, controversial developments in the genetic engineering of crop plants and animals, and the cloning of human beings on the horizon (Best and Kellner 2001).

Throughout its trajectory, *The X-Files* presented scenarios depicting fusion between humans and technology, with experiments mixing human and alien DNA, as well as portraying science and technology creating monstrous "alien" forms of life. To some extent, the alien is us, as technology invades mind and body, as we absorb ever more technologies into our bodies and minds, and as we conform and adapt to a technological universe with its own specific ways of seeing, knowing, and acting. In a sense, then, the figures of aliens and alien abduction can be read as allegorical figures representing new hybrids and unions of humans and technology. Representations of aliens in *The X-Files*, then, can be read as the depiction of new species and modifications of the human emerging out of genetic and military experimentation, out of cloning and technological amalgamation of the born and the made, creating a new species of the technohuman. From this perspective, contemporary human beings are becoming alien, exhibiting a merger of the human and technology, embodying an emergent technospecies adapting to a brave new technoworld.

The alien, consequently, can be read as a figure for what humans are becoming in an era in which individuals no longer feel that they are in command of their own destiny, in which their own bodies mutate out of control, and their minds and bodies are invaded with new societal, technological, and political forces. In exploring this new and disturbing space, *The X-Files* inhabits a liminal space between mind and body, truth and untruth, fantasy and reality, science and belief. Providing a modern mythology for our time, *The X-Files* spectacle probes our deepest fears, most disturbing fantasies, and most dramatic transformations. Whether an artifact of media culture can adequately illuminate the oncoming and overwhelming force of science and technology in every aspect of life is questionable, though *The X-Files* gains its power and effect precisely through attempting to do so.

Taken cumulatively, *The X-Files* alien conspiracy can thus be read as articulating fears of the demise of the human species through replacement of the superiority of human beings by a higher species. Recurrent images of mutant species in numerous science fiction films and shows such as *The X-Files* underscore anxieties that we are now confronting what Steven Best and I have called a "fifth discontinuity." In this scenario, once again humans are displaced from the center of the universe and are even threatened with extinction (Best and Kellner 2001). This notion builds on the framework of Bruce Mazlish (1993), who sees the multiple adventures of modern identity construction and deconstruction to involve the dramas and conflicts of crossing four "discontinuities." Beginning with Copernicus, human beings had to recognize the gulf between the earth and the universe in order to accept the fact that the sun, not the earth, is the center of our solar system. Humans had to recognize a discontinuity between humans and the universe, and that *Homo sapiens* could not control and master the entire world, nor was it the center of it. Darwin compelled humanity to examine its evolutionary past and rethink the alleged great divide between itself and animals, making humans part of the story of life and not superior to it. Freud showed that reason is not even master of its own domain, its operations being determined by the will, instincts, affects, and unconscious. And as technology advances to the point of creating human-like computers and robots, and we become ever more like cyborgs, humanity is forced to question its self-proclaimed ontological divide from machines and belief that humans are superior to machines.

Since the opening of modernity, then, human beings have had to confront four major discontinuities, which decentered and deconstructed the view that the human subject was master of the world, enjoying radical uniqueness and special status. In each case, "rational man" had to rethink its identity to overcome false dichotomies and illusions of separation from the cosmos, the animal world, the unconscious, and the machines it invented, none of which humans could master and control. Yet, against what Mazlish suggests, the process of deconstruction and decentering of human mastery prompted by scientific and technological innovations is not over: yet another yawning gulf – a *fifth discontinuity* – poses still more challenges to human identity and, perhaps, to our very survival.

The fifth discontinuity opens with the *possibility* of discovering other forms of life in the cosmos, and the *actuality* of species implosion, the creation of new life forms through genetic engineering, and widespread cloning. As of now, no signs of life in the cosmos have been detected but our own, and "contact," to the best of our knowledge, is still the stuff of science fiction narratives such as one finds in *The X-Files*. But humans have already begun to tear down species boundaries by transplanting the blood and organs of baboons, pigs, and other animals into human bodies (xenotransplantation), thereby raising the specter of new and deadly transmissible diseases like AIDS. Corporate capital has also created hundreds of transgenic plant and animal species through biotechnology and "pharming" by mixing the DNA of two different species to create an altogether new species, such as when human genes are spliced into those of a pig to make the animal grow larger and faster. Another frightening discontinuity, however, involves the production of new intelligent machines or replicants that might prove themselves superior to humans and displace the supremacy and centrality of *Homo sapiens* in the "great chain of being" (Best and Kellner 2001: Chapter 4 and Epilogue).

All of these issues are present in *The X-Files,* which is a veritable bible of prophecies of future developments that presage the overpowering of humans and potential demise of the human adventure. This theme was central to the opening episode of the seventh season "The Sixth Extinction" (7-1; 1999), the title of a book by Richard Leakey (1996), displayed in episodes in the series. Leakey postulates the possibility that a sixth great extinction of human and perhaps natural life could take place, following the five great extinctions that have already taken place on the planet in the past.

The overarching mythology of the series as a whole can be read as an articulation of the dangers of alien invasion and colonization, which can be interpreted as worries about humanity being overpowered by its technology.[17] Throughout the series, the main characters, Agent Mulder, Agent Scully, and Deputy Director Skinner, have had technological implants, which can be read as fears of the invasion of technology into the body. The pilot episode associated aliens with metallic implants, and throughout the series aliens are associated with technological implants of various sorts. Agent Scully suffered both metallic alien implants and the implantation of an egg in her womb that combined alien and human DNA, ultimately producing her baby. Scully's motherhood episodes can be read as an allegory of the technological production of children, a possibility already present in the form of *in vitro* fertilization, and one that cloning will take to new levels. And Deputy Director Skinner received a nanotechnology implant that subjects him to external control, which previews the various nanotechnologies that will no doubt inhabit our bodies in the future fast coming about us.

The X-Files mythology as a whole can also be read as displaying fears of plagues unleashed by genetic engineering. Two key story arcs present the dangers of a black oil alien virus and the spreading of an alien virus through bees and pollution. These story cycles can be read as articulating worries concerning the human creation of viruses that could create plagues destroying life on earth, a danger articulated in the studies of Laurie Garrett (1994) and others. The bee episodes express fears that the genetic engineering of food could provide substances that could also harm humans and the ecosphere.

In particular, the creation of new species and hybridization between aliens and humans was a constant motif of the story arcs of the eighth and ninth seasons, which I read as the projection of fears of merging of humans and technology and fears of cloning and the genetic engineering of human beings. "Patience" (8-3; 2000) depicts a human bat genetic anomaly preying on humans while "Alone" (8-19; 2001) depicted a scientist merging reptile and human DNA, creating a monstrosity. All of these episodes could be read as a critique of xenotransplantation, the mixing of one species with another.[18] "Salvage" (8-10; 2001) depicts a Gulf War veteran suffering from a debilitating disease that his wife fears is Gulf War syndrome, whereas the narrative depicts his illness as the result of infection with genetic material from a new strain of metal created by a biotech company that did business with the salvage yard where he worked. And "Medusa" (8-13; 2001) depicts biochemical pollution from sea algae that leaked into the Boston subway system, creating the danger of a devastating plague that could spread through the city.

The new villains of *The X-Files* spectacle during its final two seasons, replacing the Syndicate and aliens of earlier episodes, are a new race of alien/human hybrids that appear far superior to humans. These alien hybrids represent the possibility of the technological production of a new species that will overpower and control, perhaps enslaving, or eliminating, human beings. "This is Not Happening" (8-18; 2001) portrays a mass alien invasion and the abduction of members of a UFO cult, while "Vienen" (8-16; 2001) warns that "they are coming." The latter presented an oil rig in the Gulf of Mexico worked by alien/human hybrids, who are drilling oil, presumably transmitting an alien virus that will take over the human race. "Three Words" (8-16; 2001) portrays the alien attempt to use the US census to target potential takeovers of humans, warning, in the motto and title of the 1998 movie *X-Files: Fight the Future*, of the need to "fight the future," counsel that one could read as the need to fight future developments in biotechnology.

The emergence of genetically engineered and enhanced humans was the major focus of the last two episodes of the eighth season, succinctly titled "Essence" (8-20; 2001) and "Existence" (8-21; 2001). "Essence" opens with Agent Scully preparing for a baby shower, and the episode features attempts to genetically manipulate her baby. Scenes in a cloning lab portray frightening images of human fetuses in bottles supposedly injected with alien DNA, thus evoking warnings of the monstrosities of human cloning. In "Essence," Scully gives birth to her baby, the nature and destiny of which is a major theme of the ninth season. This story arc drew attention to the rapidly evolving genetic revolution and the prospects of engineering children.

The ninth season opened with a two-part story "Nothing Important Happened Today" (9-1 and 9-2; 2001). A mysterious woman drowns an Environmental Protection Agency supervisor who had discovered that a chemical is being added to the water supply that will produce genetically altered parents who will produce a generation of supersoldiers. This provides an obvious allegory for the genetic engineering of humans and the breeding of a new posthuman species, which might eliminate the human, as well as the genetic engineering of military mutants. Curiously, the theme of the genetic breeding of supersoldiers was also the key focus of another popular Fox network TV series of the era *Dark Angel* (2000 onward). The series, developed by James Cameron and Charles Eglee, pitted the escaped genetically enhanced products of a government experiment to produce a race of supersoldiers against corporate and political forces which wanted to exploit them. If one was a conspiracy theorist, one might fear that Rupert Murdoch, the militarist and rightwing owner of Fox, was preparing future generations for the breeding of a race of advanced military supermen and -women! Or, if one was charitable, Fox could be thanked for warning the human species that a new technologically engineered race threatened its dominion.

At the end of the second opening episode of "Nothing Important Happened Today" (9-2; 2001) Deputy Director Kersh tells Agent Doggett of a diary entry by George III, King of Great Britain and Ireland, on July 4, 1776: "Nothing important happened today." Kersh commented that King George had missed the significance of the revolution that was happening in front of his eyes and against his interests and that, unbeknownst to the king, everything was changing. The implication is that the genetic engineering of human beings, their cloning and DNA manipulation, and their potential remixing into novel species is a revolution with momentous implications, a time, in William Gibson's phrase in *Mona Lisa Overdrive*, "when it changed" (1989: 129).

The X-Files thus posited the danger that the human race itself could be harmed by its technologies and even engineer a posthuman species that could challenge and destroy the race. Yet hope breathes eternal, and human resurrection and salvation became an increasingly central focus of *The X-Files*. Throughout the run of *The X-Files* spectacle, disease, suffering, and healing was a major theme of the series. "The Gift" (8-11; 2001) depicted a monster that could heal illnesses by absorbing the disease and whom Mulder supposedly visited when he was suffering from a potentially deadly brain tumor produced by an alien DNA implant. "This is Not Happening" (8-18; 2001) featured the return of Jeremiah Smith, who is able to heal with touching, and he miraculously heals wounded alien abductees.

During the eighth season, death and resurrection emerged as a major subtheme, presented more in a scientific and genetic engineering register than in a theological one. In "Within" (8-1; 2000), Mulder appears in Scully's dream floating in honey-colored liquid. He is wracked by spasms and an umbilical cord is pulled from his mouth as he gasps for air. Lying down in Mulder's apartment later in the episode, Scully falls asleep and dreams of Mulder held in a chair with his head and limbs restrained, his cheeks pulled taut, and with a two-pronged metal device telescoped down into each of his nostrils while a spinning drill bit pierces the roof of his upper palate. This imagery evokes fear of technological intrusion into the human body and of medical technology, a recurrent motif in the series. Another motif shows the series' main characters in comas, trapped in paralyzed bodies, their affliction overcome through marvelous technological intervention, which I read as the projection of hopes for miracle medical cures in the present age.

"Within" also depicts the discovery of a Mulder family tombstone with a new addition: Fox Mulder 1961–2000. "DeadAlive" (8-15; 2001) opens with Mulder's funeral and his burial. Three months later Mulder's coffin is dug up after an alien/human replicant, Billy Miles, believed dead, turns up alive. Sure enough, Mulder inexplicably returns to life to play in some more episodes before disappearing again for the ninth season. Another 2001 episode showed Agent Doggett getting killed and buried, and then returning to life ("The Gift," 8-11), while Agent Reyes was apparently trapped in a coma in a 2002 episode "Audrey Pauley" (9-13; 2002), but she also, astonishingly, comes back to life.

In the season finale "The Truth" (9-19 and 9-20; 2002), Mulder returns and is accused of murdering a genetically engineered supersoldier. The episode pits Scully, Mulder, and Skinner against a formidable array of government agents who are trying to discredit and eliminate Mulder. Reprising the alien-hybrid and conspiracy motifs, the final show suggests that a vast "shadow government" threatens humanity and brings back many of the major characters, putting on display a vast conspiracy of evil forces. Yet the concluding sequence attempts to hold out hope that humans can discover the truth, fight and defeat malevolence, and come to control their destiny. Scully and Mulder's loving relationship suggests the redeeming power of love, and their quest reveals a deep need for meaning and transcendence in human life.

Thus, *The X-Files* presents a dialectic of technology, showing the dangers that technologies can create and the havoc they can wreak, while also depicting the wonders and miracles that technology can produce, including the overcoming of disease and, in its mythologies, even the overcoming of death. It puts on display hopes and fears concerning the astounding impact on human life of new technologies. The hopes displayed are often coded in a theological aura, deploying resurrection themes saturated with religious imagery and motifs. Technology itself is thus fused with a mystical and transcendental aura, and *The X-Files* spectacle is itself associated with mystery and spirituality. Thus, I conclude with some reflections on the issue of representation and the unrepresentable, a problem at the heart of *The X-Files*.

Representing the unrepresentable

Importantly, *The X-Files* is concerned with problems of representing the unrepresentable, of finding images for that which resists depiction, for articulating phenomena that cannot be readily grasped with traditional discourses and modes of representation. Typically, horror and the occult present monstrous figures for precisely those fears, fantasies, and experiences that transcend the normal and the everyday, that reside in a space outside of normality, and that demand unconventional representations for extreme experiences and possibilities. *The X-Files* regularly attempts to depict and explain the occult and the paranormal, but, more interestingly, uses these figures and phenomena to comment on contemporary fears and problems and to articulate anxieties and horrors of the present age that cannot readily fit into standard discourses and conceptual schemes.

Fredric Jameson has often written of the difficulty of representing new postmodern space (i.e. architecture, cities, cyberspace, and the global system of transnational capitalism) and suggests that popular media culture artifacts, such as conspiracy films, attempt to map these new spaces in an allegorical mode (Jameson 1991; 1992). From this perspective, *The X-Files* spectacle is a noteworthy attempt in the contemporary era to represent the unrepresentable, to put on display our deepest fears and fantasies, and to probe into the dynamics of the impact of technology on human beings, the practices of the state, and the fate of the body and individual identity in the present age. *The X-Files* thus uses the generic forms and figures of media culture to comment on some of the most frightening aspects of contemporary society. These include government conspiracies and wrongdoing, science and technology running amok, and proliferating threats to the body and individual integrity during an era of dramatic changes, which the term "postmodern" has been used to describe. Its spectacle thus represents an example of a pop postmodernism attempting to come to terms with some of the most disturbing features of the present age.

The X-Files is a particularly popular and successful show because it skillfully navigates some of the defining contradictions of contemporary hi-tech societies and taps into current experiences. While it capitalizes on popular discourses of paranoia and conspiracy, articulates negative views of government and fears of technology, and attracts an audience critical of existing institutions, one could argue that it ultimately upholds belief in authority, justice, hard work, and other dominant societal values, thus appealing to both anti-authoritarian and establishment audiences. The series navigates the conflicts between reason and anti-reason, science and faith, attracting adherents of both views, while mediating oppositions between modern science and more postmodern variants. It also combines a modern seriousness and pursuit of truth with postmodern irony, combining modernist aesthetic innovation with postmodern pastiche of traditional forms and styles. Thus, the *The X-Files* spectacle serves as a fitting icon for an age between the modern and postmodern, one that is attempting to resolve turbulent conflicts over values, culture, institutions, and the organization of society.

Notes

1 This chapter draws on several different studies that I have published over the years on *The X-Files,* including "*The X-Files* and the aesthetics and politics of postmodern pop" (*Journal of Aesthetics*, 57, 2 (spring 1999): 161–75), which focuses on its aesthetics; "*The X-Files*, paranoia, and conspiracy: From the '70s to the '90s" (*Framework*, 41 (autumn 1999): 16–36), which analyzes the series in relation to 1970s conspiracy films and associated genres of media culture; and "*The X-Files* and conspiracy: A diagnostic critique" (in P. Knight (ed.), *Conspiracy Nation. The Politics of Paranoia in Postwar America*, New York: New York University Press, 2002, pp. 205–32), which engages the political and conspiracy dimensions of the series that I expand upon here. I will combine these concerns in this study, which updates my previous articles on *The X-Files* and covers the entire run of the TV series, which came to an end in May 2002. Over the years, I have seen almost every episode of the show, either through first-run showings and TV reruns or on videocassettes and DVDs of the series. In an era of readily accessible replication of popular TV series, it is now possible to read series such as *The X-Files* as an entire text. Earlier TV research was hampered by the difficulties of seeing every episode, which often required archival research, or, in the era of the video-recorder, taping entire series. With the advent of DVDs and rental videotapes of popular series, it is now possible to do more in-depth TV research.

2 See, for example, Dean (1998) and Knight (2000), as well as the collection of articles in Knight (2002).

3 On the distinction between critical and clinical paranoia, a distinction used to read the novels of Thomas Pynchon, see Siegel (1978), Best (1991), and Best and Kellner (2001). These authors distinguish between "creative paranoia" and clinical paranoia, with the former imaginatively making connections between phenomena, seeing the hidden forces behind appearances, and ingeniously mapping a complex terrain, as does Thomas Pynchon's *Gravity's Rainbow* and his other writings. I am suggesting the term "critical paranoia" to signal a rational distrust of institutions and individuals who may be engaged in conspiracies or oppressive activities. As my study will reveal, the distinction between "critical" and "clinical" paranoia is a difficult one to make in practice. Indeed, *The X-Files* itself combines critical with projective paranoia; thus my categories are ideal types. Clinical paranoia finds provocative presentation in the academy award-winning 2001 film *A Beautiful Mind*.

4 See the discussion of political conspiracy films in Kellner and Ryan (1988) and Kellner (1995). On the earlier Hollywood film noir genre, which used paranoia and conspiracy to provide critiques of US institutions and society, see Pratt (2001).

5 On my take on the postmodern debates and claim that our current moment is in a borderland between the modern and the postmodern, see Kellner (1995) and Best and Kellner (1997; 2001).

6 In labeling the key episodes cited, I will indicate the title, the year, the season, and episode number to guide readers to the appropriate programs. Such a listing for the first three seasons is found in Lavery *et al.* (1996: 207–10), and a listing for the first five seasons in found in *The X-Files Yearbook*, Vol. 4, No. 6: 52–78. Several Internet sites list subsequent episode information, including the official Fox network *X-Files*

site (www.xfiles.com); www.pluggage.com/forums/xfiles, has plot summaries and archived fan discussion of many episodes; and www.insidethex.co.uk, collects lists and transcripts of *The X-Files* episodes.

7 On postmodern aesthetics, see Jameson (1984; 1991), Hutcheon (1988; 1989), and Best and Kellner (1997). As I will show, *The X-Files* exhibits characteristic features of a postmodern aesthetic as presented in such opposing conceptions as Hutcheon and Jameson, though on the whole the series is illuminated more by Hutcheon's conception than Jameson's.

8 Although the similarities between Scully and *The Silence of the Lambs* FBI agent Clarice Starling are often noted [see, for example, Reeves *et al.* (1996: 32), Wilcox and Williams (1996: 102f.), and Badley (1996: 163)], the differences are also quite striking. Scully is better educated, more sophisticated, and more intellectual than Starling, who is shown in her FBI training sessions generally engaged in physical activity, the scenario of the film also privileging her action sequences. *The X-Files* frequently shows Scully engaged in various forms of scientific and intellectual labor; thus, she is also portrayed as an active and competent subject (although she was more passively portrayed as an overwrought and neurotic mother in the ninth season).

9 In a March 5, 1995 symposium at the Museum of Television and Radio, the series creator, Chris Carter, described weekly battles with the standards and practices office at Fox, but claimed that Fox had been very supportive and said "I'm glad we're on it." Later clashes with Fox and the cancelation of Carter's succeeding series such as *Millennium, Harsh Realm*, and *The Lone Gunmen* have probably given Carter a more critical perspective on the Fox network.

10 A piece of history from memories of the Cold War: my first introduction to theories of aliens and flying saucers came from a book borrowed from a neighbor in Falls Church, Virginia, some time in the early 1950s. Three doors down from me on Executive Avenue lived my friend John Goeser, whose father was a liaison between the Pentagon and the CIA, or in some mode of military intelligence. I recall that the Goesers had a book by George Adamski, *Flying Saucers Have Landed*, that circulated through the neighborhood and had pictures of extraterrestrial space craft, aliens, and the like, and which eventually became a bible of alien lore. So, if indeed the government was spreading flying saucer rumors to promote a conspiracy theory, which would cover up its development of secret military technologies and perhaps its worse crimes, Mr G. might have been part of the conspiracy – or maybe he just believed …

11 As *The X-Files* evolved, more individuals began playing a creative role in the series and one can now distinguish between the more classically occultist episodes, written by Glen Morgan and James Wong (who left the series during the second season to develop and produce *Space: Above and Beyond*), the "mythology" episodes, which pursue the political conspiracy theme, often written by Carter and/or Frank Spotnitz, and the more satirical pomo episodes written by Darin Morgan. Morgan wrote "Humbug" (2-20; 1995) during the second season and such episodes during the third season as "War of the Coprophages" (3-12; 1996), "Clyde Bruckman's Final Repose," (3-4; 1995), and "José Chung's 'From Outer Space'" (3-20; 1996). Such episodes are more humorous, highly satirical, and they self-consciously exhibit postmodern pastiche, irony, and a lack of resolution in more fragmentary narratives, exhibiting what appear to be overtly postmodern aesthetic strategies. One might also cite episodes written by Vince Gilligan, which were praised for their realist evocations of Mulder and Scully.

12 For an extended reading of this episode as a postmodern play with the series' codes and conventions, see Meehan (1998).

13 Thus, books have appeared describing and extolling both the supernaturalism of *The X-Files* (Goldman 1995), as well as its science (Cavelos 1998; Simon 1999).

14 *The X-Files'* competitor in the ambiguity and genre boundary-busting TV sweepstakes is, of course, David Lynch's series *Twin Peaks,* which also exploited a high degree of postmodern generic implosion and boundary crossing, including David Duchovny

playing an FBI agent who dressed as a woman. Yet *Twin Peaks* did not carry out the ongoing social critique of *The X-Files*, or its arch and informed use of postmodern quotation and pastiche, and never became a mass pop phenomenon and example of the global popular, which fascinated and engaged audiences throughout the world, as did *The X-Files*. On *Twin Peaks*, see Lavery 1995 and the Mother of All Twin Peaks websites at www.geocities.com/Hollywood/Boulevard/1884/pg18.html.

15 Series creator, Chris Carter, reveals contradictory attitudes toward the FBI in a 1995 interview: "[I]ndividuals within the FBI have contacted us to say how much they enjoy the show. David, Gillian and I were given a red-carpet tour of both FBI headquarters in Washington, DC and their training academy in Quantico, Virginia. We learned a lot about proper FBI protocol and procedure." Shifting ideological gears, Carter then acknowledges that many Americans nowadays believe that "Government is not working in the best interests of the US public," and wryly notes that the show's freedom to criticize the FBI has less to do with the United States' current anti-statist mood than with the demise of J. Edgar Hoover: "In his day, if you criticized the FBI, you used to do it at your own risk. You would be declared Public Enemy Number One" (cited in the *Daily Telegraph*, August 28, 1995).

16 Actor David Duchovny, who played Fox Mulder, cut back his appearances in programs during the eighth season and appeared only in the finale in the ninth. Many fans obviously tuned out because of the end of the Mulder–Scully dynamic and perhaps others found the series overly complex as it developed the alien invasion mythology.

17 *The X-Files* mythology has been increasingly convoluted and murky over the past years and is impossible to summarize simply. For a heroic attempt to lay out the defining features and evolution of the series' mythology, see Daniel's Woods' detailed overview (www.cinescape.com/1/Mythology_2.asp).

18 On the dangers of xenotransplantation and genetic engineering, see Best and Kellner (2001), which includes a reading of H. G. Wells' *The Lost Island of Dr Moreau*, which projected prescient warnings of the potential ill-effects of merging humans with animals, crossing species boundaries and producing dangerous monstrosities.

6   *Presidential Politics, the Movie*

In an age of spectacle politics, presidencies in the United States are staged and presented to the public in cinematic terms, using media spectacle to sell the policies, person, and image of the president to a vast and diverse public. The media are complicit in the generation of spectacle politics, reducing politics to image, display, and story in the forms of entertainment and drama. Daily news is increasingly structured by the forms of entertainment and sound bite, as are documentaries and TV magazine-style features on politics, while fictional films or TV mini-series narrate especially dramatic events or entire presidential dynasties. Consequently, the public comes to see presidencies and politics of the day as narrative and spectacle in an era in which entertainment and information inexorably merge. In the media entertainment society, politics and everyday life are modeled on media forms, with entertainment becoming a dominant mode of media culture and a potent and seductive factor in shaping politics and everyday life.

Thus, one can depict the relationship between media and politics, from the Kennedy administration to Bush II, in terms of the narrative and cinematic spectacle that framed the presidency. From this perspective, successful presidencies presented good movies that were effective and entertaining in selling the presidency to the public. Failed presidencies, by contrast, can be characterized as bad movies, which fashioned a negative image that bombed with the public and left behind disparaging or indifferent impressions and reviews of the presidency.

In the contemporary era, politics is thus becoming a mode of spectacle in which the codes of media culture determine the form, style, and appearance of presidential politics, and party politics in turn becomes more cinematic and spectacular, in the sense of Guy Debord's concept of spectacle. Consequently, US presidential politics of the past several decades can be perceived as media spectacles, in which media politics becomes a major constituent of presidential elections, governance, and political success or failure.

In this chapter, I will examine how successive regimes of what I call *Presidential Politics, the Movie*, generated a set of the collective images, spectacles, and narratives of the administrations from Kennedy to George W. Bush. These presidencies in turn produced series of presidential narratives, some good, some bad, and some indifferent. Certain presidencies themselves engendered epic Hollywood political films, which helped to construct public images of the presidency and of recent history. The ongoing circulation and revision of representations and narratives of media-focused presidents and their specific histories helps to nurture cinematic politics and media spectacle as a basic component of political strategy and governance.[1]

JFK, the Movie

Let us start then with John Fitzgerald Kennedy (JFK), the most photogenic president in the TV era, and arguably the first to effectively use the medium of television to communicate regularly with the public. Documentary footage of JFK's press conferences show the young president's ability to totally manipulate the press, which roared at his jokes, chuckled and smiled at his sly wit, and generally were played as pawns on the set of presidential media events. Documentary footage of Kennedy also shows his handlers as extremely adept at constructing images of private and public life that were exceptionally successful in producing positive images of the Kennedy family and presidency. But the Kennedy administration also generated media spectacle brilliantly, ranging from the inauguration speech and parade, to the famous Berlin speech, to frequent presidential trips and media events such as the tragic final visit to Dallas.

Moreover, the Kennedy administration itself was of sufficient epic stature and drama to generate countless movies and TV mini-series. The Kennedy presidency can thus be seen as a movie that has created a legend, which signaled the need to dominate the media and create effective spectacle to win elections and to govern successfully. The Kennedy legend would henceforth provide the template for aspiring candidates and successful presidents, although, as we shall see, subsequent presidencies produced wildly varied media spectacles and narratives.

Cultivation of the Kennedy mystique from his first campaigns through his short presidency was not an accident. JFK's father, Joe Kennedy, was a film producer, as well as an ambassador, financier, and bootlegger. The Kennedys were always highly conscious of the cinematic quality of political campaigns, of the look and image of politicians, hence the young Kennedy was aware of the camera and the need to generate appealing images from the beginning of his career as a politician. D. A. Pennebaker made a revealing documentary, *Primary* (1960), on Kennedy and Hubert Humphrey in the Wisconsin primaries in the 1960s campaign in which one sees JFK skillfully playing to the camera and crowd.

In the 1960s presidential debates with Richard Nixon, Kennedy was extremely cool and effective, a good TV performer and personality, as opposed to the overly "hot" Richard Nixon, who tended to polarize and alienate. Kennedy, by contrast, was witty and articulate, but not too emotional or ideological. He was, as Marshall McLuhan suggested, a "corporate" man, a person that one could feel comfortable and secure with. He was tough and assertive, often taking stronger anti-communist positions than the renowned Cold Warrior Nixon advanced, but was also reasonable and reassuring, and not too aggressive or militarist.

On the whole, Kennedy effectively used the media to sell himself to the public, and once elected became one of the most effective manipulators of television and political spectacle in the contemporary era. Indeed, Camelot, a dominant metaphor for the Kennedy administration, referred to a media spectacle in the form of a play and a movie about King Arthur's court which were popular at the time. Thus, the Kennedy administration can be seen as a cinematic stage and spectacle, from the pageantry of the inauguration to the high drama of the Bay of Pigs and the Cuban missile crisis, with the epic struggles of the civil rights movement and Vietnam in the background. Countless TV movies and mini-series were made of the Kennedy presidency, and the large family created a canvas for spectacles ranging from domestic marital drama to the epics of political dynasty.

In retrospect, the Cuban missile crisis was the big movie of the pre-assassination Kennedy administration, which was dramatically mythologized in Robert Kennedy's memoir and the film *13 Days* (2000). The Cuban missile crisis presented the drama of the young Ivy League Kennedy boys and their cohorts against the older rightwing generals and hawks who wanted to launch a nuclear strike against the Soviet Union to resolve the missile crisis. The film *13 Days* used the same code as Aaron Sorkin's *A Few Good Men* (1992) in which tough and courageous young liberals exhibit restraint, rationality, and sanity in dealing with crisis and a dangerous enemy, as opposed to the patriarchal and atavistic militarism of the older conservative generation.

The Kennedy presidency, of course, had a tragic ending, the JFK assassination, spawning entire genres of conspiracy theories and political conspiracy films, ranging from Emile de Antonio's documentary *Rush to Judgment* (1968) to fictionalized views in early 1970s conspiracy films, such as *Executive Action* (1970) and *The Parallax View* (1974), to Oliver Stone's epic *JFK* (1991). These assassination films mythologized Kennedy as the noble victim of a corrupt conservative establishment, helping to mold a positive Kennedy image and to assure his inclusion in the pantheon of the great American presidents.

LBJ and Nixon: bad movies

With the Kennedy administration, the scene of US politics was set for the cinematic presidency, but Lyndon Baines Johnson (LBJ) came in and bungled up the set. While Johnson was a highly effective politician, one of the great Senate majority leaders of all time, he was a bad actor, a poor media presence, and not at all cinematic. Moreover, Johnson could not get his storyline together or across, and so he had to give up the presidency and did not run again.

In some ways, the LBJ story is a tragedy, in which a poor rural Texas boy makes good, rises to the top, and becomes the most powerful person in the world. Johnson, the southerner, was also able to put together and push through civil rights legislation that Kennedy, the northern liberal, would have had trouble getting through a largely conservative and southern-dominated Congress. Moreover, LBJ's war on poverty and his Great Society were noble programs that could have been worthy successors to Franklin D. Roosevelt's New Deal and won Johnson renown in the pantheon of great American presidents.

But, alas, LBJ's Great Society program was undone by Vietnam, and US society could not afford both guns and butter. Hence, health and welfare were sacrificed so that the military–industrial complex could try out its new weapons and counter-insurgency policies. But Vietnam technowar met a national liberation movement, and Ho Chi Minh's peasants were able to use guerilla tactics to defeat US military technology that was inappropriate for warfare in the jungles of a largely premodern society. As part of relentless globalization, the Vietnam War was able to bring the consumer society to Southeast Asia, but was not able to block the formation of a modern Vietnamese nation-state. And so *Vietnam, the Movie*, was a national tragedy and politicians associated with promoting it were destined for media damnation.

Moreover, LBJ was singularly unsuccessful in selling Vietnam to the public. Exceptionally maladroit at using television, Johnson came across on the screen as boorish, overbearing, and unpersuasive. Unable to connect with the TV and film generation, which was opposed to the war, the oversized and often crude Texan was also was unable to connect with cosmopolitan liberals. Although he did his best to court the press, Johnson just could not get through to the media and was forced to ride off into the Texan sunset, where he quickly faded from the public stage and left behind a presidency bereft of cinematic homage. Later, the release of his audiotapes would reveal that Johnson was as unpolished and vulgar as reputed, and his media afterlife continues to suffer from lack of cinematic spectacle and poor public image.

Johnson was succeeded by Richard M. Nixon (1968–73), another cinemati-cally deficient president, who, as it turned out, ended up creating the paradigm of president as villain, the man we love to hate, the very symbol of political corruption and chicanery. In fact, Nixon was a hard-working and competent politi-cian who tried to present himself as Horatio Alger, the great middle-American success story, but ended up as the butt of liberal jokes and an exemplar of a failed presidency. Nixon did manage to master television after pundits faulted a five o'clock shadow, sweat, and a poor television image in his 1960 presidential debate with Kennedy.

Indeed, JFK barely beat the experienced former congressman and senator from California and vice-president to highly popular Dwight Eisenhower. Joe McGinniss's *The Selling of the President 1968* (1970) portrayed Nixon's adept use of media events, TV advertising, and political spectacle to promote his successful 1968 campaign. Nixon clearly had a good sense of media politics and spectacle, as footage of his campaigns, conventions, and presidential events documented in Emile de Antonio's "white comedy" *Millhaus* (1972) make clear. Moreover, Nixon's political biography *Six Crises* (1969) shows that Nixon himself was clever at constructing political narratives to present himself to the American public as a man who constantly overcame hardship and crisis to triumph over adversity.

Yet, on the whole, the Nixon administration was not particularly good at constructing a cinematic or political narrative that would sell Nixon, who was highly secretive, paranoid, conspiratorial, and widely distrusted and disliked. The "president's men" were also not particularly attractive or appealing, and Nixon entered the 1972 election with a media deficit. But in the 1972 campaign, Nixon and his media team were able to successfully present Democratic candidate Gene

McGovern as a bad spectacle, as a sixties nightmare, evoking the specters of abortion, acid, and amnesty. Nixon also concocted the apparition of a "silent majority," whom he represented, simulating a fake populism, and won handily over McGovern, who was associated in the public imagination with left-wing liberalism and the anti-war movement.

The Nixon presidency never had an engaging and compelling film script or narrative to present to the public. Nixon was not widely popular, he had no great themes or appealing political dramas, and he was not successful narratively in projecting a presidential story or spectacle that could win over a large public (although he always had his supporters and even true believers). Moreover, it was Nixon's fate to suffer Watergate, a truly great film and media spectacle, which undid him, unleashing a TV and journalistic media frenzy, later memorialized in the film *All the President's Men* (1976).

In this popular political morality play, *Washington Post* journalists were celebrated as saviors of democracy, while the Nixon administration was rendered as completely corrupt and conspiratorial, a popular image that remains until this day. Although in 1995 Oliver Stone made an epic drama *Nixon* (1995) that came close to presenting Nixon as a tragic victim, and a 1998 film, *Dick,* used Nixon to stage a political comedy, the political spectacle of Watergate coded Nixon as the villain of US presidents. In this mode, Robert Altman filmed a one-man play *Secret Honor* (1984), which displayed Nixon unraveling during his last days as president, and as a pathetic drunk and near-psychotic. Hence, to this day, Nixon is seen by many as a corrupt and failed individual who was the only president of modern times forced to resign and not serve out his term. The media and their administrations' inability to construct positive presidential narratives and spectacles also helped produce the demise of Nixon's two successors.

Ford and Carter: indifferent presidencies and poor spectacle

Richard Nixon's Vice-President, Gerald Ford, assumed the presidency in 1974 after the disgraced president's resignation and thus had the bad press of the Nixon pardon to begin with. He soon presented the spectacle of a flop not up to the office. Chevy Chase on the popular TV show *Saturday Night Live!* presented Ford as a stumbling bumbler, and TV footage of a montage of him slipping and falling presented a fatally bad image. The Midwestern congressman lacked charisma and in a 1976 presidential debate with Jimmy Carter seemed not to know that Poland suffered under a communist-imposed dictatorship.

Thus, the Ford presidency was an extremely short one and provided no memorable moments or stories for Hollywood or even TV movies, with the exception of a docudrama of his wife Betty Ford's successful battle with breast cancer. The Ford administration was highly boring, and it seems that if you are unworthy of a Hollywood film, you are unworthy of the presidency in an era of cinematic politics and media spectacle. Yet Ford's predecessor, Jimmy Carter, also failed to produce a successful presidential movie and media spectacle.

Jimmy Carter, the Governor of Georgia with the big smile and twinkling eyes, beat the bumbling Ford in the 1976 election. The "man from Plains" started off with the patina of good populist Frank Capra movies such as *Mr Smith Comes to Washington* or *Mr Deeds Comes to Town,* coding Carter as the good small-town guy coming to Washington to clean up the mess. In his January 1977 inauguration walk, Carter and his wife, Rosalynn, strode down the street hand in hand, the Washington outsiders, a couple of the people who would bring a new era to Washington presidential politics.

Unfortunately for Carter, his good old boys were not so clean after all, and the early days of his presidency projected more of a Fritz Lang movie of corruption than an uplifting Frank Capra film. For Carter's close friend, Bert Lance, his brother, Billy, and advisor, Hamilton Jordan, all successively got bad press and were attacked for corruption or crimes of various sorts. Carter, in fact, was never popular with the press, which began to present him as a *Hee-Haw* hick, and this country movie did not sell well in terms of presidential image and narrative with Washington and New York media sophisticates.

Nor did Carter's moralism play well with the media or broad segments of the public. However decent and competent Carter appears in retrospect, and he looks good in comparison with what came later, his administration just did not produce a good political narrative or spectacle. Moreover, Carter was condemned by the dramatic display of the Iran hostage crisis that helped to undo his presidency. The popular TV late-night talk show *Nightline* featured a logo with dramatic music, "America held hostage! Day X." As the days went by, and the American hostages remained captives of Iranian students and radicals, Carter was portrayed as ineffectual and incompetent.

Furthermore, if you are a conspiracy buff, and US politics and cinematic culture nurtures such perspectives, Carter was ultimately dispatched by another film, a behind-the-scenes spy thriller, which never floated to mainstream media perception. In this largely untold and unknown story, the Reagan–Bush team was negotiating with the Iranians to keep the American diplomats hostage until after the election in return for payment in arms and murky diplomatic promises. There was indeed precedent for such (treasonous) behind-the-scenes skullduggery. There were reports in several later history books that in 1968, when poor, old Hubert Horatio Humphrey (HHH) was engaged in a close presidential race with Richard Nixon, the villainous Henry Kissinger, in cahoots with a Vietnamese Tiger Lady, blocked LBJ's peace negotiations with the Vietnamese. HHH barely lost the election, and the Vietnam War went on, eventually leading to the first major US military defeat. Although several books were later to document Kissinger's perfidy, and a string of other political crimes, he survived and thrived as a corporate dealmaker and political player, and so far no muckraking film has taken him down.

Cut to 1980 and another covert spy thriller: the Reagan–Bush team is worried about an "October Surprise," the release of Iranian hostages, that would give Carter a boost in popularity, overcome his biggest negatives, and win him the presidency. Consequently, the Reagan–Bush team opened up "back-door" diplomatic relations and negotiated with the Iranians to continue holding the American diplomats hostage until after the election. Several Iranians and arms dealers involved in the exchange confirmed the story, as did several foreign intelligence services, of high-level Reagan team officials, including former CIA director and candidate for the vice-presidency George H. W. Bush, meeting with Iranians. Moreover, the US hostages were released on the day of Reagan's inauguration, US arms started showing up in Iran, an Israeli plane crashed in Turkey carrying US arms, and the later events of the Iran–Contra affair situate a great crime – and a thus far unmade Oliver Stone film – at the origins of the Reagan presidency (see the appendix to Kellner 1990).

Ronald Reagan, the acting president

In any case, Carter lost in 1980 to Reagan, and so the United States had its first acting president and professional actor qua president, former movie star and Governor of California, Ronald Reagan. Not surprisingly, in an era of media saturation, Reagan was a highly effective president, despite lacking in political experience. Reflection on the Reagan presidency suggests that Hollywood is the new aristocracy, in terms of cash and lifestyle, as well as social connections and glamorous public image. Hence, it is not accidental that Hollywood would produce a president. The Reagan presidency also combined the aura of celebrity and political leader, requiring that future successful presidents also be celebrities.

The Reagan administration was one of the most successful media presidencies and set of political spectacles in US history. Michael Rogin has written a book, *Ronald Reagan the Movie* (1988), that documents the intersection of Reagan's film and political careers. Reagan, contrary to some popular misrepresentations, was a top-line A, and not a B, movie actor. His presidency was scripted to act out and play his presidential role. Reagan rehearsed his lines every day and generally gave a good performance. Every move was scripted and his media handlers had cameras on hand to provide the image, photo opportunity, and political line of the day that they wanted to convey to the media.

Reagan was also a celebrity, a superstar of media culture, an American icon and perhaps the first intersection of celebrity and politics in an era in which celebrities were increasingly not just role models but political forces who ran for office or were active politically. Like Reagan, entertainers George Murphy, Sonny Bono, Shirley Temple, Jesse Ventura, and others attained political office. A wide array of media celebrities effectively campaigned for causes and candidates, including Jane Fonda, Robert Redford, Warren Beatty, Barbra Streisand, Rob Reiner and others on the left, contrasted to Bruce Willis, Arnold Schwarzenegger, and assorted Republicans on the right.

For two administrations, the Reagan team carried out spectacle politics with co-ordinated daily political events and extravagant media spectaculars: rallies, special events, and speeches with flags, crowds, and a photogenic background. After a slow start, the new Reagan administration was given a big boost by the spectacle of his attempted assassination in 1981. The event created intense drama, but also sympathy for a man who reacted to his tragedy with humor and fortitude, and Reagan was on a media roll that would continue for years.

The Reagan administration also had a good plotline and narrative for his presidency: deregulation and the triumph of market capitalism, and the defeat of communism in the Cold War. Ultimately, the Reaganites claimed victory on both of these themes, and Reagan continues to this day to score highly in presidential ratings and receive favorable media coverage. Of course, there were significant and sometimes unperceived costs to his presidency: in his two terms, Reagan doubled the national debt and redistributed wealth upward from poor to rich, greatly increasingly the divide between haves and have-nots. His military buildup was costly and wasteful, his deregulation politics created the Savings & Loan (S&L) scandal, which cost taxpayers over a trillion dollars, and in retrospect the Clinton years were far more prosperous than the Reagan years, which were in fact an economic disaster for many.

The Reagan presidency became doomed partly by the consequences of the October Surprise and the Iran–Contra affair, and partly by the president's overly aggressive foreign and military policies, which are narratively linked. The Iran–Contra affair was itself a great political spectacle which could have made great movies, but was perhaps too complex and has never been presented in popular narrative form. Reagan's Star Wars missile defense program was broadly ridiculed, denounced by scientists, and eventually scrapped by the Clinton administration, although it is being resurrected by Bush II and especially Donald Rumsfeld, the US Secretary of Defense, a retread of the failed Ford administration. Rumsfeld was popularly referred to as "Dr Strangelove" before September 11 because of his strange faith in a missile shield and unconventional ideas on the military, although he became a respected media star in the Terror War of 2001–2.

Finally, the Reagan image has benefited in retrospect from sympathy for his suffering from Alzheimer's disease. While images of Reagan falling asleep when visiting the Pope, nodding off at a major arms negotiations meeting, or failing to distinguish between reality and some of his movie roles created a culture of Reagan ridicule and accusations of senility, the tragedy of his disease rendered it mean and unsympathetic to attack his mental failings.

Hence, although one could indeed argue that the Reagan administration was an unmitigated disaster, it was not presented in this way by the media or any films or TV programs and was thus not perceived negatively on the whole by broad sectors of the public, either then or now. In fact, generally speaking, certain types of political and economic scandals and failures do not make for good movies or coherent narratives, as these events, like the S&L scandal, the Iran–Contra affair, or the election theft of 2000, are too complex to capture in an easily consumable film. There are, arguably, great films to be made of Reagan era scandals. Yet because many of the key participants in the earlier Reagan–Bush administrations are now in the Bush II regime, and since the population is immobilized by Terror War, it is highly unlikely that there will be a cultural and political reconstruction and rethinking of the Reagan era in the near future. Thus, Reagan's acting presidency is still one of the most successful presidential narratives of recent history.

Bush I, mixed spectacle, failed presidency

In 1988, George H. W. Bush ran one of the great media campaigns of all time, as I described in my 1990 book *Television and the Crisis of Democracy*. Trailing Democratic Party candidate Michael Dukakis by 10–15 points after the late summer Democratic convention in 1988, Bush ended up winning handily, after an excellent TV campaign. The Bush I team presented positive images in its daily photo opportunities and pictures, showing Bush surrounded by flags, on stage with the police or military, and in scenes of presidential power, as he drew on his Vice-President image, and projected the impression of an experienced, energetic, and hard-working public servant. In his TV ads, there were copious pictures of his family, with Bush ladling out soup in one ad, a giving father ready to serve and provide.

Of course, Bush Daddy also ran a highly effective negative campaign, and his Willie Horton TV ads are now icons of dubious negative advertising. The Horton ads, which portrayed images of prisoners of color spilling out of open prison doors, evoked the story of a black convict whom Dukakis had released in a prison furlough program and who then had brutally beaten a Maryland couple and raped the woman. The ad insinuated that Dukakis was a liberal, soft on crime, but played on racial fears. The ad was totally unfair as many states, such as Texas, had similar furlough programs, and Dukakis's Republican predecessor had initiated the program. Another completely mendacious Bush team negative ad portrayed a polluted Boston Harbor, insinuating that Governor Dukakis was weak on the environment. In fact, it was the failure of the Reagan–Bush administration to release mandated funds to clean up Boston Harbor and other environmentally sensitive sites that was responsible for the pollution.

Bush's campaign was run by Lee Atwater and George W. Bush, both fierce attack dogs running a down-and-dirty campaign, which was one of the most negative in recent history. Roger Ailes was another top campaign official, now president of Fox TV news, where he continues his ideological service for the right wing of the Republican Party. Bush's 1988 opponent, Massachusetts governor Michael Dukakis, was highly qualified, but just could not produce strong enough positive images and sell his candidacy to the public. At times, Dukakis appeared as a doofus, as when he was photographed driving a tank, an image that Republicans used in attack ads. Using a McCarthyite tactic, Bush denounced Dukakis as a "card-carrying liberal in the ACLU," but Dukakis himself would not admit that he was a liberal until the end of the campaign. He also seemed too cold and detached in debates when he was bushwhacked with a question concerning how he would respond to his wife's rape, an incredible question that showed the tabloid nature of the media mafia that performed in presidential debates.

And, crucially, although Bush played hardball politics against Dukakis, the Democratic Party candidate, just did not respond in kind and go after Bush. Dukakis had any number of great scandals he could play against Bush, but the Democrats wimped out, refusing to go after Bush and the October Surprise, or his roles in the Iran–Contra affair, the S&L crisis, or other scandals of the Reagan era. The Democrats played softball in a hardball era, engaging in an earlier form of civil and gentlemanly politics in a smashmouth era when Republicans excelled in dirty tracks, slime, and slander, and doing everything possible to present their opponents in a negative light.

And so Dukakis lost and Bush won, after a highly effective media campaign. Moreover, Bush got off to a strong start as president with a great dramatic TV movie opener, the Panama invasion and arrest of Noriega, which created a wave of patriotism, macho assertiveness, and high ratings for the CIA president. But by 1990, the economy was crashing, taxes were going up, and Bush's popularity was heading south. Bush had pledged "Read my lips, no new taxes" and had then raised taxes, so he was losing his conservative base and looking bad in the media. Footage of his pledge not to raise taxes was repeated over and over, while economic bad news was relentless, creating an image of Bush as failed economic manager and hypocritical politician (both true).

Consequently, another great movie was needed to boost Bush I's popularity and save his presidency – the Persian Gulf TV War – a cinematic spectacle of the highest order. I am not suggesting that Bush's war movie of 1991 was merely an effort to sell the Bush presidency, as there were also geopolitical interests involved, oil interests, which have defined the Bush family politics for decades, and a desire of the military to fight and win a war to redeem its defeat in Vietnam and to increase its military budget. Major political events are always overdetermined and require multi-causal analysis. Yet, as I recount in my 1992 book *The Persian Gulf TV War*, Bush Daddy's adventure in Iraq was one of the great media spectacles and propaganda events of its era. By the time US troops returned from the Gulf after kicking Saddam Hussein out of Kuwait, Bush's popularity was soaring at 90 percent and it looked as if he would have an easy ride toward a second term.

Bush failed to follow up on the defeat of Iraq's military power and overthrow Saddam Hussein, established by Bush's propagandists as another Hitler, thus he could not claim complete triumph in the Gulf War. Moreover, images of suppressed uprisings in southern and northern Iraq, with heartbreaking images of Kurdish refugees, contrasted with Bush playing golf on vacation, made him look disengaged and heartless. These scenes, and the survival of Saddam Hussein, created a bad aftermath regarding the Gulf War, and with the economy faltering again during the later part of Bush's presidency he was vulnerable to a challenge.

Bush Daddy's opponent in 1992 was a brash young Governor of Arkansas named Bill Clinton, who was relatively unknown on the national scene. Yet he ran an excellent media campaign, like Bush's 1988 effort, one of the best in modern US political history. Clinton was self-consciously a Kennedyesque figure, a younger generation politico, who cultivated the JFK look, called attention to the lineage endlessly, repeatedly playing campaign videos of the young Bill Clinton shaking hands with Jack Kennedy in the White House.

Clinton was also entertaining as a campaigner, using every main TV genre to cultivate votes, many for the first time. Clinton played his sax on *Arsenio* and did teary and soulful melodrama and soap opera with Hillary on *60 Minutes*, as he admitted to affairs and to problems in their marriage, but stressed that they had worked hard to solve the problems and strengthen the marriage, a narrative line many in the audience could buy and identify with. Clinton bantered about underpants and boxers on MTV, he had a serious conversation about marriage with Donahue, and he was the first presidential candidate to appear on these talk shows – now a campaign necessity after Clinton's successful manipulation of popular TV genres.

Clinton also did well in debates, and had a good spectacle moment when an African American woman in the audience asked if any of the well-off candidates understood the distress of those in the underclasses. Bush was clichéd and perfunctory in his answer, but Clinton strode down the stage to eyeball the woman (and the TV audience) saying that he felt their pain, he cared, and he would work hard to improve the economy for everyone. During the same debate Bush looked bored and detached, glancing at his watch at one point, as if he just could not wait until this ordeal was over.

On the whole, Bush Daddy ran a surprisingly bad campaign in 1992. He appeared detached from everyday reality when he went into a supermarket and looked amazed at a scanner in the checkout area, obviously a chore that Bush had never performed. He seemed unhappy with having to sell himself to a fickle public, and his campaign never caught fire. His political manager, Lee Atwater, had died of cancer, his son, George W., was preoccupied with personal affairs and not yet ready for prime time, there was friction between the Bushes and long-time friend James Baker, who was running the campaign, and Bush Senior never really connected with the public.

Of course, Clinton also had issues on his side, with his team endlessly telling the public, "It's the economy stupid!," and indeed the economy was in a slump during Bush's reign. Bush doubled the national deficit while raising taxes, seemed to have no economic plan or policy other than giving big corporations whatever favors they wanted, and lost favor with the public. There was also the irritant of Ross Perot, with his nerdy charts demonstrating the economic woes under Bush, stealing votes from the center and right alike with his twangy Texas pseudo-populism.

But in a media era, it was also clear that Bush Senior just did not have the image or political skills to work the media, was a poor president, and ran a losing campaign. Although US politics are not all spectacle and image, it certainly helps, and Bill and Hillary Clinton projected more youthful, attractive, and energetic images than the Bushes. *Saturday Night Live!* made jokes about Barbara Bush as George's grandmother, and the Bushes had poor body language, always looking awkward with each other and disconnected. The more youthful and attractive Clintons made a far more appealing couple, and then provided the thrills of weekly tabloid soap opera entertainment and family melodrama that continues to the present.

The Clinton spectacle

The two Clinton terms were probably the most contested and melodramatic spectacle of any presidency in US history, with endless conflict, scandal, crisis, and their miraculous overcoming by the "comeback kid" Bill Clinton. It is almost as if Clinton needed scandal and crisis to function, requiring challenges to perform and connect with a public that ignored everyday politics but loved political battles, scandal, and spectacle. Consequently, as president, like Reagan, and unlike Bush I, Clinton gave good spectacle: sex scandals, soap opera, melodrama, impeachment, cultural war with the right, and ultimately the spectacle of survival under constant adversity.

The Clinton years were highly entertaining and unfolded during a period of unparalleled expansion of media culture and a hi-tech revolution that produced the Internet, cyberculture, and a new culture of celebrity. In this situation, the president had the potential to become First Celebrity, Top Dog in the instant recognition hall of fame sweepstakes. Kennedy had achieved positive celebrity status, as had Reagan, whereas more mundane politicians such as Johnson, Ford, Carter, and Bush I failed in the celebrity popularity race and were not able to get re-elected.

There was, however, a price to be paid for attaining a celebrity presidency. Never before had the media delved into the personal lives of a presidential couple to the extent of the media trials of Bill and Hillary Clinton. The Whitewater scandal unfolded during the first year of the Clinton presidency and there was unending media focus on every detail of the Clinton's economic, political, and, ultimately, sex and family life. No longer was the president free from the taint of scandal and tabloid journalism. The blending of information and entertainment in media culture during the Clinton years, the fierce competition for audiences, and the rise of the Internet and cyberculture all made for a volatile media mix and feeding frenzy that exploited the topic or scandal of the day to maximize audiences and profits.

In the 1996 election, Bill Clinton faced off against aging Republican Bob Dole. The election itself was purely contrived with staged town hall meetings, scripted and managed conventions, sound bite "messages" tested by polling and focus groups, and daily attempts to sell the candidates as if they were commodities. Clinton won easily, in part because the economy was relatively strong, in part because Dole was a poor candidate, and to a degree because Clinton was a good politician, in tune with many sectors of the electorate.

Clinton was seemingly able to empathize with audiences. He had highly developed social and political skills, and was, more than Reagan the old mummer, a great communicator – at least to those who were open to his communication. Precisely because of Clinton's easy-going personality, dubious morality, and pragmatic politics, conservatives deeply loathed him, and were furious when he won two presidencies and overcame scandal after scandal. The Internet burned with anti-Clinton screeds and there was a cottage industry publishing books that demonized the Clintons and cumulatively sold millions.

Indeed, the Monica Lewinsky sex scandal saga was broken on the Internet when Matt Drudge published an outline of a story, which the *Washington Post* and *Newsweek* seemed reluctant to push, concerning rumors of a sexual relationship between Clinton and a young White House intern. Eventually, the story broke and Bill and Monica were the hot item of the season. There were endless replays of the footage of the perky intern wearing a beret and hugging Clinton at a White House reception, or greeting him at another event in a cleavage-revealing dress. When Clinton insisted that he "never had sex with that woman," this image came back to haunt him and encouraged his conservative opponents that they could press on and destroy Clinton. His opponents attempted to use a videotape in which Clinton denied the sexual relation to charge him with lying under oath and then started impeachment proceedings that came close to succeeding.

Conservatives were outraged, however, that every time a new scandal broke in the Lewinsky affair Clinton's popularity went up. When Clinton's prosecutors, led by the puritanical and ultraconservative Ken Starr, released the video of Clinton lying under oath, they figured his popularity would collapse, but, no, it increased. Likewise, when Clinton's prosecutors released the Starr report detailing his sexual adventures with Lewinsky and others, once again Clinton's approval rating climbed in public polls. In the Congressional impeachment proceedings and Senate trial, yet again Clinton's ratings improved as his conservative attackers attempted to discredit and destroy him.

Clinton was fortunate that he had such unpleasant and hypocritical rightwing foes and he benefited from the political sympathies of liberals and Democrats, who did not want to see an election victory overturned and the Republicans allowed to get their way. But broad sectors of the centrist and apolitical public sympathized with Clinton, to some extent because of the obnoxiousness of his prosecutors, and in part because of empathy and identification with the spectacle of the president under attack. It seems that many in the audience had experienced similar predicaments and could empathize with Clinton and his pain.

Despite the scandals, Clinton became a celebrity and cultural icon, however tarnished, and his popularity soared, in part because his years were an entertaining spectacle and in part because of the unprecedented growth of the US and global economy. It appeared, by the end of the Clinton years, that in an age of media spectacle, possessing good looks and a pleasing personality had become important markers of a successful presidency, especially plentiful hair, a nice smile, and a good body image. The most popular presidents of the post-JFK years had abundant hair, a pleasing smile, and an engaging personality (i.e. Reagan and Clinton). LBJ and Ladybird Johnson came off as Texan Gothic types; Nixon appeared untrustworthy and shifty, someone you would hesitate to buy a used car from; Ford looked to be bumbling, unappealing, and incompetent; Carter was presented by the media as too moralistic and ineffective, as he tried to micromanage every issue and situation; Dole was perceived as unpleasant and mean; and Bush I came across as too patrician and disengaged, not really caring about ordinary people.

The presidential culture of personality and the swing toward media politics reflects in some ways shifts in the economy and culture from the post-World War II to the contemporary era, sometimes theorized as a shift to postmodern culture and society. Sociologists have argued that US culture in the twentieth century moved from a culture of individualism, with self-directed people searching for authentic meaning and shaping their own life, to an other-directed culture of conformity in which people are guided by the media and external social authorities. Further, as the economy and society moved from emphasis on production to consumption, media culture became defined by image, appearance and spectacle, requiring presidents to have a pleasing personality and to sell themselves to voters. Hence the importance of public relations, media handlers, polls, focus groups, and media spectacle in promoting candidates and policies.

To connect with audiences, politicians also have to look like just plain folks, one of the people, as well as to appear nice and attractive. Note also how recent politicians have been committed to working out and gym culture (i.e. Clinton, Gore, and Bush II), while earlier golfing was (and still is) de rigeur. All of these signs of the media president striving to make a good impression and manage his image to promote himself and his policies are evident in the ascension to power of George W. Bush.

Bush II, Grand Theft 2000, and Terror War

During Campaign 2000, the Republicans had a fourth-rate presidential candidate, the least qualified of my lifetime, but they constructed a first-rate script: Bush II was a different kind of Republican, a compassionate conservative, a uniter, not a divider, who could get Democrats and Republicans together to "get things done." Of course, none of these claims was true (see Kellner 2001), but they created a positive image and the media generally went along with them. The mainstream media, for the most part, overlooked the fact that Bush's record as Governor of Texas was not compassionate conservatism but hardright pandering to the corporate interests that funded his campaign and tax breaks for the wealthy, which bankrupted the state that had enjoyed a surplus under Democratic governors. Bush had bullied or cajoled select Democrats in Texas to go along with his rightwing corporate agenda, and was not really a consensus-builder or bipartisan.

Moreover, by and large the mainstream media neglected George W. Bush's lifetime of scandal, which was well documented on the Internet and in a series of books, but largely stayed off the media radar during the 2000 election. It was, in fact, astonishing that after eight years of scandal-mongering and mudslinging during the Clinton presidency, none of the rich history of Bush family scandal or George W. Bush's personal failings were focused on. Nor did the softball Democrats under Al Gore go after Bush's record, or personal and family history, a courtesy for which they were repaid with hardball smashmouth politics during the battle for the White House after the deadlocked 2000 election.

The battle for the White House was indeed one of the greatest political dramas and spectacles in US history, as I recount in my book, *Grand Theft 2000* (Kellner 2001). While the purloining of the presidency is arguably one of the major scandals of US political history, the story has not been told by the mainstream media, although you can find big chunks of the story on the Internet and in a series of books, including my own.

Bush's first months in office were marked by hardright conservatism, with bold payoffs to the key corporations that had supported his campaign in the form of deregulation, changing governmental rules, and tax give-aways. After the Democrats seized control of the domestic agenda in late May 2001, with the defection of Republican Senator Jim Jeffords, Bush's hardright and utterly corrupt agenda seemed sidetracked. But the September 11 terrorist attacks strengthened his hand and enabled his cronies to carry through even more radical assaults on civil liberties and the free and open society, as well as attempting more federal theft through the mechanism of an economic "stimulus" package. Such a stimulus as that proposed by the Bush administration would be composed of even greater corporate give-aways and tax breaks to the rich and his biggest contributors.[2]

The September 11 terrorist attacks, succeeding hysteria over anthrax, and war fever following the Bush administration's military intervention in Afghanistan created a situation of unparalleled media and popular support for the Bush presidency and elevated Bush into a top-tier celebrity, almost immune from criticism. In early 2002, a *USA Today* poll rated Bush as the most admired person in the United States, and he continued to enjoy high approval ratings, although economic slumps and scandals in 2002 and the unearthing of Bush and Cheney's many corporate skeletons began to focus critical media scrutiny on their pasts and their present policies.

Yet the media can destroy what they build up, and a coming Bushgate could reverse the fortunes of the Bush dynasty with a series of crime dramas, political corruption and conspiracy narratives, and family melodramas that would rival any comparative saga in US literature or history. I would indeed recommend to a future Theodore Dreiser or Oliver Stone a trilogy of books or films, starting with *Prescott*, which would detail the stunning story of Bush family patriarch Prescott Bush, who was, in effect, Adolf Hitler's financial agent. Prescott helped to manage, through the Union Banking Corporation, several key Nazi businesses in the United States and globally, including Hapag-Lloyd Shipping Lines and Thyssen United Steel Works. The Union Banking Corporation was seized by the US government in 1942 under the Trading with the Enemy Act, and Prescott Bush was listed as a top member of the board of directors. The Bushes held on to the bank through the war and sold out in the 1950s, making their family fortune through an institution that had helped to finance national socialism. But somehow the scandal never came out during Prescott's Senate campaigns and he died a respected family patriarch.

This epic history of ruling-class scoundrels would also present the story of Herbert Walker, Prescott Bush's close business associate and father of his wife, Dorothy Walker. George Herbert Walker Bush and George Walker Bush were named after the man who helped run businesses for Stalin's Russia, Mussolini's Italy, and Hitler's Germany. The secretive wheeler-dealer is perhaps best known for his golf spectacle, the Walker Cup, and the construction of Madison Square Garden, while his son Herbert Walker Jr. ("Uncle Herbie") was one of the owners of the New York Mets, a sports spectacle that helped get George W. Bush interested in baseball. The Walker–Bush alliance is one of the shadiest and most scandalous in US economic and political history and uncovering this story will be one of the great spectacles of the new millennium.

The second part of the trilogy would tell the remarkable saga of *George* (Herbert Walker Bush), detailing an astonishing life of intrigue in economic and political scandals, including a stint as director of the CIA, which involved interesting but largely unknown relations with scoundrels such as Saddam Hussein and Manuel Noriega. *George* would also include engaging spy thriller episodes such as the October Surprise, the Iran–Contra scandal, and the support of Islamic fundamentalist groups in Afghanistan, which later helped to form the al-Qaeda network and the

Taliban regime. This monumental epic would include scandals of the Reagan era, such as the S&L crisis and the tremendous increase in the global drugs business when George was given the responsibilities of the drugs czar during the Reagan years. It would include some curious business relations with the bin Laden family, strange relations with the Rev. Moon and some other sinister figures on the right, and would delve into the affairs of the Carlyle Fund. This was one of the biggest holders of military stocks at a time when the bin Laden family and Bush–Baker cliques were the chief investors and managers of the fund. At the same time, their sons George Jr. and Osama bin Laden were the main protagonists in the Terror War, which so far has been the defining spectacle of the new millennium, and a source of great profit for the Bush–Baker alliance and bin Laden family.

The Bush family saga could also present the remarkable business careers of George H. W. Bush's three sons, looking into the Silverado S&L scandal and the involvement of Neil Bush; it could examine how Jeb Bush was involved in businesses with rightwing Cuban crooks who scammed HUD and Medicare for millions, and made a fortune for Jeb, who became Governor of Florida and one of the architects of the theft of the White House in the 2000 election. And it would require an entire separate study of how George W. made his fortune and then succeeded in state and presidential politics. This story, found in a series of books and Internet sources, but generally left out of mainstream media, would tell the remarkable tale of how George W. Bush made his fortune, gained the presidency through "Grand Theft 2000," and fronted the Terror War, which saved his failing presidency and enriched his family, friends, and wealthiest supporters.

The *W.* story would recount how, after years of frat-boy ribaldry at Yale, George W. Bush got his father to pull strings so that he would not have to go to Vietnam, and then got into the Texas National Guard Air Reserves. During his lost years in the 1970s, George W. reportedly went AWOL for a year from military duty, was a heavy alcohol and drug abuser, and a ne'er do well, who finally decided to put together an oil company when he was already well into his thirties. Investors reportedly included the bin Laden family and other unsavory types. His initial company, Arbusto, went bust and was eventually taken over by Harken Energy Corporation, with family friends again jumping in to bail George Jr. out. Harken soon after received a lucrative Bahrain oil contract, in part as a result of Bush family connections, and the Harken stock went up.

In summer 2002, there were copious allegations of insider stock trading and corporate scandals following the Enron, Worldcom, and other corporate crises, and the media for the first time focused on Bush's Harken energy record and the allegations of insider trading. It was documented that, as a member of the board of directors, George W. knew that figures showing declining profits for the previous quarter, about to be released, would depress the value of the stock, and so he unloaded his stock, in what some see as an illegal insider-trading dump. Moreover, young Bush failed to register his questionable sale with the Securities and Exchange Commission, although later a paper was produced indicating that he had eventually registered the sale, some eight months after he dumped his stock (it maybe helped that his father was president when George Jr. should have been investigated for his questionable business dealings).[3]

With the money made from his Harken disinvesture, George W. invested in the Texas Rangers baseball team and was made general manager when some other Texas good old boys put up the money. Using a public bond issue, which he pushed upon voters to finance construction of a new Rangers stadium, the stock value of the baseball team went up. Once again, Bush sold out for a hefty profit and then ran for Governor of Texas, despite no political experience and a shaky business history. His two terms in office wrecked the state economy as it went from surplus to deficit, thanks to a tax bill that gave favors to the wealthiest and sweetheart deals and deregulation bonanzas to his biggest campaign contributors. Governor Bush helped make Texas the site of the most toxic environmental pollution and outrageous corporate skullduggery in the country. Bush provided questionable favors to a nursing home corporation facing state investigation and strong support for the wheeling and dealing Enron company, one of the major financial contributors to Bush's campaigns and a corporation that later underwent one of the the biggest collapses of any US company in history, under highly questionable circumstances.

The Bush spectacle is therefore far from over and it will be highly instructive to see how the family history continues to be constructed and perceived in the media and by the general public. It will also be interesting to see if the Internet spectacle replaces television and Hollywood spectacle as the foremost conveyer of news, information, entertainment, and politics as the millennium proceeds, providing multiple sources of information and entertainment that will be impossible for the Bush clique to control. Or will the Terror War provide a spectacle that will enable the Bush administration to close the open society and create a military and police state? How will the Bush–Cheney gang manage a US and global economy in crisis, in which, as of Fall 2002, more than 2,000,000 jobs in the United States have been lost since Bush stole the presidency and a healthy surplus was replaced by a spiraling deficit? Will US democracy and the global economy survive the Bush spectacle, or is a new form of military police state and an Orwellian nightmare the coming spectacle of the new millennium? Whatever the answers to these questions, it is clear that the forthcoming narratives of the Bush presidency will be among the most interesting and fateful in US history.

Conclusion: democratic politics and spectacle culture in the new millennium

The US presidency, from John F. Kennedy to Bush II, has produced a series of political narratives, some of which were successful and others unsuccessful. In the age of media spectacle, politics is mediated more and more by the forms of spectacle culture and, in particular, by appearance, image, style, and presentation, but also narrative. What sort of stories a presidential administration generates determines success from failure, and a positive from an ambiguous or negative legacy.

The centrality of media spectacle and political narrative to contemporary politics means that making sense of the current era requires the tools of a critical social theory and cultural studies in order to analyze the images, discourses, events, and narratives of presidential politics. Of course, politics is more than merely narrative, there are real events with material interests and consequences, and often behind the scenes maneuvering that is not part of the public record. Yet the public sees presidencies and administrations in terms of narrative and spectacle, so that theorizing the cinematic and narrative nature of contemporary politics can help us to understand, analyze, and transform our political system.

Spectator politics, in which viewers/citizens contemplate political spectacles, undermines a participatory democracy in which individuals actively engage in political movements and struggles. Political movements since the 1960s have actively engaged the media and produced an oppositional spectacle politics to counter the spectacles of the mainstream. In the 1960s, the events of May 1968, when student and worker rebellion almost overthrew the establishment, were influenced by the theories of the Situationist International and Guy Debord, who sketched out ways in which oppositional groups could produce counter-spectacles. In the United States and other countries, a spectacle politics flourished in the 1960s, often with mixed results, as when the New Left acted out for television cameras, rather than organizing for change, or when fantasies of violent revolution led to terrorism.[4]

The anti-globalization movement in the present day has also engaged in spectacle politics in spectacular demonstrations from the "Battle of Seattle" in 1999 to the April 2002 demonstrations in Washington against the IMF, World Bank, and other instruments of capitalist globalization. The Internet too provides a new realm of interactive spectacle for oppositional politics, although it is also becoming colonized by capitalist corporations (Kellner 1999; Best and Kellner 2001).

Political battles of the future will thus be fought out, in part, on the terrain of media spectacle. In the new millennium, terrorist groups, such as the al-Qaeda network, have engaged in spectacle politics, of which the September 11 attacks on the World Trade Center and the Pentagon were the most stunning. To the spectacle of terror, the Bush administration has offered the spectacle of Terror War. Likewise, the Israel–Palestine conflict is increasingly fought out on the sphere of terrorism and the terror spectacle. A democratic politics of the future must invent a progressive spectacle politics that will further the goals of democracy, justice, human rights, environmental protection, and a progressive agenda. Understanding media spectacle is thus a requirement for both understanding and transforming the existing society. The future of democracy rests on how spectacle politics plays out in the future and what sort of oppositional politics progressive groups will invent.[5] As I have documented in this book, media spectacle has emerged as a major social, political, and cultural force in the contemporary era, and the future will depend upon what spectacles will emerge and how democracy can be reconstructed and reinvented in the face of the continuing reign of the spectacle.

Note

1 I first gave a talk on this topic at the American Political Science Association convention in August 2001 and thank panelists and the audience for discussion. The paper will be published in the *Western Behaviorial Science Journal* and I would like to thank Lauren Langman for comments on the text and discussion of the topics. I am also indebted to Rhonda Hammer for many comments that helped with revision of this study. In this

study, I draw on a series of books that I have published, including Kellner and Ryan (1988), Kellner (1990; 1992; 2001), and Kellner and Streible (2000).

2 For the astonishing story of the Bush gang's election theft, see Kellner (2001), which also cites documents grounding the thumbnail sketch of Bush's life presented above. All of these stories are well documented in websites such as www.bushwatch.com and Kellner (2001), but the mainstream media prefer to neglect the more unsavory aspects of the life and times of George W. Bush in favor of puff pieces on the rascal.

3 For the insider trading allegations, widely circulated in the Texas press during Bush's first run for Governor against Ann Richards, see Hatfield (2000) and Ivins and Dubose (2000); for an update on the story by investigative reporter Knut Royce, released on the Center for Public Integrity website, see "Bush's insider connections preceded huge profit on stock deal," www.public-i.org/story_01_040400.htm. During the summer of 2002, there was intense media focus on the Bush insider trading allegations in the light of corporate scandals in which other executives and celebrities, such as Martha Stewart, were accused of insider trading.

4 On the May 1968 events, see Feenberg and Freedman (2001), and on the media politics of the movement in the United States, see Gitlin (1980).

5 I will take on Terror War and the terror spectacle in a forthcoming study, and I am also working on a future book on technopolitics, which will develop the perspectives on new technology and oppositional politics sketched out in Kellner (1999) and Best and Kellner (2001).

References

Adorno, T. W. (1991) *The Culture Industry*, London: Routledge.

——(1994) *The Stars Down to Earth and Other Essays on the Irrational in Culture*, London: Routledge.

Alfino, M., J. S. Caputo, and R. Wynyard (eds) (1998) *McDonaldization Revisited: Critical Essay in Consumer Culture*, Westport, CT: Praeger.

Andrews, D. L. (1996) "The fact(s) of Michael Jordan's blackness: Excavating a floating racial signifier," *Sociology of Sport Journal*, 13, 2: 125–58 (reprinted in Andrews 2001).

——(1997) "The (Trans)National Basketball Association: America's commodity sign culture and global localization," in A. Cvetovitch and D. Kellner (eds), *Articulating the Global and the Local. Globalization and Cultural Studies*, Boulder, CO: Westview Press.

——(ed.) (2001) *Michael Jordan, Inc. Corporate Sport, Media Culture, and Late Modern America*, Albany, NY: State University of New York Press.

Andrews, D., B. Carrington, Z. Mazur, and S. J. Jackson (1996) "Jordanscapes: A preliminary analysis of the global popular," *Sociology of Sport Journal*, 13, 4: 428–57.

Antonio, R. J. and R. Glassman (eds) (1985) *The Weber–Marx Dialogue*, Lawrence, KS: University of Kansas Press.

Badley, L. (1996) "The rebirth of the clinic," in D. Lavery, A. Hague, and M. Cartwright (eds), *Reading The X-Files*, Syracuse, NY: Syracuse University Press, pp. 148–67.

Barber, B. R. (1996) *Jihad vs. McWorld*, New York: Ballatine Books.

Barthes, R. (1983) *Mythologies* (translated by Annette Lavers), New York: Hill and Wang.

Baudrillard, J. (1981) *For a Critique of the Political Economy of the Sign*, St Louis: Telos Press.

——(1983a) "The ecstacy of communication," in H. Foster (ed.), *The Anti-Aesthetic*, Washington, DC: Bay Press.

——(1983b) *Simulations*, New York: Semiotext(e).

——(1983c) *In the Shadow of the Silent Majorities*, New York: Semiotext(e).

——(1986) *Forgetting Foucault*, New York, Semiotext(e).

——(1993) *Symbolic Exchange and Death*. London: Sage.

——(1976) *The Coming of Post-Industrial Society*, New York: Basic Books.

Benjamin, W. (1969) *Illuminations*, New York: Shocken.

Berger, P. and T. Luckmann (1967) *The Social Construction of Reality*, New York: Doubleday.

Berlant, L. (1994) *The Anatomy of National Fantasy*, Chicago: University of Chicago Press.

Best, S. (1991) "Creative paranoia: A postmodern aesthetic of cognitive mapping in *Gravity's Rainbow*," *Centennial Review*, 36, 1: 59–88.

Best, S. and D. Kellner (1991) *Postmodern Theory: Critical Interrogations*, London: Macmillan.

——(1997) *The Postmodern Turn*, London: Routledge and New York: Guilford Press.

—— (2001) *The Postmodern Adventure*, London: Routledge and New York: Guilford Press.

Blumenberg, H. (1983) *The Legitimacy of the Modern Age*, Cambridge, MA: MIT Press.

Boggs, C. (2000) *The End of Politics*, New York: Guilford Press.

Boorstin, D. (1961) *The Image*, New York: Random House.

Bové, J. and F. Dufour (2001) *The World is Not For Sale: Farmers Against Junk Food*, London: Verso.

Boyd, Todd (1997a) *Am I Black Enough for You? Popular Culture From the 'Hood and Beyond*, Bloomington, IN: Indiana University Press.

—— (1997b) "Hoopology 101. Professor Todd Boyd deconstructs the game," *LA Weekly*, May 23–29: 49.

Braverman, H. (1974) *Labor and Monopoly Capital*, New York: Monthly Review Press.

Bugliosi, V. (1996) *Outrage. The Given Reasons Why O. J. Simpson Got Away With Murder*, New York: Norton.

Castells, M. (1997) *The Power of Identity*, Malden, MA: Blackwell.

Cavelos, J. (1998) *The Science of The X-Files*, New York: Berkeley Books.

Clark, M. (1998) *Beyond a Doubt*, New York: Penguin Books.

Cole, C. L. (1996) "American Jordan: PLAY, consensus, and punishment," *Sociology of Sport Journal*, 13, 4: 366–97.

Coplon, J. (1996) "The best. Ever. Anywhere," *New York Times Magazine*, April 21: 32–7, 44, and 54.

Cose, E. (1997) *The Darden Dilemma: 12 Black Writers on Justice, Race, and Conflicting Loyalties*, New York: HarperPerennial.

Cvetkovich, A. and D. Kellner (eds) (1997) *Articulating the Global and the Local. Globalization and Cultural Studies*, Boulder, CO: Westview.

Darden, C. with J. Walter (1996) *In Contempt*, New York: Regan Books.

Dean, J. (1998) *Aliens in America. Conspiracy Cultures from Outerspace to Cyberspace*, Ithaca, NY: Cornell University Press.

Dear, W. C. (2000) *OJ Is Guilty But Not of Murder*, Dear Overseas Production.

Debord, G. (1967) *Society of the Spectacle*, Detroit: Black and Red.

——(1990) *Comments on the Society of the Spectacle*, London: Verso.

DeBord, M. (1999) "Children of the Jordan age," *Feed*, January 29 (www.feedmag.com/essay/es167.shtml).

Denzin, N. K. (1998) "More Rare Air: Michael Jordan on Michael Jordan," *Sociology of Sport Journal*, 13, 4: 319–24 (reprinted in Andrews 2001, pp. 3–14).

Dershowitz, A. (1996) *Reasonable Doubts: The O. J. Simpson Case and the Criminal Justice System*, New York: Simon & Schuster.

Durham, M. G. and D. Kellner (eds) (2001) *Media and Cultural Studies: KeyWorks*, Malden, MA: Blackwell.

Dyson, M. (1993) *Reflecting Black*, Minneapolis: University of Minnesota Press.

Eco, U. (1986) *Travels in Hyperreality*, New York: Harcourt, Brace and Jovanovich.

Elias, T. and D. Schatzman, *The Simpson Trial in Black and White*, Los Angeles: General Publishing Group.

Enloe, C. (1995) "The globetrotting sneaker," *Ms.*, March/April: 10–15.

Farrand, P. (1997) *The Nitpicker's Guide for X-Philes*, New York: Dell Trade.

Feenberg, A. and J. Freedman (2001) *When Poetry Ruled the Streets: The French May Events of 1968*, Albany, NY: State University of New York Press.

Fiske, J. (1996) *Media Matters. Everyday Life and Political Change*, Minneapolis: University of Minnesota Press.

Foster, H. (ed.) (1983) *The Anti-Aesthetic*, Washington, Bay Press.

Fox, N. (1998) *Spoiled: Why Our Food is Making Us Sick and What We can Do About It*, Baltimore, MD: Penguin Books.

Freire, P. (1972) *Pedagogy of the Oppressed*, New York: Herder & Herder.

——(1998) *A Paulo Freire Reader*, New York: Herder & Herder.

Gabler, Neil (1998) *Life the Movie. How Entertainment Conquered Reality*, New York: Alfred A. Knopf.

Garrett, L. (1994) *The Coming Plague: Newly Emerging Diseases in a World Out of Balance*, New York: Penguin.

Gates, B. (1995) *The Road Ahead*, New York: Viking.

——(1999) *Business@The Speed of Thought*, New York: Viking.

Gibson, N. and A. Rubin (2002) *Adorno. A Critical Reader,* Malden, MA: Blackwell.

Gibson, W. (1989) *Mona Lisa Overdrive*, New York: Dell.

Giedion, S. (1969) [1948] *Mechanization Takes Command*, New York: Norton.

Gilder, G. (1989) *Microcosm*, New York: Touchstone.

——(2000) *Telecosm*, New York: Free Press.

Giroux, H. (1994) *Disturbing Pleasures*, New York: Routledge.

Gitlin, T. (1980) *The Whole World is Watching*, Berkeley, CA: University of California Press.

——(2002) *Media Unlimited. How the Torrent of Images and Sounds Overwhelms Our Lives*, New York: Metropolitan Books.

Goldman, J. (1995) *The X-Files Book of the Unexplained*, New York: HarperPrism.

Goldman, R. (1992) *Readings Ads Critically*, London: Routledge.

Goldman, R. and S. Papson (1998) *Sign Wars*, New York: Guilford Press.

Gouldner, A. (1976) *The Dialectic of Ideology and Technology*, New York: Seabury Books.

Graham, A. (1996) "'Are you now or have you ever been?' Conspiracy theory and the *X-Files*," in D. Lavery, A. Hague, and M. Cartwright (eds), *Reading The X-Files*, Syracuse, NY: Syracuse University Press, pp. 52–62.

Gramsci, A. (1971) *Prison Notebooks*, New York: International Publishers.

Glass, S. (1997) "Blood, sweat and shears. The young and the feckless," *New Republic*, September 15.

Greider, W. (1994) "The global sweatshop," *Rolling Stone*, June 30: 43–4.

Habermas, J. (1984) *The Theory of Communicative Action*, Vol. 1, *Reason and the Rationalization of Society*, Boston: Beacon Press.

——(1987) *The Theory of Communicative Action*, Vol. 2, *Lifeworld and System: A Critique of Functionalist Reason*, Boston: Beacon Press.

Halberstam, D. (1999) *Playing for Keeps: Michael Jordan and the World He Made*, New York: Random House.

Hammato, D. (1995) "All seeing eye: TV and the People vs. O. J. Simpson," *LA Village View,* February.

Hammer, R. (2002) *Antifeminism and Family Terrorism*, Lanham, MD: Rowman & Littlefield.

Hall, S. (1986) "On postmodernism and articulation: An interview with Stuart Hall," *Journal of Communication Inquiry*, 10, 2: 45–60.

——(2001) "Encoding/Decoding," Durham, M. G. and D. Kellner (eds) (2001) *Media and Cultural Studies: KeyWorks*, Malden, MA: Blackwell, pp. 166–76.

Harvey, D. (1989) *The Condition of Postmodernity*, Oxford: Basil Blackwell.

Hatfield, J. H. (2000) *Fortunate Son: George W. Bush and the Making of An American President*, New York: Soft Skull Press.

Heller, C. (2002) "From scientific risk to paysan savoir-faire: Peasant expertise in the French and global debate over GM crops," *Science as Culture*, 11, 1: 5–37.

Herbert, B. (1996) "Nike's Pyramid Scheme," *New York Times*, June 10: A19.

Herbert, B. (1997) "Nike's boot camps," *New York Times*, March 31: A16.

Hirschberg, L. (1996) "The big man can deal," *New York Times Magazine*, November 17: 46–51, 62–5, 77–8, 82, and 88.

Hofstadter, R. (1996) [1962] *The Paranoid Style in American Politics and Other Essays*, Cambridge, MA: Harvard University Press.

Horkheimer, M. and T. W. Adorno (1972) *Dialectic of Enlightenment*, New York: Continuum.

Huizinga, J. (1986) *Homo Ludens: A Study of the Play-Element in Culture*, Boston: Beacon Press.

——(1997) *The Autumn of the Middle Ages*, Chicago: University of Chicago Press.

Hutcheon, L. (1988) *A Poetics of Postmodernism*, New York: Routledge.

——(1989) The Politics of Postmodernism, New York: Routledge.

Hutchinson, E. O. (1996) *Beyond OJ. Race, Sex, and Class Lessons for America,* Los Angeles: Middle Passages Press.

Ivins, M., and L. Dubose (2000) *Shrub: The Short but Happy Political Life of George W. Bush*, New York: Random House.

Jameson, F. (1984) "Postmodernism – the cultural logic of late capitalism," *New Left Review*, 146: 59–92.

——(1991) *Postmodernism, or, the Cultural Logic of Late Capitalism*, Durham, NC: Duke University Press.

——(1992) *The Geopolitical Aesthetic*, Bloomington, IN: Indianan University Press.

Jeffords, S. (1994) *Hard Bodies: Hollywood Masculinity in the Age of Reagan*, New Brunswick, NJ: Rutgers University Press.

Johnson, L. and D. Roediger (1997) " 'Hertz, don't it?' Becoming colorless and staying black in the crossover of O. J. Simpson," in T. Morrison and C. B. Lacour (eds), *Birth of a Nation'Hood: Gaze, Script, and Spectacle in the O. J. Simpson Case*, New York: Pantheon, pp. 197–240.

Kant, I. (1999) *Critique of Pure Reason*, Cambridge: Cambridge University Press.

Kellner, D. (1985) "Critical theory, Max Weber, and the dialectics of domination," in R. J. Antonio and R. M. Glassman, (eds), *A Weber–Marx Dialogue*, Lawrence, KS: University Press of Kansas, pp. 89–116.

——(1989a) *Critical Theory, Marxism, and Modernity*, Cambridge, UK: Polity Press and Baltimore: Johns Hopkins University Press.

——(1989b) *Jean Baudrillard: From Marxism to Postmodernism and Beyond*, Cambridge, UK: Polity Press and Palo Alto, CA: Stanford University Press.

——(1990) *Television and the Crisis of Democracy*, Boulder, CO: Westview Press.

——(1992) *The Persian Gulf TV War*, Boulder, CO: Westview Press.

——(1995) *Media Culture*, London: Routledge.

—— (1999) "Globalization from below? Toward a radical democratic technopolitics," *Angelaki*, 4, 2: 101–13.

—— (2000a) "New technologies/new literacies: reconstructing education for the new millennium," *Teaching Education*, 11, 3: 245–65.

—— (2000b) "Theorizing globalization critically," in A. Suess (ed.), *Globalisierung. Ein wissenschaftlicher Diskurs?*, Vienna: Passagen Verlag, pp. 73–108.

—— (2001) *Grand Theft 2000*, Lanham, MD: Rowman & Littlefield.

—— (forthcoming) *September 11 and Terror War: The Dangers of the Bush Legacy*.

Kellner, D. and M. Ryan (1988) *Camera Politica: The Politics and Ideologies of Contemporary Hollywood Film*, Bloomington, IN: Indiana University Press.

Kellner, D. and D. Streible (2000) *Film, Art and Politics: An Emile de Antonio Reader*, Minneapolis: University of Minnesota Press.

Kincheloe, J. (1997) "McDonald's, power, and children: Ronald McDonald (aka Ray Kroc) does it all for you," in S. Steinberg and J. Kincheloe (eds), *Kinderculture. The Corporate Construction of Childhood*, Boulder, CO: Westview Press, pp. 249–66.

—— (2002) *The Sign of the Burger: McDonald's and the Culture of Power*, Boulder, CO: Temple University Press.

Kirshenbaum, G. (1996) "Nike's nemesis," *Ms.*, November/December: 23.

Knight, P. (2001) *Conspiracy Culture: From Kennedy to 'The X-Files'*, New York: Routledge.

Knight, P. (ed.) (2002) *Conspiracy Nation. The Politics of Paranoia in Postwar America*, New York: New York University Press.

Kovel, J. (1997) "Bad news for fast food. What's wrong with McDonald's?" *Z Magazine*, September: 26–31.

Kracauer, S. (1966) *From Caligari to Hitler*, Princeton, NJ: Princeton University Press.

Kracauer, S. (1995) *The Mass Ornament*, Cambridge, MA: Harvard University Press.

Kroc, R. (1977) *Grinding It Out. The Making of McDonald's*, New York: St Martin's Press.

Kroker, A. and D. Cook (1986) *The Postmodern Scene*, New York: St Martin's Press.

Lavery, D. (ed.) (1995) *Full of Secrets: Critical Approaches to Twin Peaks*. Detroit: Wayne State University Press.

Lavery, D., A. Hague, and M. Cartwright (1996) "Deny all knowledge," in D. Lavery, A. Hague, and M. Cartwright (eds), *Reading The X-Files*, Syracuse, NY: Syracuse University Press.

LeFeber, W. (1999) *Michael Jordan and the New Global Capitalism*, New York: Norton.

Lipsitz, G. (1997) "The greatest story ever sold: Marketing and the O. J. Simpson trial," in T. Morrison and C. B. Lacour (eds), *Birth of a Nation'Hood: Gaze, Script, and Spectacle in the O. J. Simpson Case*, New York: Pantheon, pp. 3–30.

Lipsyte, R. (1996) "Pay for play: Jordan vs. Old-Timers," *New York Times*, July 14: B2.

Love, J. F. (1986) *McDonald's: Behind the Arches*, New York: Bantam Books.

Lyotard, J. F. (1984) *The Postmodern Condition*, Minneapolis: University of Minnesota Press.

—— (1985) "The sublime and the avante-garde," *Paragraph* 6: 1–18.

McDonald, M. G. (2001) "Safe sex symbol? Michael Jordan and the politics of representation," in Andrews, D. L. (ed.), *Michael Jordan, Inc. Corporate Sport, Media Culture, and Late Modern America*, Albany, NY: State University of New York Press.

McGinniss, J. (1970) *The Selling of the President 1968*, New York: Pocket Books.

Malach, M. (1996) "I Want to Believe … in the FBI," in D. Lavery, A. Hague, and M.

Cartwright (eds), *Reading The X-Files*, Syracuse, NY: Syracuse University Press, pp. 63–76.

Marcuse, H. (1964) *One-Dimensional Man*, Boston: Beacon Press.

Mazlish, B. (1993) *The Fourth Discontinuity*, New Haven, CT: Yale University Press.

Meehan, E. R. (1998) "Not your parents' FBI: *The X-Files* and 'Jose Chung's *From Outer Space*'," in A. A. Berger (ed.), *The Postmodern Presence*, Walnut Creek, CA: Alta Mira Press, pp. 125–56.

Mercer, K. (1994) *Welcome to the Jungle: New Positions in Black Cultural Studies*, London: Routledge.

Mitchell, W. J. T. (1998) *The Last Dinosaur Book: The Life and Times of a Cultural Icon*, Chicago: University of Chicago Press.

Morrison, T. and C. B. Lacour (eds) (1997) *Birth of a Nation'Hood: Gaze, Script, and Spectacle in the O. J. Simpson Case*, New York: Pantheon.

Nixon, R. M. (1969) *Six Crises*, New York: Doubleday.

Novak, R. (1999) "Riding the Air," *Washington Post*, January 31: X3

Parker, M. (1998) "Nostalgia and mass culture: McDonaldization and cultural elitism," in M. Alfino, J. S. Caputo, and R. Wynyard (eds), *McDonaldization Revisited: Critical Essay in Consumer Culture*, Westport, CT: Praeger, pp. 1–19.

Petrocelli, D. (1988) *Triumph of Justice: the Final Judgment on the Simpson Saga*, New York: Crown Publishers.

Pratt, R. (2001) *Projecting Paranoia. Conspiratorial Visions in American Film*, Lawrence, KA: University of Kansas Press.

Reel, Michael (1977) *Mass-Mediated Culture*, Englewood Cliffs, NJ: Prentice-Hall.

Reeves, J. L., M. C. Rogers, and M. Epstein (1996) "Rewriting popularity," in D. Lavery, A. Hague, and M. Cartwright (eds), *Reading The X-Files*, Syracuse, NY: Syracuse University Press, pp. 22–35.

Reilly, R. (1991) "Gotta pitch it," *Sports Illustrated*, May 27: 74–86.

Resnick, F.D. with M. Walker (1994) *Nicole Brown Simpson, the Private Diary of a Life Interrupted*, New York: Dove Books.

Rifkin, J. (1992) *Beyond Beef. The Rise and Fall of Cattle Culture*, New York: Plume.

Rinehart, J. (1998) "It may be polar night of icy darkness, but feminists are building a fire," in M. Alfino, J. S. Caputo, and R. Wynyard (eds), *McDonaldization Revisited: Critical Essay in Consumer Culture*, Westport, CT: Praeger, pp. 19–38.

Ritzer, G. (1996) [1993] *The McDonaldization of Society*, Thousand Oaks, CA: Pine Forge Press.

—— (1998) *The McDonaldization Thesis: Explorations and Extensions*, Thousand Oaks, CA: Sage.

——(2002) *McDonaldization. The Reader*, Thousand Oaks, CA: Pine Forge Press.

Roberts, P. (1995) *OJ: 101 Theories, Conspiracies and Alibis*, Diamond Bar, CA: Goldtree Press.

Rogin, M. (1988) *Ronald Reagan, the Movie: And Other Episodes of Political Demonology*, Berkeley: University of California Press.

Schlosser, E. (2001) *Fast Food Nation. The Dark Side of the All-American Meal*, Boston: Houghton Mifflin.

Schulman, J. N. (1999) *The Frame of the Century*, Pahrump, NV: Pulpless.com.

Shelton, A. (1995) "Where the Big Mac is king: McDonald's, USA," *Taboo*, II (Fall): 138ff.

Siegel, M. R. (1978) *Pynchon: Creative Paranoia in Gravity's Rainbow*, New York: Kennikat Press.

Simon, A. E. (1999) *The Real Science Behind The X-Files: Microbes, Meteorites, and Mutants*, New York: Simon & Schuster.

Sinclair, U. (1981) [1906] *The Jungle*, New York: Bantam.

Smart, B. (ed.) (1998) *Resisting McDonaldization*, London: Sage.

Smith, S. (1995) *Second Coming. The Strange Odyssey of Michael Jordan – From Courtside to Home Plate and Back Again*, New York: HarperCollins.

Taylor, S., S. Smith, and P. Lyon (1998) "McDonaldization and consumer choice in the future: An illusion or the next marketing revolution?" in M. Alfino, J. S. Caputo, and R. Wynyard (eds), *McDonaldization Revisited: Critical Essay in Consumer Culture*, Westport, CT: Praeger, pp. 105–20.

Toobin, J. (1996) *The Run of His Life: The People vs. O. J. Simpson*, New York: Random House.

Vidal, J. (1997) *McLibel. Burger Culture on Trial*, New York: The New Press.

Walker, S. (2001) "To play, or not to play," *Esquire*, November.

Watson, J. L. (ed) (1997) *Golden Arches East: McDonald's in East Asia*, Palo Alto, CA: Stanford University Press.

Watson, J. (2000) "China's Big Mac Attack," *Foreign Affairs*, May–June: 120ff.

Webster, F. (1995) *Theories of the Information Society*, London: Routledge.

Weller, S. (1995) *Raging Heart*, New York: Pocket Books.

Wilcox, R. and J. P. Williams (1996) "What do you think?" in D. Lavery, A. Hague, and M. Cartwright (eds), *Reading The X-Files*, Syracuse, NY: Syracuse University Press, pp. 99–120.

Williams, L. (2001) *Playing the Race Card: Melodrama of Black and White from Uncle Tom to O. J. Simpson*, Princeton, NJ: Princeton University Press.

Wilson, B. and R. Sparks (1996) "'It's gotta be the shoes': Youth, race, and sneaker commercials," *Sociology of Sport Journal*, 13, 4: 428–57.

Wolf, M. J. (1999) *Entertainment Economy: How Mega-Media Forces are Transforming Our Lives*, New York: Times Books.

Index